A

MYSTERIO'S ENCYCLOPEDIA OF MAGIC AND CONJURING

MYSTERIO'S ENCYCLOPEDIA OF
MAGIC AND CONJURING

GABE FAJURI

QUIRK BOOKS

Library of Congress Cataloging in Publication Number:
2008932811

ISBN: 978-1-59474-496-9
Printed in China

Typeset in Adobe Caslon, Algerian Condensed, and Rosewood

A Quirk Packaging Book
Cover designed by Doogie Horner
Interior designed by Stislow Design + Illustration
Cover illustration by Jeff Foster
Interior illustrations by Tony Dunn
Project management by Eloise Flood
Copyedited by Liana Krissoff

Distributed in North America by Chronicle Books
680 Second Street
San Francisco, CA 94107

10 9 8 7 6 5 4 3 2 1

Quirk Books
215 Church Street
Philadelphia, PA 19106
www.irreference.com
www.quirkbooks.com

FOR MY MOTHER

CONTENTS

CHAPTER IV
CUPS AND BALLS 125
THE OLDEST DECEPTION

CHAPTER VII

MAGIC OF THE MIND 221
MENTAL MARVELS

CHAPTER VIII

PARLOR MAGIC 253
CONJURING ON STAGE

INTRODUCTION

A REMARKABLE DISCOVERY LED TO THE COMPILATION, PRODUCTION, EDITING, AND COMPLETION OF THIS EXTRAORDINARY BOOK.

A T HIS UNTIMELY DEATH IN 1936, Mr. Mysterio stood at the pinnacle of his profession. The preeminent theatrical wonder worker of his generation, Mysterio's career had taken him to every corner of the globe. Appearances before the public were punctuated with prestigious command performances before royalty, heads of state, emperors, and celebrities of the era. Mr. Mysterio was both the public's favorite prestidigitator and mystery maker to the stars.

In January 1936, Mysterio began, in fits and starts, to outline and roughly draft a large book of trade secrets, a tome of tricks and methods he planned to publish upon his retirement from the stage. Though the vast majority of Mysterio's work on the project was in sketch and note form (having been jotted down in between performances, on trains and in dressing rooms), brief fragments and passages of his prose, in plain English, have survived the years. It was in late 2007 that I discovered, in a musty corner of a Chicago warehouse, the great magician's wardrobe trunk. Along with a host of notebooks and theatrical papers, the vestiges of that manuscript were revealed in the trunk's bottom-most drawer.

Never one to spare an audience a healthy dose of bombast, in a suitably grandiose and whorled script, the first page of Mysterio's notes bore the following title:

Mr. Mysterio's Stupendous, Incredible, Gigantic, Unparalleled, and Not–to–Be–Equaled Encyclopedia of Magic and Conjuring Secrets / Embracing the whole calendar of sleights, tips, tactics, tricks, dodges, and swindles essential to the education of a professional prestidigitator.

Clearly, the conjurer had set forth an ambitious project for himself. But, sadly, it was not to be. Mysterio, as we all know, died later that year in a tragic accident during one of his performances. His grand encyclopedia was left to molder—until now. For as I studied the yellowed pages, it occurred to me that it would be not only a fitting tribute to Mr. Mysterio, but also a great gift to the aspiring magicians of today if I were to complete the project Mysterio began.

The distillation, clarification, and refinement of Mysterio's scribbling, notes, and ideas has yielded, years later, two things: a choice selection of secrets, sleights, and tricks, and a shorter title for the book: *Mysterio's Encyclopedia of Magic and Conjuring.*

In many cases, I employed Mysterio's notes, patter suggestions, and choreographic suggestions to fully describe the miracles that follow. Data drawn from his diaries (also found in the wardrobe trunk) were used to supplement information gleaned from his notebooks. However, in the years since Mysterio's passing, modern materials and ideas have filtered into the ever-changing marketplace of magical ideas. With a nod to the master mystifier's original intent, the flavor of his manuscript has, I hope, been retained while taking into account more recent developments in conjuring technology.

That said, rather than concluding these introductory remarks on a more contemporary note, I will step out of the limelight and set in my place the rightful star of this literary magic show: Mr. Mysterio. What follows is a passage drawn directly from the leger-de-mainiac's book-in-progress. Though written over half a century ago, the advice offered is as relevant and vibrant today as it was then.

"Had I been alerted to four basic rules upon my entrance into the world of magic I now inhabit, my meteoric rise to stardom would have been much smoother. These rules are iron-clad, and can either be learned by reading and study, from the pages of this illustrious volume, or in a manner much more difficult: through trial and error. Take my advice, dear readers, and commit the following precepts to memory. If you aspire to tread the boards, to spend your life before the footlights, then heed this, my hard-won advice.

"First and foremost, pay court to your audience. Woo it. Make your spectators your accomplices. Though the people before whom you perform may have no knowledge of your methods, and no inkling as to "how you do that," they still wield power—ultimate power, in fact. With no audience, you have no show; you have nothing. And a magician who treats his audience as a panel of experts who exist merely to be confounded by the latest puzzle is a magician who will never advance his career beyond the level of dilettante.

"Nearly as important as wooing one's audience is choosing the appropriate method whereby your magic is presented. As Albert Einstein once opined, 'The most beautiful experience one can have is the mysterious.' Deliver your magic graciously, with humor, thoughtfulness, and elegance. Welcome your audience not only with your words, but with your attitude. If the tricks in your repertoire seem remarkable and surprising to you, so will they appear to others.

"Furthermore, rehearse and polish your magic. When presented properly, conjuring, like any other entertainment, can approach art. But the only way to perform artistically is to methodically and repeatedly practice both the technical aspects and the presentational nuances of each effect in your program. Sleight-of-hand should be made silky-smooth by repeated drilling. To labor over a movement or motion for hundreds of hours is not enough. The secret actions of each trick must become second nature. In performance, there is no leeway, no room for half-measures or fumbling. Your goal is to conceal the methods of your magic. Exposure of even the smallest secret is tantamount to utter failure. No effect should be presented before its time, before it has been carefully scripted, rehearsed, and rehearsed again. Boiled down to a single word, this rule can be described, simply, as "practice."

The fourth and most overlooked essential of the mystic arts is the element of surprise. Except under certain specific circumstances, tricks should not be repeated for the same audience. Not knowing what comes next in a performance of magic is where much of the delight lies."

His points, laid bare, are simple: Respect your audience, practice your magic and do not present it as a challenge, and use the element of surprise to your advantage.

Heed the great wizard's advice and study these pages with some care. Though the journey you take will be a self-guided one, the master will be with you every step of the way. He set out the road map. Follow it, and you may find yourself on a path to magical success, fame, and fortune as an entertainer.

Welcome to *Mysterio's Encyclopedia of Magic and Conjuring*.

Gabe Fajuri
Chicago
2008

CHAPTER I

BODY MAGIC

PROPLESS WONDERS

· ~∘⊙∘~ ·

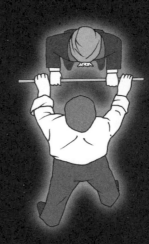

"YOU'RE A MAGICIAN? LET'S SEE A TRICK!"

I T'S EASY TO THINK OF EXCUSES when a curious potential spectator requests an impromptu magic show. Perhaps you're unprepared, or have no props available for an on-the-spot performance.

This chapter prepares you to handle such requests with aplomb. The effects outlined here require no special props or gimmicks—at least not as far as the audience is concerned. Almost all of them can be performed with little or no preparation, and few properties. Also, remember that almost any magic trick—simple or complex—can be made more effective by the appropriate witty banter, known in magicians' circles as "patter." Suggested patter lines are provided throughout the chapter.

If you feel your confidence wavering, take a cue from the masters. "Alexander Herrmann created a reputation for himself by making miracles wherever he went," Mysterio wrote. "Herrmann's reputation off the stage was nearly as gigantic as it was on the boards. When he discovered gold doubloons in raw eggs sold on street corners and extracted live geese from the collars of unsuspecting pedestrians, it was only natural that the waves of interest created followed him to the theater. The lesson to be learned here is that the conjurer should never turn down a request for a performance. He should always be at the ready—even when he is 'unarmed,' so to speak."

BOY, ARE MY ARMS TIRED!

This trick practically works itself; all the more reason to develop and practice a convincing—but not hokey—presentation for it. Properly staged, tricks like this can transform you from a mere magician to something approaching superhuman.

EFFECT: The magician offers a demonstration of invisible physical influence over a volunteer. Standing in a doorway, the spectator is told by the magician to clear his mind of all intrusions. Next, the volunteer is instructed to press the backs of his hands firmly against the frame of the door for 30 or 45 seconds.

"Imagine that strings are tied to your fingers, and that a flock of sparrows are tugging on those strings," the magician chatters. "Imagine that you cannot control your arms, that the birds are lifting the arms up, up, and away."

When the volunteer steps out of the doorjamb, he will find the magician's patter to have influenced him significantly—his arms will rise up nearly to shoulder height, seemingly of their own accord!

REQUIRED: Nothing.

PREPARATION: None.

PERFORMANCE: Other than developing an appropriate story, something similar to the brief outline provided above, there is no preparation or special apparatus required to perform this quick trick. In fact, you can test the results on yourself.

Stand in a doorjamb and press the backs of your hands against the frame, firmly, for approximately 30 seconds. See **Figure 1.** When you step out of the jamb, your arms, conditioned to the pressure they have been exerting, will rise, slowly and steadily, seemingly pulled toward the sky.

All that's required is a steady line of chatter and a willing volunteer. With the right dramatic flair, you'll have them believing in your "invisible influence" in no time.

FIGURE 1

FINGER FINDER

Though a spectator may attempt to hide information from you, if you employ some simple techniques, he will be unable to do so. In this demonstration of apparent mind reading, you use the unconscious reactions of a spectator's body to read his thoughts.

EFFECT: A spectator extends one of his hands out in front of his body and spreads his fingers wide apart. The magician asks him to concentrate on one digit of the five, and do so intently. Amazingly, the magician determines—without asking leading questions—which finger the spectator is thinking of!

REQUIRED: Nothing.

PREPARATION: None.

PERFORMANCE: Instruct a spectator to stand directly in front of you and to hold his arm out and away from his chest. "Open your hand, please, and spread your fingers apart, palm out." Once he has complied with this request, give him further instructions: "Concentrate on—make a definite mental selection of—one of your fingers. Think of it, and nothing else. It's a funny thing to concentrate on, I know, but please pick one of your digits and home in on it. Block everything else out of your mind."

Now use your index finger to push against the tip of each finger in his extended hand. The finger that gives you the most resistance will be the one he is concentrating on.

To conclude the demonstration announce his mental selection.

RUBBER DIGIT

The commonly known version of this trick (the old detachable thumb gag, which uses a virtually identical method) can't hold a candle to this one.

EFFECT: The magician grasps his left thumb with his left fist, and stretches it out, until it's six or seven inches (15–18 cm) long!

REQUIRED: Your hands.

PREPARATION: None.

FIGURE 2

PERFORMANCE: Extend your left thumb away from your fist, as if giving the traditional "thumbs up" sign. Make your right hand into a fist, and as you do, place the tip of your right thumb between the right index and middle finger, as shown in **Figure 2**. Bring your right fist over your left thumb, placing the extended opposable digit into the right fist, as shown in **Figure 3**. The tip of your right thumb appears to be the tip of your left thumb, sticking up through your right fingers.

With a screwing action, twist your "left" thumb back and forth, and as you do, slowly pull your right hand upward, along the length of your left thumb, as shown in **Figure 4**. Apparently, you are stretching your left thumb with considerable force! Continue pulling and stretching your thumb until the tip of your real left thumb is just inside the right palm, as shown in **Figure 5**. To add a convincing layer of deception to the effect, wiggle the exposed thumb tip before, during, and after the stretching.

"I can't keep the poor thing in this condition," you tell the audience as you exert an apparently Herculean amount of pressure on the extended digit and return it to its regular state. Remove the death grip of your right hand from what is apparently a very fatigued and very stretched left thumb, which you then wiggle vigorously, proving it's none the worse for the wear.

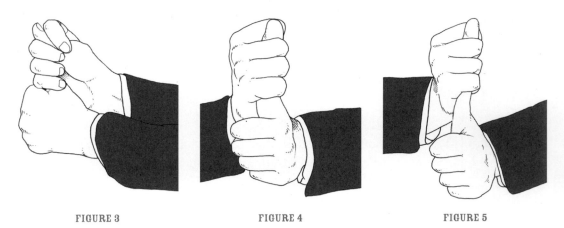

FIGURE 3   FIGURE 4   FIGURE 5

LENGTHENED LIMB

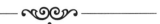

Mr. Mysterio once worked in American vaudeville with a unique act billed as "Willard, the Man Who Grows." Clarence Willard's turn on the vaudeville stage featured a demonstration of his ability to grow several inches in height over the course of ten minutes—and prove it!

EFFECT: The magician's arm visibly and slowly stretches. As if fueled by some mysterious elixir, it grows apparently as much as 12 inches (30 cm) in a matter of moments.

REQUIRED: You must be wearing a jacket to perform this effect. No props are required.

PREPARATION: When ready to present this stunt, pull the sleeve of your jacket down so that the cuff covers the base of your right hand.

PERFORMANCE: If seated, set your right arm on the table in front of you. "Alterations can get expensive," you say, indicating the poor fit of your suit coat. "I've devised a way to get around the poor workmanship of my tailor…lengthening my arms."

Begin by tugging on your right fingers with your left hand, *very* gradually extending your arm from your coat sleeve as you do. Then, as best you can, pantomime the action of pushing your arm out of the sleeve. The right combination of acting and subtle motion from your right arm will produce a visually arresting effect—that of your arm gradually growing out of your sleeve.

Continue tugging and pushing on the arm until is has reached its "full-grown length." Admire your handiwork, adjust your sleeve to the appropriate length, and go on about your business.

The effect can also be performed standing, with the magician's right side turned toward the audience.

FOUR OUT OF FIVE

Of this feat, Mysterio noted: "I've gleaned many a laugh and gasp with this bit. When worked smartly, and not made into a big 'production,' this mini-mystery can flummox nearly any onlooker."

EFFECT: The magician's middle finger is removed from his hand. Though from one angle the feat looks like a gag, when the magician's hand is turned over, the spectators see that the finger really is gone! The hand is then restored to its natural, original state.

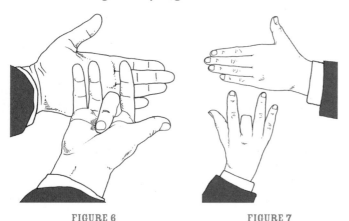

FIGURE 6   FIGURE 7

REQUIRED: A hand with five fingers.

PREPARATION: None.

PERFORMANCE: Hold your right hand in front of you, and cover it momentarily with your left hand. When the middle finger is covered, bend down its top two joints only, as shown in **Figure 6.**

The audience view is shown in **Figure 7.** Remove your left hand and show that the top of your middle finger has apparently vanished.

To "prove" that the finger is gone, flip the palm of your right hand toward the audience, and at the same time, spread your fingers apart so that the hand looks like **Figure 8.** A wide gap between your ring and middle finger helps create the illusion that your middle finger really *is* gone. You can now rotate your hand back and forth, switching between the two positions, showing the altered state of your hand. Finally, return every-thing to normal by holding your left hand in front of your right. When you remove it, your fingers are spread wide apart and all of them are where they're supposed to be.

FIGURE 8

D.O.S. (DEAD ON STAGE)

Here, effective staging is also crucial. While a strong trick one-on-one, this effect can be made to play for larger groups as well.

EFFECT: The magician demonstrates his ability to control his biorhythms. Inviting a spectator with medical experience on stage, the performer's pulse is taken. It is steady and strong. The spectator counts out each beat of the performer's heart, so everyone in the crowd has an audible record of the performer's vital sign. "And now for the astonishing demonstration," the magician says. "This yogic technique is rarely seen today. But after years of practice and self-denial, I have mastered it. I now present it for you—for your entertainment pleasure."

As he utters these words, the spectator, who has been counting aloud all along, begins to slow her pace. Apparently, the magician's pulse is slowing. After a short period, his pulse stops. "Check again…just to be sure," the magician says in an anemic, weak voice. Repeated attempts to locate the magician's pulse fail. Then, as if snapping out of a trance, the magician snaps his fingers, and his heartbeat slowly and steadily returns to normal, his heart apparently thumping and bumping at its usual pace after only ten or twenty seconds have passed. He has returned to the land of the living!

REQUIRED: A small, hard rubber ball (a racquetball or even a large Super Ball works well). If a ball is not available, a balled-up pocket handkerchief can be used.

PREPARATION: Place the ball in the pit of whichever arm your spectator will take your pulse on. Hold it there loosely.

PERFORMANCE: As with the other feats of body magic Mysterio presents in this chapter, the secret has very little to do with the mechanics of the trick. Showmanship is the key—building up the appropriate (but not too hokey) story about your rare "yogic" abilities and your years of practice.

Once you have found a spectator who can take a pulse accurately, proceed as outlined above. Have her locate your pulse on your wrist. Everything should seem aboveboard; your heartbeat should be easy to locate. Have the spectator call out or count out each beat of your heart so that everyone in the audience can hear her.

As you deliver your monologue about mind over body, increase the pressure on the ball in your armpit. To the assisting spectator, your pulse will apparently begin to slow.

This should be reflected by a slowing of her counting. Eventually, if enough pressure is exerted by your arm, your pulse will be impossible to find (on the wrist she is holding). To restore your pulse—and, apparently, your life—gradually relax your pressure on the ball. When sufficiently "revived," take a bow—if you have the strength.

SLIGHT ADJUSTMENT

This is as much a visual and auditory gag as a trick—making it a perfect interlude between other body tricks. "Accent your impromptu performances with bits of stage business in between," Mysterio once wrote a colleague, "and your reputation will grow exponentially."

EFFECT: Grabbing hold of his head, the magician gives it a quick sideways twist. A loud and certainly unnatural "CRACK!" is heard, as if his impromptu demonstration of chiropractics has gone wrong. After the laughter and worried expressions subside, the entertainer grins, and continues his performance.

REQUIRED: A jacket and a hard plastic drinking glass. The cup must be stiff, so that when squeezed it will crack. Many plastic tumblers will not crack sharply. Experiment with a variety of goblets to find one that cracks easily—and loudly.

PRESENTATION: Place the cup in your armpit, under your jacket. Do not place it next to your skin.

PERFORMANCE: As you address your audience, feign a cramp in your neck. "Give me a moment to work this out," you say, as you grab the sides of your face with your hands. Giving your head what appears to be a firm twist, squeeze the concealed cup with the inside of your arm, causing it to crack as you complete the twisting action. It will crack, with luck (and practice) loudly, and everyone will hear it.

Shake off the apparent readjustment. "It's only an upper vertebra," you say, as you continue with your performance. At an opportune moment—perhaps in preparation for your next trick—reach into your coat, ostensibly to remove something from your inner breast pocket. Instead, remove the broken cup from its hiding place and dispose of it by dropping it to the floor behind your table.

TRIPLE-JOINTED

This participatory piece of body magic can effectively play for a crowd of five or five thousand.

EFFECT: The audience members are invited to clasp their hands together, with arms twisted. The magician then untwists his arms (since he has been providing an example to the spectators of how to arrange their arms) and asks the audience to do the same. Even though the performer is able to easily untangle his arms, the audience can't!

REQUIRED: Nothing.

PREPARATION: None.

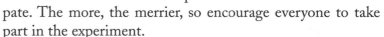

FIGURE 9

PERFORMANCE: "Everyone follow along with me, please." As you say this, extend both hands out from your body, and turn your thumbs down, toward the floor, as shown in **Figure 9.** "Follow along, please!" Inevitably, someone in the audience will not want to partici-pate. The more, the merrier, so encourage everyone to take part in the experiment.

FIGURE 10

Cross your hands and clasp them together, fingers inter-locked, as shown in **Figure 10.** Now for the crucial moment, which allows you to make the magic happen and which will leave the spectators flummoxed.

Study your audience and pretend that one of the spectators has not followed directions. "Sir, you need to clasp your hands the way I have." As you say this, attention is drawn from your arms and hands to your face, since you are addressing a member of the audience. Take advantage of this misdirection and unclasp your hands momentarily. Continue pattering ("Make sure you're holding on tightly"), and then reclasp your hands, but *not* in the same way. Instead, your right hand is turned thumb down as before, but is rotated *clockwise* to do so. Then, your left hand is turned over on

FIGURE 11

top of it as before, as shown in **Figure 11.** If your hands are held in position and you don't call attention to the difference between your arms and the audience's, no one will notice the difference.

"Now for the funny part," you continue. "With enough practice, you can give your arms a rotation of approximately 180 degrees…like this!" Do as you say, rotating your arms in a counterclockwise circle, as in

FIGURE 12

Figure 12. "Now everyone give it a try!" Try though they will, no one in the audience will be able to do as you have. The result will be laughter and surprise.

MODERN-DAY GEORGIA MAGNET

Lulu Hearst was a diminutive vaudevillian from Georgia. Though short in stature, her act went over in a big way. After seeing her on the Keith-Orpheum circuit, Mysterio noted, "The lady appears to have the strength of twenty men while on stage, and had the audience in hysterics with her remarkable turn. She deserves the star spot on the bill."

EFFECT: Bracing yourself against a wall, you challenge a group of five, ten, or even twenty people to squash you flat against the wall. Even though you are clearly outnumbered and out-muscled, your super-strength is just that: super enough to resist the most earnest efforts of the volunteers who are trying to flatten you. No matter how hard they try, you are able to resist their pressure without so much as batting an eye.

REQUIRED: A sturdy wall—the sturdier the better.

PREPARATION: None.

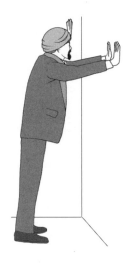

FIGURE 13

PERFORMANCE: "What is about to transpire will seem impossible," you say, "but I assure you it is not. I require the assistance of ten men." Once the willing subjects have joined you, line them up in a row, and assume the position shown in **Figure 13,** the palms of your hands flat against the wall, fingers up, arms straight.

"The challenge, gentlemen, is to sap you of your strength, to incapacitate your rippling muscles and make you as weak as a mouse. Though you may not realize it yet, I have already done so." At this point, invite your assistants to pile on, as shown in **Figure 14.** The first spectator, whose hands end up on your shoulders as shown, should be the weakest one of the group, so choose wisely. Because of the physical law in play, the force the men are about to exert on you will feel like nothing more than the force of *one* person. That is the secret to your super-strength. If you can withstand the force he exerts on you, you can beat the rest of them, too.

"Gentlemen, your challenge is to exert as much pressure as possible on the shoulders of the man in front of you, and to, with your collective might, mash me against the wall. On the count of three, do your best to flatten me. One…two…three!"

Though the men will grunt and groan and make every attempt to slam you face-first into the wall, no amount of energy can make it so. Tell everyone to stop pushing, then wipe your brow as if you've just exerted a great amount of energy, and thank the crowd for its participation in the demonstration. "I promise to use my powers exclusively for the forces of good," you tell them as they exit the stage.

FIGURE 14

STAY PUT!

Another Lulu Hearst-ian stunt, this one creates the impression of super-strength over a single person. As Mysterio remarked, "It is most impressive if put into practice by a female Svengali or even a child."

EFFECT: An audience volunteer, seated in a chair, is immobilized by the performer, as if by magic. "Though the action you are about to attempt is one of the simplest, and something you do each and every day, it takes only a moment of magnetic influence from me to render you helpless as a newborn. Observe!" After this introductory spiel, the spectator truly is incapacitated; he cannot rise from the chair when only one hand (and sometimes only one finger) of the performer's is pressed against his forehead.

REQUIRED: Nothing.

PREPARATION: None.

PERFORMANCE: Ask for an audience volunteer—one who looks big and burly, if you can find such a subject—to sit forward in a chair, as if he were slouching and had bad posture. His back should *not* touch the back of the chair.

FIGURE 15

"Remarkable though the following statement may sound, it is entirely true. The moment you sat down, you came under an imperceptible, subtle power of mine. You have been rendered nearly helpless and will be virtually incapacitated. Please, lean back in the chair so that I can demonstrate this unique situation to the audience."

Have the subject lean back in the chair and tilt his head backward so that he is looking toward the ceiling. As shown in **Figure 15,** tell him to cross his arms in front of him. Now, with your index finger, press firmly (but not too hard) in the center of your subject's forehead.

"Try though you may, you will be unable to even rise from this chair," you say. "Make an attempt, sir." When he tries to stand up, the pressure of your index finger on his forehead does exactly what you say it will: The subject is unable to stand up.

Remove your index finger from his forehead and say, "And now, the spell is broken. Rise, sir, and return to your seat and please accept this round of applause from the audience for your willing participation in this strange experiment." He stands up; the audience claps as he returns to his seat and the test is concluded.

THE WHY: After witnessing the above experiment in the act of vaudeville and lyceum performer C. A. George Newmann, Mysterio correctly divined its secret, and recorded it in his diary on July 3, 1913: "To stand up from a seated position, the first thing required of the human body is the establishment of a center of gravity. Pressure from the performer's index finger that keeps the subject's head tilted backward keeps him off balance, and makes standing up impossible, no matter how much effort he exerts. The subject's arms must remain folded in front of him as the experiment takes place, lest he use them as an aid to establishing that center of gravity."

FLOATING FINGER

This quick optical illusion can be an effective warm-up for a longer magic show. It won't fool anyone, per se, but will offer everyone who tries the experiment a new illusory perspective on his surroundings.

EFFECT: In an effect of mass hypnosis, everyone in the magician's entire audience causes a miniature finger, approximately ³/₄ inch (2 cm) long, to float between outstretched index fingers!

REQUIRED: Nothing.

PREPARATION: None.

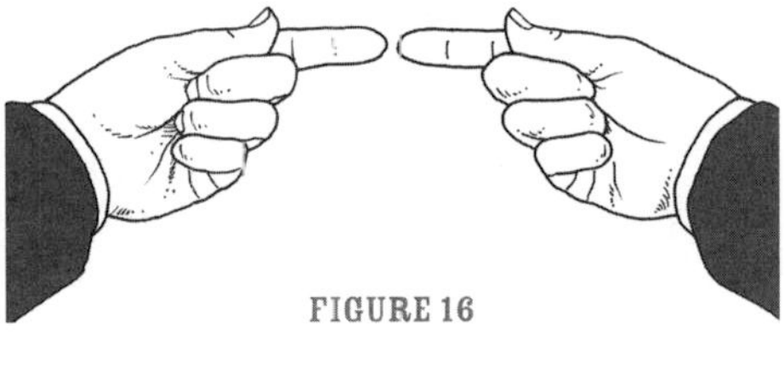

FIGURE 16

PERFORMANCE: "As a prelude to the illusions you will witness this evening," the magician says, "I'd like everyone in the audience to participate in the following optical experiment."

Have your spectators hold their hands out in front of them, with both index fingers pointing at each other, as shown in **Figure 16.**

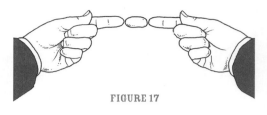

FIGURE 17

"What is about to happen is nothing more than an optical illusion. But it is a powerful one, and looks very, very real. Slowly move your hands toward the bridge of your nose. Don't try to focus on your fingers; keep your gaze on me. As your hands approach your nose, you'll notice something curious floating in between the tips of your extended index fingers."

Indeed, when the spectators' fingers approach their noses, they will all see a small, stubby mutant digit floating in between their index fingers, as shown in **Figure 17.**

STUCK LIKE GLUE

Properly presented, arcane knowledge can be used to great advantage by the resourceful magician. This feat takes advantage of a little-known physical fact, cloaked in an air of mystery.

EFFECT: A spectator is asked to hold his hands together, fingers extended and touching. His middle fingers are folded down over the backs of his hands, and a coin is placed between his ring fingers. After a few incantations are uttered over the spectator's hands, it becomes impossible for him to release his hold on the coin. It is as if his hands have been stuck to each other with a strong adhesive.

REQUIRED: A coin, which may be borrowed.

PREPARATION: None.

PERFORMANCE: The essence of this effect is in the build-up and presentation. "Develop a tale that seems plausible and scientific and you will go far on the stage," Mysterio wrote. This feat, simple as it is, requires window dressing.

Addressing your volunteer, you say, "Sir, can you please wiggle your fingers for me? Good. They all work."

Next, instruct him to clasp his hands together and bend down his middle fingers, as shown in **Figure 18.** Place the

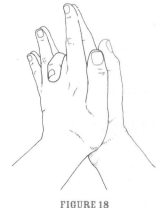

FIGURE 18

coin between his ring fingers—see **Figure 19**—and say, "Your fingers all work. We've just established that fact. Even so, I will now sap your hands of their mobility—without even touching them." Challenge the spectator to drop the coin from between his ring fingers into your cupped hands. Because the muscles of the ring fingers are the most under-developed of all the digits, he will find this simple request impossible. As he tries, continue building up the effect by saying something like, "Your fingers—indeed, your hands—feel bound together, as if joined by some invisible, spectral glue. Is that correct?" Asking the spectator to confirm your statement heightens the effect immeasurably for those viewing the performance.

FIGURE 19

To conclude, remove the coin from between his fingers, and hand it to him "for being a good sport and participating in our little psychological, magical experiment."

PINKIES, TOO: The effect can be repeated with pinkies: Ask the spectator to fold over his little fingers instead of the middle fingers.

SKEWED SENSE OF TOUCH

This feat is perfect for when someone presses you to perform a stunt or two at a party.

EFFECT: The magician alters a spectator's sense of touch, so that what was once hot feels cold and vice versa.

REQUIRED: Three glasses of water, one hot, one cold, and one at room temperature.

PREPARATION: None.

PERFORMANCE: Comment on the water in each glass: "The one on the left is hot, but not scalding hot. The one on the right is cold, but not ice cold. And the center glass is full of tepid water."

Invite a spectator to assist. Have her dip her left index finger into the cold water and her right index finger into the hot water at the same time. Tell her to hold her fingers there for at least a minute, maybe two. (According to Mysterio's notes on this stunt, "This fatigues the nerve endings in the fingers.")

"It's easy to tell the difference between the two temperatures, isn't it?" Look intently at the spectator and then say, "And now to alter your reality, if only momentarily. I will confuse your sense of touch. Please place both fingers into the center glass of water, and when you do, tell us what your left hand feels. Then tell us what your right hand feels."

Amazingly, the finger that was placed in the cold water will now feel as if it is immersed in hot water, and the finger just placed in the hot water will feel as if it is in cold water!

PERCEPTIVE PULSATION

Mysterio's notebook entry for January 15, 1935, states: "Though seemingly simple enough for a child to perform, the pulse-detection stunt I unveiled tonight at Windsor Castle created a sensation with each repetition. I performed this trick twenty-five times for the king and queen, with each revelation more perplexing than the last."

EFFECT: The magician grasps the wrists of a subject and asks her to think of one of her two arms. After she does so, the performer immediately raises the arm she is thinking of, without fail!

REQUIRED: You must be able to find the spectator's pulse on both of her wrists, at the same time.

PREPARATION: None.

PERFORMANCE: The secret of this effect—the spectator's pulse—is the tiniest element of the bigger picture. As with many body tricks, the key is to veil a simple secret in a large, theatrical presentation.

Stand in front of a spectator and grip her wrists, finding her pulse as you do so. Ask her to concentrate on her hands, and, eventually, to mentally select one of them. Amazingly, you will be able to tell which hand she is concentrating on by the pulse in its corresponding wrist. The pulse will first slow down, and then speed up in the wrist that your spectator is thinking of. Once you have felt the difference in pulses, raise the hand that the spectator is concentrating on. If both pulses waver or change, then the subject cannot make up her mind, a fact that you can announce as well (and which may receive a strong reaction, since the feat seems even more like genuine thought reading).

The test can now be repeated with the same or different spectators ad infinitum—though you should know when to quit. The other key to repeating the effect is being certain that the spectator's pulse returns to normal before beginning again. Tell her to clear her mind before continuing with round two or three. "The old adage 'Always leave them wanting more' is an important one to remember," Mysterio wrote.

ROOTED
— ❦ —

This feat was Lulu Hearst's most famous. "It was particularly effective," Mysterio wrote, "because of her stature and her femininity."

EFFECT: No matter how hard they try, the strongest men in the audience cannot lift the performer (or, preferably, his trim and tiny female assistant) from the ground. Grunt and groan though they will, no amount of force is able to lift the tiny enchantress from the floor of the stage.

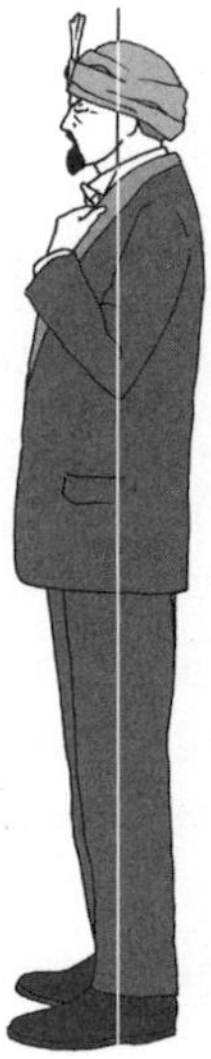

REQUIRED: Nothing.

PREPARATION: None.

PERFORMANCE: Stand squarely on the floor and have the challenger—an audience volunteer, one who's big and strong-looking, face you. Tell him that the challenge is simple: He is to exert all of the energy he has, using every muscle in his being, to lift you (or your assistant, if you prefer) off the floor. The only rule—and it is an important one—is that he must lift you by your elbows.

Hold your elbows at your side, tightly against your body, and fold your arms upward, as in **Figure 20**. Tell your volunteer to grab you by your elbows

FIGURE 20

and to lift you up. This should be a relatively easy task to fulfill.

Now you will make it impossible for him to repeat the lifting. This is accomplished by changing your center of gravity, though apparently you change nothing about your stance or body.

The secret is to very slightly move your shoulders and elbows forward, away from the center line of your body, as in **Figure 21.** This shifts your center of gravity and makes the challenger before you work not only against the weight of your body, but against the force of gravity as well. Unless the volunteer trying to lift you is incredibly strong, making you budge from your position will feel equivalent to an attempt to uproot a tree.

If your shoulders and elbows are kept loose and flexible during the experiment, lifting you becomes even *more* difficult, if that is at all possible.

FIGURE 21

Embellish the presentation of this gravity-defying feat by training an assistant to be your own "Georgia Magnet" (see page 14) and make sure that this helper is preferably a lightweight subject; a girl or a teenager would be perfectly suited to the role.

Furthermore, much fun can be had with a burly spectator who takes on the challenge of lifting your assistant if, on his first attempt, he *is* able to lift her off of the ground. After his success, put him in a trance (or at least pretend to put him in a trance) or pretend to sap his power with a mesmeric, magical pass of your hand, and then show that he cannot lift the girl who only moments before was as light as a feather.

One of Mysterio's favorite tales relates to the above feat of legerdemain and can be used as an excellent patter story to accompany the trick. "Jean Eugene Robert-Houdin, known to all magicians as the Father of Modern Magic, performed a Georgia Magnet–like feat in Algiers in 1856, but used a small wooden chest in place of the girl. Robert-Houdin invited a Marabout warrior to lift the chest from the stage, an easy task for the strapping tribesman. Then, with little more than a few cabalistic words, Robert-Houdin apparently deprived the man of all of his strength, for when he next attempted to lift the box from the stage, he found it impossible to move! Even when assisted by a rope and pulley, the man was powerless; he found himself as weak as an infant.

"In a final, brilliant moment, Robert-Houdin made one last incantation over the chest, as the Marabout warrior struggled with it. Suddenly, the man cried out in pain, released his grip on the box and ran, shrieking all the way, from the theater. This demonstration, among others, helped Robert-Houdin quell an Algerian rebellion on behalf of the French government, which had sent him there expressly for that purpose.

"I believe I have divined the secret behind this astounding feat, but as it is not mine I shall not reveal it."

MAKE LIKE A TREE

This effect was another of Lulu Hearst's favorites. "She blended the tests together into a series of bewildering demonstrations, using little by way of props," Mysterio reported in the pages of *The Sphinx*, a trade journal for magicians. "The experiments with a broom were particularly effective."

FIGURE 22

EFFECT: The performer challenges a strong man, a member of the audience, to knock him off balance by pushing against a broom held in the performer's hands. No matter how strong the audience volunteer, the magician cannot be uprooted from his position on the stage. Even when the performer stands on one foot, knocking him off balance is proven impossible!

REQUIRED: A broom and a willing spectator.

PREPARATION: None.

PERFORMANCE: Holding your arms at your sides, bend them at the elbows, almost at a right angle to your chest. With your palms down and approximately 12 to 18 inches (30 to 45 cm) apart, grip the handle of a broom securely between them, as shown in **Figure 22.**

Invite a spectator to the stage and ask him to hold the broom in a similar fashion, as in **Figure 23.** His hands should be outside of yours. Instruct the spectator to apply steady, even pressure. "Try as hard as you can to knock me off balance. Put your back into it. Really make an effort." Build up how much strength he will use and how much he *should* use to try to knock you over. "Put everything you have into the effort," you say.

The key is to not allow the spectator to make any sudden, jerky movements. If he does so, you *will* lose your balance and you *will* fall. Steady, even pressure is essential from your challenger.

FIGURE 23

Once you have mastered the stunt as described above, with both feet planted on the floor, the ability to perform it while standing on one foot becomes easy. Practice with an understanding friend away from the prying eyes of the public and you'll quickly develop the necessary script and stance to make this challenge both puzzling and impossible-looking.

STIFF AS A BOARD

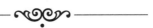

This effect and the follow-up have been featured, on and off, as a sensational, publicity-grabbing stunt since the 1930s. Its effectiveness has not been diminished by time.

EFFECT: The magician is balanced between two chairs, head on one, feet on the other. The performer then utters a spell over himself, saying that his physical abilities have been transformed. "I am now impossibly resistant to the force of gravity," the performer states. This fact is demonstrated when a spectator steps up on a chair, and then on to the magician's chest. The spectator, without any assistance, is supported effortlessly by the performer's body!

REQUIRED: Three identical chairs and at least two spectators, though three are preferable.

PREPARATION: None.

FIGURE 24

PERFORMANCE: Place two chairs on the stage, their seats facing each other, and at a distance approximately 18 inches (45 cm) less than your height. Finding the correct distance will require a little experimentation. Lie on the floor, and have your assisting spectators lift you by your shoulders and ankles and place you on the chairs, as shown in **Figure 24.** Your ankles are on one chair and your shoulders are on the other. You span the space between the seats like a human suspension bridge.

Now explain—as best you can from your awkward position, which can be the source of some comedy—your intentions. "I offer a demonstration of impossible, superhuman strength," you say. Invite a spectator to sit on your chest. You will find that, as long as she does not sit in the center (pit) of your stomach, you will be able to support her full weight without any trouble.

"Let's take things one step further—literally," you say. Invite the spectator to stand on your chest (again, off center). Tell her to use the free chair as a step stool, and ask the other spectator to assist her in standing up.

Make sure that the spectator stands with one foot (preferably clean and free of shoes) on your chest and the other on your upper thigh. If she follows these instructions, you will have no trouble supporting her weight. In fact, burlier performers should be able to support the weight of two spectators—one standing on the chest and the other on the thighs—if those spectators weigh 150 pounds (68 kg) or less.

IMPROMPTU LEVITATION

Suited only for the "right moment," this impromptu levitation lasts just seconds. Even so, when performed with panache, the impression it makes will last a lifetime. The originator of the effect is unknown.

EFFECT: The magician stands well away from two or three spectators. He turns his back on the small audience, extends his arms, and breathes deeply. After a moment of what appears to be extreme mental concentration and strain, the magician begins to rise up, several inches from the ground! He is levitating! Just as quickly, the performer descends to the ground.

REQUIRED: Nothing.

PREPARATION: None.

PERFORMANCE: The secret to this effect is rather disappointing, from the perspective of the magician, since, in essence, you stand on the toes of one foot to effect the levitation. The real secret of the trick, more than anything, is the way you present it and the way you position your audience.

FIGURE 25

Perform the levitation for no more than four people. As shown in **Figure 25,** the audience should stand together in a tight group. The psychology involved in performing this effect is nearly as important as the performance itself, so before you levitate, deliver a suitably grandiose preamble along the lines of "What I am about to attempt can be dangerous, and only lasts for a few moments. I'm going to try to levitate for you…to lift myself off the ground with no visible means of support."

Explicitly telling the audience that you are about to levitate goes a long way to selling the effect to them and helping them build up what you are about to do in their minds.

"I need a perfectly solid piece of ground to take off from," you continue. Walk directly away from the spectators approximately ten paces, and then study the ground on either side of you. Take approximately three or four steps to your left, so you are in the position shown in **Figure 26.** The key is to end up at an angle that will obscure the view of your left foot from the spectators.

FIGURE 26

Now more acting comes into play. Breathe deeply. Shake out your arms and stretch slightly, as if preparing for a difficult task. Bring your feet together and then say to the audience, "I ask only one thing of the three of you. Please remain still during this demonstration. What I'm attempting here requires great concentration on my part."

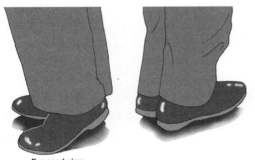

Exposed view

FIGURE 27   FIGURE 28

Bend at the knees and then, as shown in **Figure 27,** slowly lift your right foot off the ground, as your left foot flexes, supporting all of your weight on its ball and toes. From the angle the spectators are viewing the action, it appears as if you are rising up off the ground, as shown in **Figure 28.**

Your work is not done, however. Remain in this levitated position for approximately ten seconds (or less), and then "land" by *quickly* dropping both feet to the ground and spreading them wide apart, as shown in **Figure 29.** Exaggerate your landing as much as possible to overemphasize the fact that you were in the air. Separating your feet makes the landing appear much more haphazard and creates the impression that you were higher in the air than you actually were.

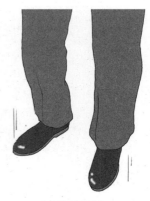

FIGURE 29

ANOTHER WAY TO LIFT OFF: Though the above levitation has much to recommend it (it is an entirely impromptu effect), another way to perform the effect is with a prepared pair of shoes.

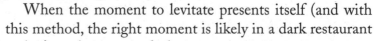

Cut most of the sole out of one shoe in a pair, leaving 2 to 3 inches (5 to 8 cm) intact near the toes, as shown in **Figure 30.** You can now walk (albeit uncomfortably) in the shoes without your foot falling entirely out of the shoe.

When the moment to levitate presents itself (and with this method, the right moment is likely in a dark restaurant or bar), gather a crowd close to you

FIGURE 30

and place your feet together. The closer the crowd, the better.

Slip your foot out of the cut-out shoe and begin to rise up on the ball of your foot, as shown in **Figure 31.** Depending on the strength of your ankle and the amount of time you have devoted to practicing this effect, you should be able to "levitate" several inches off of the ground. Conclude your flight, return to the ground, and replace your foot in the cut-out shoe. The flight has come to an end! ⌇

Exposed view

FIGURE 31

CHAPTER II

CARD MAGIC

PASTEBOARD PRESTIDIGITATION

· ~⚬⚬⚬~ ·

SINCE THE INVENTION OF PLAYING CARDS themselves, people have used them to perform tricks. Card magic is perhaps the most expansive and endlessly fascinating branch of the art of conjuring.

"Hofzinser's dictum rings true for me, even today," Mysterio wrote in the margin of one of the manuscript pages concerning card magic for this book. The comment is a reference to Johann Nepomuk Hofzinser, the great nineteenth-century Viennese conjurer who termed conjuring with cards "the poetry of magic."

It is not the intention of the chapter that follows to give the reader a complete, be-all, end-all course in card magic. A compilation of every move and trick in the canon would require thousands of pages—and, indeed, thousands of books have already been written on the subject.

Instead, working from Mysterio's notes on the subject, these pages offer a succinct overview of card magic. Study and learn the material and you will have an above-average understanding of how card magic works, why it works, and different ways to accomplish effects—not to mention a healthy number of excellent tricks in your repertoire.

Pay particular attention to the different ways in which the same goal—for example, secretly bringing a chosen card to the top of the deck—can be accomplished, and learn them all. Very often, card magic is performed under informal, impromptu circumstances. Having a large arsenal of sleights and techniques to draw on will allow you to adapt to the situation at hand.

The diagram below, a version of which appeared in Mysterio's notebook, provides a map by which a deck of cards can be navigated while learning card sleights, subtleties, and tricks. "Many of the terms I have sketched out are intuitive," Mysterio noted in his characteristic whorled script, "but are not apparent until studied. The student should note the various positions and nomenclature, which will become second nature after only brief consideration."

Hold a deck of cards in your hand as you study the illustration. Note the positions that correspond to each of the terms outlined and familiarize yourself with each one. This will greatly aid you in understanding the tricks, sleights, and moves in the following pages.

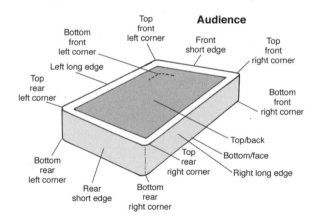

Most of the specialized terms used for card magic will be defined throughout the chapter. The one exception is the "overhand shuffle." This is the shuffle commonly used by magicians, except where a trick specifically calls for something different. In the overhand shuffle, the deck is held by the short edges in the right hand, as shown in **Figure 1**. The left hand is cupped under the deck and the left thumb strips small packets of cards off the top of the deck into the left palm as in **Figure 2**.

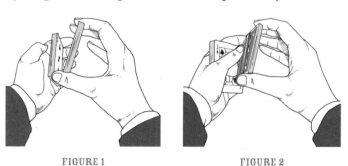

FIGURE 1   FIGURE 2

SELF-WORKING CARD TRICKS

THE TRICKS DESCRIBED IN THIS SECTION require virtually no prior knowledge of cards or card magic. Though prearrangement of some of the cards is required for the effects to operate, many of them require no preparation at all. Follow the directions outlined below, and the magic virtually works itself.

ODD MAN OUT

Don't let the super-simple secret of this trick fool you. Played appropriately, this effect can have a powerful impact.

EFFECT: The deck is divided into two piles, and each one is handed to a separate spectator. Both volunteers are asked to shuffle their cards, select one, and memorize it. Then, "to make the proceedings even more fair," the magician says, "I want you to trade cards, replace each other's cards in your respective halves of the deck, and shuffle your cards thoroughly." The spectators follow instructions, and the magician reassembles the deck. Quickly, he scans the faces of the cards and removes two. They prove to be the spectators' selections!

REQUIRED: A deck of cards.

PREPARATION: Before performing, separate the cards into two piles; one is composed of all of the red cards, the other of all the blacks. Stack one pile on top of the other.

PERFORMANCE: Explain to your spectators that you are about to perform a very fair trick. "There won't be any undue manipulation of the cards on my part." With the faces of the cards toward you, run through them quickly, separating the deck between the red and black packets. Hand one packet to a spectator on your right and the other to a spectator on your left.

Instruct the spectators to shuffle the cards and to remove one—face down. You don't want anyone to know that the deck has been prearranged. After each spectator has noted and remembered his card, have it placed in the *opposite* packet. In other words, a red card is placed in the black half of the deck and the black card in the red half.

Reassemble the deck and scan the faces of the cards quickly, removing the selections when you come to them. Of course, the selected cards will be the only odd-colored cards in their respective groups—the only red card amid the blacks and the only black amid the reds. Set the cards on the table, face down. Dramatically announce the names of the cards on the table and have the spectators turn them over. As your spectators react, casually shuffle the deck, destroying all evidence of your setup.

OTHER ODD BALLS: Some magicians feel that the red and black piles are too obvious a method for this trick. Other prearrangements work too. For example, you could separate the deck into piles of odd and even cards (irrespective of color), and proceed as above. Or the top half of the deck can be composed of clubs and diamonds, while the bottom half is made up of hearts and spades. With these arrangements, the faces of the cards can be casually flashed during the proceedings without fear of detection. Of course, locating the selected cards won't be nearly as easy, but with a modicum of practice, this, too, should become second nature.

FURTHER THAN THAT

This trick is considered by many professional magicians to be one of the finest card tricks ever conceived. It was devised by Canadian magician Stewart James in 1940, and has as powerful an effect today as it did at the time of its conception. Had the effect been invented in Mysterio's lifetime, it would certainly have become part of his regular repertoire of card miracles.

EFFECT: "Magicians need to update their tricks, to stay in tune with the times," the performer says. After that, a card is selected in a "modern" manner.

REQUIRED: A deck of cards.

PREPARATION: A simple stack is placed on top of the deck before you begin. From the top down, the spades and aces are arranged in the following order: 2 3 4 5 6 7 A A A A (spades) 8 9 10 J Q K (**Figure 3**). Follow along with the stacked deck in hand and prepare to be amazed. This trick works itself.

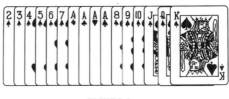

FIGURE 3

PERFORMANCE: The magician says, "I would like to perform for you a streamlined, modern card trick of the future—something entirely unlike the card tricks of the recent past. To start, I would like you to select a card in a new, modern manner. None of this 'pick-a-card' business." The spectator takes the deck in her hands and names *any* number between ten and twenty. For the purpose of this description, assume she names sixteen.

"Perfect. Please count sixteen cards, one at a time, into a face-down pile on the table. Set the balance of the deck aside for now.

"Magicians of yesteryear might ask you to take the top card of the pile, but my version of this effect goes *further than that*. I'm going to have you choose one of those sixteen cards entirely by chance." Have the spectator add together the digits of the number she selected: in this case, 1 + 6 = 7. "The total of the digits is seven. Pick up the packet and count seven cards face down onto the table. Look at and remember the seventh card, and drop it back onto the tabled cards. Then, drop the cards in your hand on top of the tabled cards. When you're done, drop everything back on top of the deck."

Instead of searching the deck and trying to locate the spectator's card, you continue with your story about the "new, streamlined and modern" magic trick in progress. Say, "I'm not going to hunt for your card or resort to sleight-of-hand to find it. This trick goes *further than that*." Hold the deck to your forehead and boldly announce that the card she chose was the ace of spades (you know this because you have forced her to pick the ace—more on this later).

"Not a bad trick," you say. "But I'm going to take it *further than that*. I spell A-C-E, dealing one card off the top of the deck for each letter. In this next pile I deal cards for each of the letters in S-P-A-D-E-S." Turn over the top card of the portion of the deck that's still in your hand to reveal that it is the ace of spades!

The trick, however, is not over. "I can—and will—take things *further than that*," you continue. On turning over the ace pile, the other three aces are revealed. When the spade pile is turned over, all of the cards it contains are spades!

"*Further than that,*" your patter continues, "the spades are in order: two, three, four, five, six, and seven." Display the cards and show this to be the case.

"Believe it or not, this effect is so modern as to go one step *further than that*. Here are the rest of the spades." Deal the next six cards off the top of the deck to reveal the eight, nine, ten, jack, queen, and king of spades, in order.

"I can't go further than that!"

FURTHER INSTRUCTIONS: The ace of spades will *always* be chosen by your spectator, no matter what number she selects at the outset, so long as that number is between ten and twenty. A mathematical principle is at work, and it forces the tenth card from the top of the deck.

Once you master the presentation above and master some of the other techniques described in "Card Sleights and Their Uses" (page 40) and "Shortcuts" (page 53), experiment with ways to apparently shuffle or cut the deck prior to performing Further than That. A crimped card (see "Crimps," page 60) on the bottom of the deck will allow you to cut the cards ad infinitum and later bring the stack back to the top when you're ready to perform.

DOUBLE REVERSE

The magician Paul Rosini headlined America's leading nightclubs and hotels in the 1930s and '40s, just as Mysterio's star began to fade from prominence due to his untimely death. Rosini's charming "Italian" accent (his real name was Paul Vucic) and the intimate nature of his performances made tricks like Double Reverse even more entertaining.

EFFECT: The magician hands half the deck to a spectator. She selects a card from her half, while the magician selects a card from his. The cards are traded, the magician's card being inserted among the spectator's cards and the spectator's among the magician's. Next, the entire deck is reassembled—in a haphazard fashion. Some of the cards are face down and some are face up. "Let's try to make some sense out of this mishmash of cards," the magician says. He spreads the cards in a wide arc on the table and shows that, magically, the entire deck has righted itself—with the exception of two cards. They are, of course, the selections!

REQUIRED: A deck of cards.

PREPARATION: Reverse the bottom (face-out) card of the deck and memorize it. In this case, let's assume it is the jack of spades (**Figure 4**).

FIGURE 4

PERFORMANCE: "Normally, only spectators select a card in a magic show," you say. "Here, let's try something a little bit different." Offer the deck to a spectator and have her cut half of the cards off the top. Ask her to pull out and memorize a card from her half, and tell her you will take one too. As she pulls a card out, you do too, but you *don't* memorize its value or suit. Tell the spectator to show her selected card around, and as she does so, you do one simple but important move.

FIGURE 5

Drop the hand holding the deck to your side and turn it over, as in **Figure 5,** so that the card you previously reversed and memorized (the jack of spades) is now uppermost. As you do this, ask the spectator, "Will you remember the card you picked if you see it again?" Whatever her response, answer appropriately. Then set your "selected" card on the table, face down, and ask her to do the same. "We're going to trade cards," you say.

Pick up her card, and without looking at it, place it face down into your (apparently) face-down half of the deck. "I didn't look at your card, so don't look at mine," you say. "Put it back in your half somewhere, so neither of us knows its location."

Now ask your spectator for *half* of her half of the deck. Take it from her, turn it face up, and place it underneath the cards you're holding. "We're going to mix up the deck in an unusual way," you say. "Let me have the rest of your cards." Take what's left in her hand and place it, face up, on top of the cards in your hand (**Figure 6**). Apparently, the deck has been reassembled in a face-up/face-down/face-up fashion.

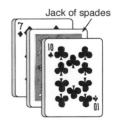

Jack of spades

FIGURE 6

"This is incredible," you say. "I've trained the cards to do back flips. Watch!" As you say this, square the cards in your hand and spread them in a wide arc on the table. The entire deck will be in order, with the exception of two cards (**Figure 7**). Here's where the final deception takes place.

FIGURE 7

"I picked the jack of spades," you say, naming the card you reversed at the outset of the trick. "What card did you select?" The spectator will name her card. "It happens every time I do this. Turn them over and take a look." Of course, when she does, she discovers that her card and the jack of spades are the only two reversed cards in the deck.

FOUR BULLETS THE HARD WAY

The secret of this effect is painfully simple, but the effect on an audience is staggering.

EFFECT: The performer hands out a deck of cards and requests that it be shuffled thoroughly. After the cards are returned, the magician places them in his inner coat pocket and offers to demonstrate his ability to track the location of four important cards in the deck: the aces. Reaching inside his coat, the magician removes, one at a time and in rapid succession, all four aces!

REQUIRED: A deck of cards. You must be wearing a shirt with a breast pocket and a jacket with an inside pocket to perform this effect.

PREPARATION: Remove the four aces from the deck and place them in the breast pocket of your shirt.

PERFORMANCE: The bulk of the work involved in this trick is presentational. Make a spectacle of the effect's difficulty with the appropriate patter: "Some scientists have called this demonstration 'seeing with the fingertips.' Others have labeled my sense of touch unique, and well trained. I prefer the latter explanation. Allow me to demonstrate." Hand out the deck of cards (which lacks the aces) and have it thoroughly shuffled.

"Now that the cards are well mixed, please drop them into my jacket pocket." Here, a spectator confirms that there is nothing else in your inside jacket pocket, and complies with your request.

It is now a simple matter to produce the aces "from the shuffled deck" one at a time. Simply plunge your hand into your jacket pocket (really into the breast pocket of your shirt) and reveal the aces, one at a time.

"Though spectators and scientists have yet to agree on a name for my talent," you say as you produce the last ace, "I have settled on one: sleight-of-hand."

EXTRA WORK, ADDED EFFECT: If, before your performance, you place the aces in your breast pocket in a known order, they can later be produced in any order, or in a sequence decided upon by your audience.

SIMPLICITY FOUR-ACE TRICK

The "Ace Assembly" plot, as this type of trick is known to magicians, is extremely popular, with both conjurers and laymen. This no-sleights, no-frills version was invented by enigmatic Canadian wizard Stewart James.

EFFECT: The magician lays four aces on the table, in a row. Three cards are placed on top of each ace. The piles are gathered up, and dealt out on the table again. "There's an old saying that goes, 'Birds of a feather flock together,'" you say. "Watch this." An ace is removed from the pile containing all of the aces, and switched with an indifferent card—a card that's unimportant to the trick—in another pile. As if that old, tired phrase were composed of magic words, the aces mysteriously assemble in the other pile, following the leader! Everything can be examined.

REQUIRED: A deck of cards.

PREPARATION: None.

PERFORMANCE: Remove the four aces from the deck and lay them on the table in a row, face down. "Allow me to demonstrate a strange principle of sympathy that not many card players have discov-

FIGURE 8

ered," you explain. Deal three cards face down on top of each ace. You now have four piles in front of you, each one made up of four cards, and the bottom-most card of each pile is an ace (**Figure 8**). Place the remainder of the deck to one side.

Gather up the piles, one on top of the other. Say, "Because I've placed three cards on top of each ace, when I redeal the cards in a row, the aces will end up in the fourth pile. Correct?" As you ask this question, deal the top four cards of the packet onto the table in a row, face down. The fourth card is an ace.

Remove the top card of the packet and use it as a pointer, gesturing as you say, "Here are three indifferent cards," tapping the first three cards in the row as you say this, "and the last card is an ace." Use the card in your hand to help you flip over the last card in the row, which is an ace.

As you continue your patter, saying, "So, every fourth card I deal will be an ace…" perform a bold yet sneaky move: Place the pointer card in your hand *underneath* the packet of cards you're holding.

Continue dealing the cards into four piles until there are four in each pile. "What I've discovered," you say, "is that, as the old saying goes, 'Birds of a feather flock together.' This is particularly true of the aces. Let me show you what I mean."

Remove the bottom-most card from the far right packet and turn it face up—this is the ace you showed just moments ago. Also remove the bottom card from the packet second from the right and turn it face up. This will be an indifferent card (the rest of the cards in the packet, however, are aces). "Watch the aces follow their leader." Transpose the position of the two cards, so that the ace is now in the packet second from the right and the indifferent card is underneath the heap on the far right.

Though you've done very little work, you should still play up what is about to happen. "It happens very slowly," you say, as you dramatically gesture at the pile of cards on the right. Slowly turn over the three face-down cards there to reveal, not three aces, but three indifferent cards. Have a spectator turn over the cards in the heap of cards second to the right to discover that the aces have magically assembled there, following their leader as you promised.

MIRASKILL

This card prediction, another brainchild of Canadian magic genius Stewart James, has been canonized by more than one author as one of the greatest card tricks of all time. While not recorded in Mysterio's notebooks (as the effect was first published in 1935), Miraskill is important enough for inclusion in this, his *Encyclopedia*.

EFFECT: The magician and spectator play a game with the red and black cards. The spectator shuffles and deals, precluding any tampering with the cards by the magician. "You will make all of the moves and all of the choices," he instructs, "and yet, I will exert total control over the cards. My prediction is predestined." And it is so—the prestidigitator accurately and infallibly predicts the outcome of the game. He always knows its outcome—who will win, who will lose, and by how much!

REQUIRED: A deck of cards, a slip of paper, and a pencil.

PREPARATION: Hide four black cards in your pocket, and make sure there is no joker in the deck.

PERFORMANCE: Have the deck shuffled, and ask your volunteer to choose one of the colors: red or black. If he selects red, write the following prediction: "You will have four more cards than I." If black is picked, write: "I will have four more cards than you." After folding the slip of paper into quarters, place it on the table.

For this example, assume the spectator selected the red cards. Tell him, "Deal two cards at a time from the top of the deck and turn them face up. If both of the cards are red, put them in a face-up pile in front of you. If both of them are black, put them in a pile in front of me. If the cards are red *and* black, put them in a third pile—a discard pile."

After he has dealt through the entire deck, casually pick up the discard pile as if to get it out of the way. "Count the cards in your pile," you say, "then count the cards in the black pile." As he does this, remove the four black cards from your pocket and quietly add them to the top of the discard group already in your hand.

Next, the spectator opens the slip and reads your prediction. You are correct! "Here… reassemble the deck and shuffle it again," you say as you hand him the discard pile. "I will make another prediction." Again, ask him which color he prefers, then write: "Our piles will be even."

The volunteer goes through the identical procedure a second time and your second prediction proves to be correct!

CARD SLEIGHTS AND THEIR USES

SLEIGHT-OF-HAND WITH CARDS SEEMS DAUNTING. To the uninitiated, phrases like "double lift," "diagonal palm shift," and "Erdnase color change" seem to be written in indecipherable magician-speak.

In Mysterio's notebook, the following sage advice to prospective students is tendered about card sleights: "Do not overwhelm the student with verbiage in order to discourage. No! In fact, the exact opposite should be the teacher's goal: welcome new and earnest students to the fold and lay bare the secrets of the conjuring craft." With that spirit in mind, we turn to sleights with cards.

Matt Schulien was an accomplished magician who hailed from Chicago. He entertained at his family saloon and eatery, Schulien's, performing practical jokes, stunts, and world-class magic. In fact, Matt's magic gave Schulien's an international reputation.

Card tricks were appetizers, main courses, and desserts at Schulien's, and to Matt's way of thinking there were three essential sleight-of-hand moves with cards that should be in every magician's repertoire:

1. **CONTROL:** a means whereby the magician can control the position of a selected card even though, to a spectator, the card has apparently been lost in the deck.
2. **FORCE:** to make a spectator unknowingly select a specific card, even though he believes he has a free choice.
3. **PALM:** a way to hide a card in the magician's hand without anyone knowing it is there.

Though Mysterio and Schulien never met, it is clear from the entries in Mysterio's notebooks that he would have thoroughly approved of the Chicago restaurateur-cum-magician's dictum regarding card sleights. However, there is one more move that Mysterio viewed as essential to any magician working with the pasteboards, namely:

4. **THE DOUBLE LIFT:** a method whereby two cards are lifted off of the deck, yet the audience is aware of only one.

Each of these sleights—and various methods for accomplishing them—will be discussed in this section.

Before methods of card control can be taught, the concept of a break in the deck must be understood.

Assume a card has been selected by a spectator and remembered, and the deck has been separated by the magician. The card is returned to the lower half of the deck, as in **Figure 9,** and the upper half is placed back on top, apparently burying the selection near the center of the deck.

FIGURE 9

To keep control of the selected card, so it can later be located, the magician uses the fleshy pad of his little finger to secure a break above it, as in **Figure 10.** In short, a break is created by sticking a portion of the little finger between the halves of the deck at its rear right corner.

Though few spectators will suspect you are keeping track of a selected card by securing a break above it, be sure that the distance between the halves of the deck is kept to a minimum, and that the front end of the deck is nearly square. With a modicum of practice, both of these goals are easily attained.

FIGURE 10

CONTROLLING A CARD

THE DOUBLE UNDERCUT

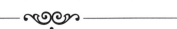

FIGURE 11

This useful sleight will bring a desired card from the top of the deck to the bottom (or vice versa) in the action of apparently cutting the deck. It was invented by Dai Vernon.

With the selected card on top, obtain a break below it with your right thumb, as in **Figure 11.** The left hand cuts off the lower half of the deck and places it on top, the right thumb maintaining its break below the selected card

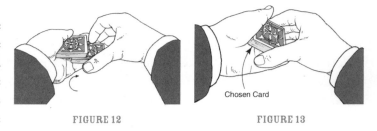

(Figure 12). Now all of the cards *below* the break are cut off by the left hand, and transferred to the top of the deck. The selected card is now on the bottom of the deck, as in **Figure 13.**

FIGURE 12   FIGURE 13

Chosen Card

THE HINDU SHUFFLE CONTROL

In the process of shuffling the cards, a selected card is replaced, yet the magician can control it to the top of the deck using this deceptive technique.

Have a spectator select, note, and remove a card from the deck. Gripping the deck from above in the right hand with your thumb on the left long side and your fingers on the right, approach the deck with your left hand, from underneath, as in **Figure 14.** Strip off a small packet of cards—say five or ten, though the number need not be exact—from the top of the deck into your left hand, which catches them as they clear the deck (**Figure 15**).

Strip off several packets in this manner, adding them to the cards already in your left hand. When approximately half of the cards have been shuffled off into the left hand, ask the spectator to place the selected card on top of the left-hand packet.

When this has been done, again approach the right hand's cards from underneath with your left hand, ostensibly to continue the shuffle. As you strip off the next packet of cards from the top of the right hand's portion, your right thumb and middle finger steal the top card (or cards) of the left hand's packet underneath the right hand's cards. A break should be maintained between the selected card and the cards that remain in the right hand. (See **Figure 16,** which shows the selection being stolen, and the gap between it and the cards that remain in the right hand.)

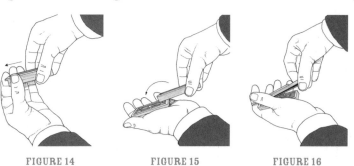

FIGURE 14   FIGURE 15   FIGURE 16

Continue stripping off packets with your left hand until you reach the break, and then set the card or cards that remain in your right hand on top of the left hand's packet. The selected card is now on top of the deck.

According to Mysterio's notes, "this simple control must be practiced until the steal of the selected card looks like nothing more than the continuation of the Hindu shuffle after the spectator's card has been returned to the lower half of the deck."

JOG SHUFFLE CONTROL

This method of controlling a selected card is performed during an apparently fair overhand shuffle of the deck.

Have a spectator select, note, and remove a card from the deck. Then begin shuffling the deck into your left hand via the traditional overhand shuffle.

To use this shuffle to control a selected card, shuffle off approximately half the cards,

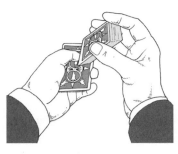

FIGURE 17

then have the spectator place the selection on top of the left hand's portion. Now, instead of shuffling off a packet of cards on top of the spectator's chosen card, shuffle only one card onto it, and jog this card back approximately half an inch, toward the heel of your hand as you do so, as in **Figure 17.** Continue shuffling off the rest of the deck on top of the jogged card. Make a messy job of it so the out-jogged card is not obvious to anyone staring at the deck; cards should be shuffled in a careless manner.

At this point, the deck is held in the left hand, and one card is outjogged from the end of the deck.

Re-grip the deck with your right hand for another overhand shuffle, contacting the face of the outjogged card with the tip of your right thumb. The right thumb presses up on the jogged card, creating a break between it and the cards above it, and the remainder of the deck, as in **Figure 18.**

To complete the control, shuffle off all of the cards above your break, and throw the balance of the deck on top. The spectator's selection is now the top card of the deck.

FIGURE 18

While this maneuver may seem bold ("and it certainly is," according to Mysterio's notes), the practical experience of several modern working professionals, including Tom Mullica and Eddie Tullock, indicates that this method of card control is certainly as effective—and easier to execute—than the standard pass, taught in many conjuring texts (but performed well by very few).

Have a spectator select and note a card, then have him replace it in the middle of the deck. Secure a break above it, as described previously in this chapter. The cards are held in the left hand, in standard dealing position, as this break is held.

Now, in the action of shuffling the cards in the traditional overhand style, the selected card is brought to the top.

Your right hand seizes all the cards above the break, and at the same time, your left hand levers over its half of the deck (with the selected card on top) so that they are perpendicular to the floor. See **Figure 19,** which shows the position of the left hand's cards, and the right's cards above it, in preparation for the shuffle.

FIGURE 19

The right hand's cards are now rapidly shuffled off onto the *face* of the left hand's packet. In other words, the cards that formerly buried the selection in the center of the deck are now being added to what was, moments before, the *bottom* of the deck. **Figure 20** shows the shuffle in action, the left thumb repeatedly pulling off small batches of cards from the right hand's packet, and indicates the position of the selected card.

At the conclusion of this shuffle, the selected card will be on top of the deck.

FIGURE 20

THE FLEXIBLE SWITCHOUT

Invented for other purposes by Chicago card technician Edward Marlo, this easy sleight can be used to control a card in an apparently fair manner. In the act of showing a selected card to a spectator or group "one last time," you secretly add another card on top of it, allowing you to control the selection's position in the deck.

Have a spectator remove and note a card from the deck. Now spread the cards between your hands in a slightly fanned position, and remove the upper half of the deck from the lower half. Be certain that the cards are spread so that the upper cards are to the right and the lower ones are to the left. Have the spectator return his selection to the top of the lower half of the deck, as in **Figure 21.**

FIGURE 21

Say something like, "I don't want you to forget the identity of your card—and I don't want anyone else to forget it either. So I'll give you one last look." This justifies the actions that are about to take place.

Thumb the selection to the right, and grip it from below with the fingers of the right hand, which pulls it underneath the cards the right hand holds. Raise this portion of the deck to the eye level of your audience, as in **Figure 22.** The selected card will be staring at them, as it is now the lowermost card of this group.

FIGURE 22

Bring your right hand and its cards up toward the left hand's packet, to re-take the selected card. However, as the hands come together, use your left thumb to take two cards instead of one, as in **Figure 23.** This steal of two cards takes place with the deck at an angle to the spectators, and the fact that a second card is taken on top of the selection is virtually impossible to perceive.

FIGURE 23

Continue lowering your hands, and as you do, push over the top card of the left hand's portion of the deck with your left thumb. Insert this card—apparently the selection—anywhere in the right hand's packet, as in **Figure 24.** Place the left hand's packet on top of the right hand's cards. The selection is now on top.

FIGURE 24

FORCING A CARD

CROSS CUT FORCE

Even though this is one of the easiest of all card forces, it is still effective. It is used to force the top card of the deck.

Discreetly note the card on top of the deck. This is the force card. Now invite an audience member to cut the cards. Complete the cut yourself by placing the lower portion of the deck onto the cut-off portion, forming a cross, as in **Figure 25.** "Let's mark the spot you cut to," you say, as you form the cross.

FIGURE 25

All that remains is for the spectator to look at the "spot they cut to." The card they are actually looking at, of course, is the original top card of the deck. Before telling them to look at the card, however, it's necessary to kill a moment or two, thereby allowing the audience to forget what has just happened. After you have pattered about the spectator's "random" selection or simply complimented his haircut, refocus all attention on the cards and have the force removed from beneath the upper portion of the cross, and noted by your spectator. Unbeknownst to him, you already know the selected card's identity.

PSEUDO-HINDU SHUFFLE FORCE

FIGURE 26

This technique forces the spectator to select the bottom card of the deck, and in some ways imitates the mechanics of the venerable Hindu shuffle.

Discreetly note the card on the bottom of the deck. Hold the deck in the right hand at one short end, so the long edges of the cards are parallel with the edge of the table. With the left fingers, strip off a small packet of cards (five or seven) from the top of the deck, as in **Figure 26,** and drop it onto the table. Repeat this action, which shuffles the deck, yet retains the position of the bottom card.

As you strip off the packets, ask the spectator to call out "Stop!" at any point during the shuffle. When she does, raise your right hand, flashing the bottom-most card to her. "Remember the card you stopped me at," you say as you drop the right hand's cards on top of those already on the table. You have just forced the bottom card on her.

If the spectator does not stop you before the cards in your right hand are exhausted, simply slip the last packet of cards in the right hand (the packet containing your force card) under the cards already on the table, and repeat the shuffle until you are able to successfully execute the force.

According to Mysterio's notes on this force, "it is a simple matter, in the course of shuffling a deck, to glimpse the bottom or top card, thus preparing you for the force."

RIFFLE FORCE

As the magician riffles down the edge of the deck, a spectator calls out "Stop!" Even though the spectator stops at an apparently random location, the performer is able to force a specific card on her.

Note the card on top of the deck. The mechanics of this force are as follows: Cut the top card (your known force card) into the center of the deck and hold a break above it. The cards should be in the left-hand dealing position. With the second and third fingers of your right hand, riffle through the deck from bottom to top. Say, "I'm going to run through the cards again. Next time, call out 'Stop!' any time you like."

On the next riffle, when the spectator stops you, do so. All the while, however, your break has been maintained above the force card. No matter where the spectator stops you, what happens next is simple: Look up at the spectator and ask her a question (such as "How's that?" or "That seemed fair, didn't it?") as you lift off the cards above the break.

Asking a question directs attention away from the cards and the sleight. To mask the deception further, it is advisable to lift the cards off the deck at an angle that blocks the spectator's view of the spot they stopped you at.

SLIP FORCE

Note the card on top of the deck. The force card starts on top of the deck, which is in the left-hand dealing position. With the first finger underneath the deck and the thumb on the outer left corner, riffle down the edge of the deck once with your right hand. On your second riffle, tell the spectator to call out "Stop!" at any point.

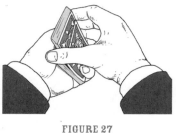

FIGURE 27

When he stops you, your right second finger grasps the outer short edge of the deck and the thumb grabs the inner short edge. The left third and fourth fingers apply pressure to the top (force) card of the deck as the right hand draws the top half of the deck away, as shown in **Figure 27.** This allows the top card of the deck to be slipped onto the bottom half of the deck, so that the force card is now on top of the packet in your left hand. This move is covered by the following action.

As the top half is drawn away (to the right), both hands turn over, exposing the bottom card of the deck and the face card of those now in the right hand. When the hands turn over, the left first finger points to the bottom card of the top half. You comment, "This is the card you could have stopped me at, but didn't." You then turn your hands back over and offer the top card of the portion of the deck in your left hand to the spectator. This, of course, is the force card that you have slipped from the top of the deck to the point at which they stopped you.

This method can be used to force a small number of cards stacked on top of the deck in quick succession. After forcing the first card, replace the right hand's portion of the deck on top of the left hand's portion and repeat the force as described.

PALMING A CARD

Dozens, if not hundreds of methods of palming cards exist. Cards can be palmed from the bottom of the deck, the center, or the top and concealed in myriad ways. Three basic methods of palming from the top of the deck are taught here. "Lulu Hearst once complained to me that her hands were simply too small to conceal a card," wrote Mysterio. "However, in the case of Max Malini, whose hands were tinier than most mystifiers I knew, size was never an issue. It always seemed to me that the cards were bigger than Malini's palms. But that never kept him from using palming to great advantage."

PALMING POINTERS

1. **ACT NATURAL.** Though a card is concealed in your hand, the "guilty" hand should never look guilty. Curl the fingers around the concealed pasteboard naturally, as if

the hand contained nothing. If the performer believes his hand is empty, there is a much better chance that his audience will believe it to be empty too.

2. **ALLOW THE THUMB TO HANG LOOSELY.** When palming, the thumb should never jut straight out from the hand as if you are hitchhiking. The jutting hitchhiker's thumb serves as a warning sign—a flag, of sorts—for the observant spectator. It says, "Look here! Here I am! The card!"

3. **PALMED CARDS ARE NOT HELD IN PLACE BY THE ENTIRE HAND.** When palming, the concealed card should only contact the hand in two spots; at the base of the thumb, and the pad of the little finger, as in **Figure 28.**

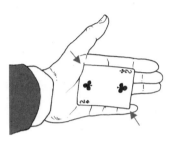

FIGURE 28

BASIC TOP PALM

To execute this sleight, hold the cards in the left hand with the thumb on the left side, the middle, third, and little fingers at the right, and the index finger curled gently

underneath. With the right fingertips, upjog the top card approximately ¼ inch (²/₃ cm), as in **Figure 29.**

The right hand will now press down on the upjogged card and lever it into the palm of the hand. Contact the left edge of the card with the second joint of the right index finger, and its right edge with the first joint of the pinky finger. With minimal downward pressure from the right hand, the card will spring into the right hand.

FIGURE 29

CLASSIC TOP PALM

The deck is held in the left hand, in dealing position. The right hand comes over the deck, nearly screening the top of the cards from view, fingers at the front edge and thumb at the rear. As it does, the left thumb pushes the top card to the right approximately ½ inch (1³/₄ cm). From beneath, the left ring finger, assisted by the middle finger, contacts the top

FIGURE 30

card and pushes it gently into the waiting right palm, as in **Figure 30.** The left thumb, from above, assists in guiding the card into the proper position in the right hand. The right hand, holding the palm card, now drops to the side.

THE DOUBLE LIFT

In the world of sleight-of-hand, the double lift is a more recent development than the palm or the force. First introduced to the magic fraternity in the early twentieth century, its invention opened an entirely new world of possibilities to the clever card conjurer. Previously unimagined avenues for controlling, changing, and switching cards were developed with this indispensable sleight-of-hand tool.

BASIC DOUBLE LIFT

Hold the cards in dealing position in the left hand. Prior to performing the lift, use the pad of your right thumb to riffle up the back of the deck until only two cards remain above it, as in **Figure 31.** The left little finger then holds a break below these two cards.

When the moment arrives to show both cards together as one, the right hand approaches the top of the deck from above. The thumb grasps the cards at the rear, and the middle finger contacts them at the front, as in **Figure 32.** The right hand lifts these cards up and away from the deck and shows them to the spectators, as in **Figure 33.** The cards are then replaced or dropped back on top of the deck.

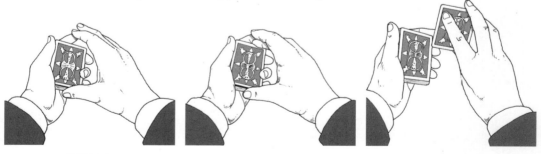

FIGURE 31   FIGURE 32   FIGURE 33

FIGURE 34

ANOTHER BREAK: Instead of using the right thumb to riffle up the back of the deck to obtain the break, the following method is far more elegant and subtle.

With the deck in left-hand dealing position, the left thumb pushes the top two cards of the deck to the right approximately ½ inch (1¾ cm), as shown in **Figure 34.** The left little finger is then inserted underneath the second card, in preparation for holding the break. To complete the move, pull back on the top two cards with the left thumb so that they are again square with the top of the deck, as in **Figure 35.** The break is now held by the little finger.

FIGURE 35

DOUBLE TURNOVER

This is a much more casual, professional, and convincing method for showing the top two cards of the deck together as one.

With a break held by the left little finger below the top two cards of the deck, the right index finger contacts the center of the long side of the top two cards and gently flips them over onto the top of the deck, as one card, as shown in **Figures 36 and 37.** As the cards fall, they naturally line up with the top of the deck and the left little finger has every opportunity to maintain a break under them, as shown in **Figure 38.** The move can now be repeated to turn the cards face down again.

FIGURE 36

FIGURE 37

FIGURE 38

QUICK DOUBLE TRICK

According to Mysterio's notebook, "This startling card revelation may be quickly described, but produces untold levels of astonishment when performed."

EFFECT: The magician attempts to reveal a spectator's selected card. "It's this one, right?" he says as he turns the top card of the deck over. Sadly, the performer has missed the mark, and the spectator tells him so. The card is set on the table and the problem is fixed by magic—the wrong card becomes the right card in the blink of an eye!

REQUIRED: A deck of cards and mastery of one form of card control.

PREPARATION: None.

PERFORMANCE: Have a card selected, noted, and returned to the deck. Control it to the top with any one of the methods described in this chapter (the overhand shuffle control works well for this effect), then make the following statement as grandly as you can: "Your selection, believe it or not, has been controlled, through my masterful handling of the cards, to the top of the deck!"

Perform the double turnover described above and proudly point to the face-up card on "top" of the deck. The spectator will, eventually, point out that this is not the right card.

Look embarrassed as you turn the card (in reality, two cards) back over. Place the true top card of the deck onto the table (or into the spectator's hand, if you're feeling daring) and say, "I must have missed a riffle or some such thing. I apologize for the oversight. Let me try a magic spell."

Utter the appropriate incantation over the card, ask the spectator to name his selection, then turn it over. The card has changed into the selection!

· SHORTCUTS: ·
GIMMICKS, GAFFS, AND SUBTLETIES

WHILE THERE IS A CERTAIN SATISFACTION derived from performing self-working tricks and those that rely on clever sleight-of-hand, there is perhaps more satisfaction derived from the unsuspected use of the shortcuts about to be described. In fact, the various tactics and subtleties you will learn in this section were selected by Mr. Mysterio for their clandestine yet utilitarian nature. Properly employed, they can make your card magic cleaner and more impossible-seeming than you ever imagined.

THE KEY CARD

This principle is an effective method for secretly discovering the identity of a chosen card.

The basic concept is that a known card—a "key card" on the top or bottom of the deck, for example—can be placed next to an unknown card. Later, when looking through the deck, the card next to the key will be the previously unknown (selected) card.

A good way to understand the use of the key card principle is through the following trick.

THE NEXT CARD I TURN OVER...

The key card principle is put to work in a simple trick that makes it look like the magician is in trouble.

EFFECT: A card is chosen and returned to the deck, which is cut several times by the spectator. The magician deals cards face up, telling the spectator not to give away the location of his selection. Apparently unbeknownst to the performer, the selected card is passed by. Apparently frustrated, the magician makes an announcement to the spectator, "The next card I turn over will, without a doubt, be your selection!" It looks like the magician is about to make a wrong move when, instead of turning over the next card in the deck, he dips down into the discard pile, picks up the selected card, and triumphantly turns it over!

REQUIRED: A deck of cards.

PREPARATION: None.

PERFORMANCE: Shuffle the deck and, when you're done, secretly note the bottom card. You can also sneak a glimpse at the bottom card while casually talking to your spectators. This will be your key card.

Have a card selected and noted by a spectator, and ask her to return it to the top of the deck. Then say, "Bury your card in the middle of the deck by cutting the cards." When the cut is complete and the bottom half of the deck is placed on the top half, your key card—let's assume it is the five of spades in this case—will be placed directly on top of the selected card.

The deck can now be cut (though not shuffled, since you need the key card to remain on top of the selection) as many times as you like, "to mix the cards well," you say.

Once the spectator is satisfied that the cards have been mixed, begin dealing from the top, so the cards land in a face-up pile on the table. Look for your key card, the five of spades. The *next* card you deal will be the spectator's selection. Deal past it five or ten cards, and then pause. Say, "This isn't easy, but I think I've got it." Grasp the top card of the deck with your dealing hand and say, "I bet the next card I turn over will be yours. Hard to believe, isn't it?" Undoubtedly, since you have already passed her card, the spectator will agree that it *is* hard to believe.

To conclude the trick successfully, replace the card you were about to turn over and, instead, search through the pile of discards already on the table. Turn the selected card—the card on top of the five of spades—face down. Smile as you say, "I didn't say *where* the card would be turned over, did I?"

DO AS I DO

This is a classic piece of card magic—a demonstration of magical sympathy between two decks of cards.

EFFECT: The magician and a spectator each shuffle a deck of cards thoroughly, and each selects a card from the center of the deck. "I don't want the mixing to end here," the performer says. The cards are cut and the selections are lost in each deck. When the magician and spectator trade decks, and find their own cards, they discover that they both selected the same one!

REQUIRED: Two decks of cards.

PREPARATION: None.

PERFORMANCE: The mixing and selection of each of the decks is legitimate. Instruct a spectator to follow your actions exactly. When you shuffle, he shuffles. When you cut, he cuts. And when you select a card, he selects one too.

"Whatever I do, you imitate exactly," you say. "If you're not able to follow my exact actions with the deck, the trick won't work." Great fun can be had by performing non-sensical actions with the cards that the spectator believes he has to imitate. Have fun with this, but don't make him look foolish in the process.

Trade decks with the spectator several times during the shuffling procedure, saying, "You can shuffle my cards and I can shuffle yours. That way we keep each other honest." When you hand a deck back to the spectator, note the bottom card of the deck and then tell him to select a card from the center, memorize it (but without revealing it to you or anyone else), and place it on top. Tell him to then cut the cards. This places your key card on top of his selection. Do the same with the deck in your hand. Do *not* memorize the card you've selected.

Trade decks with the spectator again and spread them out face up in front of you. Tell the spectator to do the same, and explain: "I'm going to locate the card I selected in this deck. You look for the card you selected among the other deck."

Instead of looking for the card you selected (which you've forgotten), seek out the key card you memorized earlier. The card to its right will be the spectator's selection. When you have found this card, place it on the table face down. "Here's mine," you say.

"When you've found yours, place it here, next to mine." When the two cards are on the table, have the spectator name his selection out loud. "Funny," you say, "it must have something to do with the fact that we both were doing the same thing at the same time. I picked the same card you did!" Turn over the cards on the table to show that they match perfectly.

THE SHORT CARD

There are countless subtle ways to make one card in a deck stand out from the rest. The concept of making one card minutely shorter than the others is very old, and very useful in helping the conjurer locate a selected card in a very straightforward and fair manner. There are several ways of "shorting" a card. Here are three methods. In his notebooks, Mr. Mysterio outlined the corner short (the second method described) as his favorite sleight-free method of card control.

BASIC SHORT CARD

The short card concept is self-explanatory. One card in the deck is shorter than the others, which allows the prestidigitator to locate it by riffling down the edge of the deck. To make a short card, carefully trim off $^1/_{16}$ inch ($^1/_4$ cm) from one of the short ends of a card in your deck. Then, with a nail clipper or fine pair of scissors, re-round the corners of the card so that it looks ordinary. See **Figure 39.**

FIGURE 39

CORNER SHORT

Many professional magicians, including the late S. Leo Horowitz (whose *nom de theatre* was Mohammed Bey), preferred to shorten only the corner of a card, as opposed to the entire short edge. Using a nail clipper, a fine piece of a card's corner can be trimmed off, thus turning it into a short card. See **Figure 40.** Nail clippers are,

FIGURE 40

needless to say, easy to carry, and can therefore be put to use at a moment's notice, turning even a card from a borrowed deck into a short card. "Many a time, when performing at a private function, I would excuse myself from the company prior to my performance, and, having stolen a card from the host's deck, would retire to the powder room where it could be quickly transformed into a corner short," Mysterio wrote. "It was then a simple matter to reintroduce the card to the deck in the midst of a performance with the audience none the wiser."

VERNON'S SHORT CARD

Dai Vernon preferred to trim a small concave piece from each end of a card to create a very subtle short card. See **Figure 41,** which shows an exaggerated view of the cut. In Vernon's published work, this cut was described as being no thicker than a "coarse hair."

FIGURE 41

EYE-SPY SHORT LOCATION

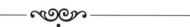

This effect gives the beginning student a simple yet effective use (other than card control) for a short card.

EFFECT: A card is selected, noted, and returned to the deck, which is mixed. "Indulge me, if you will, in a character-reading experiment," the magician says. The performer studies the face of the spectator who, moments ago, selected and memorized the card. Then, in the action of riffling through the deck, the performer, staring into the eyes of the audience volunteer, is able to stop directly at the selected card!

REQUIRED: A deck that contains a short card.

PREPARATION: Begin with the short card on top of the deck.

PERFORMANCE: Have a card—any card but the short card—selected. Tell the spectator who chose it, "Concentrate on it intently. Stare at the card, and burn it into your memory. Stare at the card for a minimum of fifteen seconds. As you do, I will observe the dilation of your pupils, the actions of your eyes, and the way your brow furrows. Concentrate on the card."

The spectator does so, and finally averts her gaze from the card, which is placed on top of the deck (and, incidentally, on top of the short card). The deck is now cut as many times as you like, ostensibly "losing" the selection amid the rest of the deck.

"I will now attempt a difficult feat—a trick based solely on my powers of observation and my ability to read your face. As I riffle through the deck, I will attempt to determine, by reading your reaction to what you see, the location of your card."

Hold the deck high in your left hand, and with your right fingertips riffle through it from face to back, at the upper right corner, as in **Figure 42.** Stop the riffle at the short card (an easy matter, since you will feel a noticeable "click" when you arrive at this card). Outjog the card above it, which is the selected card!

FIGURE 42

THE MISSING CARD

Paul Rosini was an accomplished and entertaining magician who specialized in close-up and parlor magic. This trick was a highlight of his intimate performances.

EFFECT: A spectator removes a group of cards from the center of the deck, notes the bottom-most card of the bunch, and drops the packet back on top of the deck. He then gives the cards several cuts. The performer places the deck behind his back. "Astoundingly," the magician states, "even though I cannot see the deck, I can still work miracles. Observe!" The deck is brought back into view. When searched, the selected card is missing. The performer removes it from the inside breast pocket of his jacket.

REQUIRED: A deck that contains a corner short card.

PREPARATION: Begin with the corner short on top of the deck.

PERFORMANCE: As outlined in the description of the effect above, instruct a spectator to remove a batch of cards from the center of the deck, note the bottom-most card of the group, and drop the packet back on top of the deck. "You can then cut the cards to further lose your selection in the deck," you tell him. The selected card is now on top of the corner short, and no amount of cutting will separate the two cards.

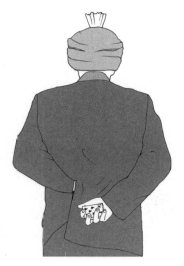

Take the cards back from your volunteer and place them behind your back. "I can still perform miracles, even with both hands behind my back!" Riffle down the edge of the deck to the corner short and cut it to the top of the deck. This brings the selection to the bottom of the deck. Pull the selected card into your left hand and bring the deck forward with your right hand, offering it to a spectator and asking him directly, "What card did you select?"

As he looks at you to answer the question, reach up and under the back of your jacket with your left hand and shove the selected card into your right armpit, as in **Figure 43**. A modicum of practice will be required to perform this maneuver deceptively, but it is not as hard as it may appear on first read-through.

FIGURE 43

When the spectator answers your question, ask him another: "How's that possible? That card is not in the deck!" Prove the veracity of your statement by having the cards examined. The selection is gone.

To successfully conclude the experiment, dive into your coat with your left hand and simulate the action of removing the card from your inner breast pocket. Of course, you simply reach into your armpit and remove the card that was loaded there only moments before.

BAKER'S VERSION: Al Baker used the same method of stealing a card from the deck and loading it into his inner breast pocket, but with one important twist. The selected card, which Baker often had the selectee sign on its face, was reproduced not only from the magician's inner breast pocket, but from his wallet! "Mr. Baker's performance at the Hotel McAlpin left me speechless," Mysterio wrote in a letter to a confidant on May 15, 1929. "There are dozens of ways to spirit a selected pasteboard from the deck, but to have it appear in the performer's billfold was a masterful touch! I begin work on my own version of the effect tomorrow."

CRIMPS

To crimp a card is to bend it or dog-ear it in some subtle fashion so that it can be easily located no matter where in the deck it lies. Even after a spectator has shuffled the cards, a crimped card can be cut to by sense of touch alone. This makes the crimp a powerful secret tool with which a selected card can be located or controlled to the top or bottom of the deck.

BASIC CRIMP

The most basic crimp is a bent corner. See **Figure 44** for an example of how this looks (the bend has been exaggerated for clarity) and **Figure 45** for an example of how this crimped card looks when shuffled into the deck at random. By cutting at the crimp, it is easy to bring either it, or the cards above or below it, to the top or the bottom of the deck.

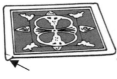

FIGURE 44

FIGURE 45

RIDGED CARD CRIMP

Instead of dog-earing a card, this method of preparing a card, which is essentially a form of crimping, is much more discreet.

Prepare a card from the deck by placing a coin on the table and pressing the face-down card onto it, creating an impression of the coin on the face of the card, as shown in **Figure 46.** This creates a subtle locator card. A card placed on top of the crimp can be cut to without looking at the deck.

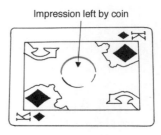

Impression left by coin

FIGURE 46

Remove a card from the deck and set it aside. Shuffle the cards thoroughly, then set the deck face down on the table. Pick up the deck from its ends with the right hand (from above) and with a light touch, allow the cards to drop as a block from the hands at the natural break created by the crimped card. Incredibly, the cards will always break at the same spot—at the crimp. Place the card you set aside on top of the lower portion of the deck and then replace the balance of the cards on top of it. Now whenever you cut the deck, you will cut directly to the selected card, which can then be brought to the top or bottom of the deck as you see fit.

CUTTING TO THE QUEENS

EFFECT: The magician loses the four queens in the deck and then explains that he can find them again with his highly trained fingers. "I can tell where the ladies lie based on sense of touch alone," he explains. True to his word, the magician quickly and effortlessly cuts directly to all four queens, even though they have been lost in the deck.

REQUIRED: A deck of cards.

PREPARATION: Before performing, crimp one of the cards in the deck.

PERFORMANCE: Remove the four queens from the deck and display them to the audience. Shuffle the deck thoroughly as you explain that the queens are four of the most powerful cards in the deck, and also the easiest to locate by sense of touch.

As you patter, cut the crimp card to the top of the deck and then replace the queens, face down, on top of it. Cut the deck to apparently lose the queens in the center.

"I've trained my fingers to find the queens based on weight alone," you say. "Just don't tell the ladies that's how I know which of the cards they are. No woman likes a man to know how much she weighs."

Locate the queens by cutting directly to the crimped card. Be sure not to reveal the fact that directly next to each queen are her sisters. To do this, hold the deck in your left hand. With your right hand, cut to the crimp, then display the bottom, face-out card of the portion of the deck that's in your right hand. Turn the hand palm down again and deal the queen just displayed to the table, effectively shielding the spectators' view of the bottom of the cut-off packet.

Cut the cards several more times, then cut to another queen. "The color of ink on the cards does not matter," you explain as you cut to both red and black queens with relative ease. Continue the apparent mixing of the cards and cutting to the queens until you have revealed all four.

If you are feeling daring, you can allow a spectator to cut to the last queen. Because of the presence of the crimped card, if the spectator cuts the deck from the ends as you have, he is almost certain to cut directly to the card you desire him to! Alternatively, you could cut to the first queen as an example to your spectators and then have three different individuals cut to the queens in turn.

ADVANCED HANDLING: Instead of placing the queens on top of the deck and cutting them to the center, try placing them in the center of the deck one at a time. Make sure the crimped card is somewhere near the center of the deck. Cut to it and place the first queen on top of it. Then mix the cards again (cutting them) and repeat this procedure of cutting to the crimp, placing a queen on top, and assembling the deck again. Once the queens have apparently been lost in the deck, go into the routine as described above.

SPECIALLY PRINTED CARDS

A host of specially printed cards have been devised for magical purposes. Among these are the creations of Theodore Deland, Jr. (the most famous printer and inventor of special cards for magicians who made his reputation during Mysterio's early years on the boards, in the mid- and late teens). Prior to Deland, J. N. Hofzinser devised many of the standard trick cards still in use today. These include double-backed cards, which can be the same color on both sides, or contrasting colors, which can allow for a number of fascinating effects. Double-face cards, which are most often printed with different cards on either side, though occasionally are produced for other tricks that require the same card on each face. Blank-face, blank-back, and blank-both-sides cards have been used by magicians for years to perform effects in which cards are magically printed or erased on one or both sides.

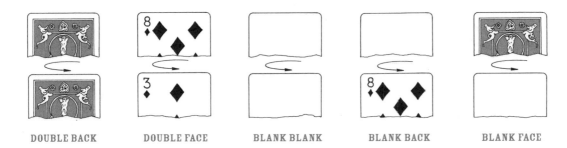

DOUBLE BACK   DOUBLE FACE   BLANK BLANK   BLANK BACK   BLANK FACE

Mr. Mysterio himself created his own set of specially printed cards, which, in addition to the ones mentioned above, included unusual specimens like the trap-door jack, which had a small flap in the middle, and the death-defying ace of clubs, which had a ragged hole in its center that looked as if it might have been made by a bullet.

While all of these specially printed cards can be purchased from emporiums that sell supplies for magicians, in the case of double-back and double-face cards, it is a simple matter to make up the requisite cards from a matching deck and a pot of rubber cement.

HANDS-OFF TRANSPOSITION

This effect uses a double-face card to great advantage.

EFFECT: "This trick happens under test conditions," the magician says. He shows two cards, one a face card and the other a spot card. Even though one card is placed in a spectator's pocket and the other is placed in the magician's pocket, they transpose locations in the blink of an eye.

REQUIRED: One regular court card, one regular spot card, one double-faced card that matches the regular cards, and the deck from which the regular cards were removed. In this example, the two regular cards will be the five of spades and jack of hearts.

PREPARATION: Place the double-face card in your pocket.

PERFORMANCE: The five of spades and jack of hearts are removed from the deck and placed in a willing spectator's pocket.

Reaching into the spectator's pocket, the performer removes a card. Assuming it is the five of spades, the magician shows it to the spectator and says, "If I place this card in my pocket, what does that leave in yours?" Undoubtedly, the spectator will answer, "The jack of hearts." Have him remove the card and make sure. At this point, the regular five of spades is in your pocket, and the regular jack of hearts is in the spectator's pocket.

"Let's try it again—in your pocket, so there's no funny business." Remove the double-face card from your pocket with the five of spades showing, and place it in the spectator's pocket (which holds the regular jack of hearts already).

"Look—my hands are empty." Reaching into the spectator's pocket again, you remove the double-face card, this time showing the jack of hearts, then put it in your pocket. "What card does that leave in your pocket?" you ask. The spectator will say, "The five of spades."

Have the spectator remove his card—which is in fact the jack of hearts—as you remove the ordinary five of spades from your pocket, saying, "I'm as confused as you are. I could have sworn it was the other way around!"

DOUBLE-BACKER BEHIND THE BACK

This card location happens—for the most part—in the spectator's hands. "When a spectator is convinced he 'has the power,'" Mysterio said, "the effect is heightened twenty-fold."

EFFECT: The magician and a spectator each select a card at random by placing cards behind their backs and choosing one. The spectator then reverses the magician's selected card and places it, face up, anywhere in the center of the deck. The spectator does this with the cards behind his back. Even so, he places the magician's selection directly above his own!

REQUIRED: A deck of cards and a matching double-back card.

PREPARATION: Place the double-back card under your belt, behind your back.

PERFORMANCE: Have the deck shuffled by a spectator, then ask him to hand you half of the cards. After he has done so, tell him to do as you do. Place your cards behind your back and say, "Remove one random card, note its identity, and then replace it on top of the cards behind your back." You do this, and show him the face of the card you remove, but instead of returning it to the top of your cards, you place it face up on the *bottom* of your portion, and add the double-backed card to the *top* of your cards.

"Now let's reassemble the deck." You both bring your cards forward, and his portion is placed underneath yours, burying his selected card somewhere in the center of the deck. "You don't know where it is, do you? Even so, you're going to find it. Here's how."

Tell him to place the deck behind his back and to turn *your* selection, "which is on top of the deck," face up, and then place it anywhere in the center of the deck.

If your instructions are followed explicitly, the double-backed card will be the card turned over and placed in the center of the deck. Your card is already face up, on top of the spectator's selection. Have the cards spread on the table, face down. One card—your selection—will be face up. The card next to it is the spectator's chosen card.

SKILLED CARD TRICKS

Now that you've mastered the skills of a pasteboard prestidigitator, put them to use in the tricks that follow.

THE TRIPLE-SPELLER

This effect puts the power in the hands of the spectator, which always heightens the climax of a magic trick.

EFFECT: A card is selected, remembered, and lost in the deck. "Fair though everything may have seemed up to this point," the magician states, "I already know the identity of your card." Spelling out the name of a card (not the spectator's selection), while dealing one card to the table for each letter in the card's name, the magician produces the named card on the last letter of the deal! The magician spells out another card in the same fashion, dealing one card to the table for each letter in its name. At the conclusion of this spelling, the second card is shown—and proves to be the second named card. "Here, you try," the magician says. He hands the card to the spectator, who spells out the name of his selection. Lo and behold, the card dealt down on the last letter is none other than that which was previously selected.

REQUIRED: A deck of cards, which may be borrowed.

PREPARATION: None.

PERFORMANCE: Begin by forcing a spectator to choose a card known to you. For this example, let's say the forced selection is the six of hearts. Since the card is known to you, the deck can be shuffled after the selection is returned to the deck.

"Cards can be made to do surprising things," you say, as you fan through the face-up deck. "Let me find a few likely candidates." When you spot the six of hearts, cut the cards, bringing it near the face of the deck. If you are adept at card control, this step can be eliminated by controlling the card to a position near the face of the deck.

Briefly place the cards under the table (or behind your back or in your pocket, if standing) and say, "Just now, when I placed the cards under the table, you may think I did something sneaky. Maybe your card is no longer in the deck. Let's take a look, just to be sure. If you see it, don't say anything. I don't want to know your card's identity."

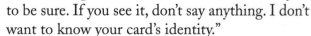

Chosen card

FIGURE 47

Spread the cards left to right, face up. When you reach the six of hearts, begin silently counting from right to left, one card for each letter in the name of the selection (S-I-X-O-F-H-E-A-R-T-S). The first card in your count will be the six of hearts itself. See **Figure 47.**

When you reach the end of the selection's name, begin the counting/spelling process again, starting with the next card in the spread, and spelling out its name. Repeat this process one more time, so that you have spelled out three cards in a row, the first of which is the spectator's selected card. When you reach the last letter of the last card, cut the remaining cards from the top of the deck to the bottom.

Turn the deck face down as you ask, "Did you see your card in there? I didn't do anything suspicious, I promise. Let's get back to what I was saying about cards doing surprising things."

Call out the name of the last card you spelled out—let's say it's the nine of hearts. Deal down one card to the table for each letter, spelling out N-I-N-E-O-F-H-E-A-R-T-S. Turn over the card dealt on the letter "S." It is the nine of hearts!

"Let's try it again," you say. Now spell out the second card (in our example, the six of diamonds). The six makes its appearance as you say the last letter.

"Now you try," you say, handing the cards to the person who selected the ace of clubs at the outset of the trick. "Deal down one card for each letter in the name of your selection, and turn over the last card." He does so, and finds the six of hearts!

THE ALLERTON VERSION: Chicago magician Bert Allerton performed a variant of the spelling trick with a more startling climax. He called it Surprise Spelling.

A spectator chooses and notes a card. It is returned and brought to the position second from the top of the deck (this can be done with a quick overhand shuffle, or by adding a single card on top of the selection prior to the control).

The top card is then turned over and shown to the audience. As it is displayed, a break is secured under the top card (in other words, under the selection). The face-up card is then dropped on top of the deck, and the top two cards are re-gripped by the right hand, with the fingers at the front short edge and the thumb at the inner end. Lift these two cards from the top of the deck slightly, and then turn the entire deck face up. Place the deck proper on top of the double card, as in **Figure 48.** The selection is now face down on the bottom of an otherwise face-up deck of cards.

FIGURE 48

It is now an easy matter to glimpse the selection in the act of squaring up the deck. Then the spelling procedure begins as the magician "looks for" the selection, asking his audience if the selection is anywhere to be found. They will not see it, since it is on top of the deck and reversed. The spelling begins at the face of the deck, with the name of the selected card, one card being counted off for each letter. The card next in the spread is noted, and its name is spelled out in the same manner as previously described. At the conclusion of the count the cards are cut, bringing the batch of counted-off cards to the top of the deck.

Now the magician announces the name of the second card, and spells it out, producing it as the last letter is called off. The cards are next handed to the spectator, who spells out the name of his selection. On the last letter of the deal, he will find the selected card staring him in the face, face up in the deck!

DEUCE SANDWICH

Magicians have invented myriad methods of locating a selected card in a manner similar to the approach described here. Myriad methods for the effect have been created for a singular reason: The trick is an entertaining one.

EFFECT: After a card has been selected, noted, and returned to the deck, the magician offers the two red deuces to a spectator. "Place them anywhere in the deck you like, face up," the performer says. The spectator does so. "What's about to take place is a demonstration of ten of the most nimble fingers in the universe. In a flash, faster than you can perceive, I will cause those two twos, which only a moment ago were inserted in the deck at random, to mysteriously meet, one on top of the other." The edge of the deck is riffled and when spread, the two face-up twos have met—almost. One card is between them, face down. It is, of course, the spectator's selection!

REQUIRED: A deck of cards.

PREPARATION: A red deuce must be on the bottom (face) of the deck. Remember which one it is.

PERFORMANCE: After a card has been selected and memorized by the spectator, have it returned to the deck in the midst of a Hindu shuffle. When the card has been returned on the lower half (held in the left hand), drop the balance of the cards in the right hand on top. This places the red deuce, formerly the bottom card, on top of the selection.

"For the purposes of this demonstration of my fancy fingerwork, I require the two red twos from this deck," you say. Turning the faces of the cards toward you, remove the two red deuces, at the same time noting the selected card (which is immediately underneath the deuce that was originally on the bottom of the deck), and cutting it to the top of the deck.

"Turn either one of the deuces face down," you tell the volunteer. As he does this, turn the cards face up and begin another Hindu shuffle, further instructing him to "return the face-down deuce anywhere you'd like in the face-up deck." He stops your shuffle wherever he likes, sets down the face-down two, and you drop the balance of the deck on top (placing the selection directly above the face-down card).

Turn the deck face down and spread through it to display one face-up red two in the center, "at an entirely random location, which you selected." As you close the spread, slip the tip of your left little finger under the card directly under the two. This is the selection. "Please pick the other card up off of the table," you ask the spectator politely.

As he does, casually cut the cards at the little finger break, bringing the selected card to the bottom of the deck. One red deuce is now on top of it.

Perform another Hindu shuffle, and ask the spectator to "stop me wherever you'd like, and then return the other deuce, face up, to the deck." He does so, and you drop the cards that remain in your right hand, as before, on top of those in your left. Square the deck.

Now explain the challenge: After years of practice and self-denial, you have trained your "ten assistants" (your fingers) to do remarkable things. In this instance, in under two seconds, they will locate the red deuces and cause them to join one another at a position in the deck.

Riffle the edges of the cards smartly and then spread the deck between your hands. "So close!" you announce, as you spot the lone face-down pasteboard between the two face-up twos. "However, there's a reason for my slip-up. It's no slip-up, after all." Turn over the sandwiched card to reveal it as the spectator's selection.

FOLLOW YOUR CARD

This effect is not difficult to perform, but is not self-working, either. Neatly handled, it can produce a startling effect, since everything happens out in the open, while the spectators stare at the cards.

EFFECT: "This is an observation test, and not an easy one," the performer comments, while offering a shuffled deck to a spectator, who is instructed to select a card. The selection is put through a quick and deliberate series of twists and turns, and its location seems obvious. Yet when asked where the chosen card lies in the deck, the spectator never sees the big finish coming. Instead of being on top of the deck as he suspected, the selection is found reversed in the center of the deck!

REQUIRED: A deck of cards.

PREPARATION: Reverse the second card from the top.

PERFORMANCE: Spread the deck in the traditional "please take a card" gesture, taking care not to expose the reversed card second from the top as you do so. As the chosen card is being shown around to the audience by its selector, secure a break with the left little finger under the top two cards of the deck.

"Rarely does a magician ask his audience to stare directly at his hands," the magician states, "but in this instance, I'm going to break the usual rules and specifically request that you do just that."

Take back the spectator's card and ask him to "follow its position in the deck very carefully." Set the selection on top of the deck, then push it back toward your body approximately half of its length. With the right thumb on the back of the selected card and the tips of the right fingers on the back of the next card down, push forward on the selection and the next card at the same time, squaring the selection with the deck and outjogging the card below it at the same time, as shown in **Figure 49.** Remove the protruding card and place it face up on top of the deck. "This will be my card," you say.

FIGURE 49

Next, turn over the top three cards (all of which are above your little finger break) as one. It appears as if you simply removed your card from the top, turned it over, and then turned it back down, on top of the selection. In reality, however, the selection is now second from the top, and face up.

Take the top two cards off of the deck as one and push them into the center of the deck, then ask the spectator a direct question: "I moved slowly and deliberately. Where is your card?" Undoubtedly, he will say that it is on top. "No, *my* card is on top," you say as you turn over the uppermost card of the deck to prove your statement. "Your card is here." Spread the deck on the table to show the selected card in the center of the deck, face up!

TRICK OF THE YEAR

The presentational theme of this trick makes what might otherwise be a boring, procedural trick a charming, clever, quick trick.

EFFECT: A card is selected, noted, and returned to the deck by a spectator. "I'm about to ask you a series of ridiculously simple questions," the magician says. "Please answer me honestly when I ask them of you, and you'll be surprised at the result, I promise." True to his word, the card conjurer asks his volunteer a number of questions, all of them having to do with time: how many days in a year, days in a week, and so on. At the conclusion of the Q&A session, the spectator's selection is dealt from the top of the deck!

REQUIRED: A deck of cards.

PREPARATION: None.

PERFORMANCE: Have a spectator select a card, note it, and return it to the deck. Control it to the top of the deck, then slip one more card on top of it.

"Forgive me for the questions I am about to ask you," you say, addressing your spectator. "They are all obvious and easy to answer. But the end result of this line of questioning will be worth it. We are going to locate your card based on data about the calendar year."

Hand the cards to the spectator and ask him how many weeks are in a year. The answer is fifty-two. At this point, you instruct him to deal off two piles from the top of the deck, the first containing five cards and the second containing two. Tell him to drop the pile of two cards on top of the pile of five. The seven cards are placed back on top of the deck.

"How many months are in a year?" Twelve will be the response. Have him count twelve cards off the top of the deck, one at a time, into a pile on the table. These cards are replaced on top of the deck. The next question: "How many days are in a week?" After hearing the answer, have him count seven cards off the top of the deck into a pile on the table, then replace them on top of the deck, as before.

"Stay with me," you say. "I only have one more question to ask. A leap year adds how many days to a year?" One, of course.

Receiving this response, tell him to remove the top card from the deck, to hold it face down, and then ask for the name of his selection. After he answers, tell him to turn over the card in his hand—it is the selection!

BUSINESS CARD PROPHECY

This trick is actually a two-card force disguised as a prediction effect. It was invented in the 1950s by New York card magician Bill Simon.

EFFECT: The magician writes a prediction on the blank side of his business card. This card is handed to a spectator, who inserts it into the deck at any position he chooses. The performer spreads the deck, and reveals the cards on either side of the prediction. The spectator then reads the prediction aloud, proving that the magician knew which cards it would be placed between before the spectator even held the prediction!

REQUIRED: A deck of cards, a business card (one side of which is blank), and a pencil.

PREPARATION: Secretly note the top and bottom cards of the deck.

PERFORMANCE: "I'm going to make a prediction of something that will happen in a moment or two," you state, "and I'm going to write down my thoughts on the blank side of this business card." Saying so, you scribble a quick prediction on your card: the names of the two cards on the top and bottom of the deck.

Hand the business card to a spectator, prediction-side down, and have him insert it in the deck anywhere. "Put it in the center, please. Any random location will do."

After he has done so, ask the assisting spectator a question. "Did you, sir, know which spot in the deck you would place that business card before you volunteered to help me today?" Whatever his response, continue by saying, "Believe it or not, I did. I knew where the business card would be placed—even before you did." Pause, then say, "I seem to be the only one who believes that last statement. Let me prove it to you. I'll show you that I wrote something on the other side of that business card."

FIGURE 50

Now for the sleight-of-hand. With the cards in your left hand, in dealing position, spread through them, stopping at the business card. Hold it on the lower half of the deck with the left thumb and as you do, use the right hand to turn over the portion of the deck it holds, to assist in flipping over the business card, as in **Figure 50.** With the right thumb, take hold of the business card, clipping it against the cards it holds, and rotate the cards in the right hand back to rest position. Quickly place the cards that remain in the left on top of the business card as shown in **Figure 51.** You have just sandwiched the business card between the two force cards (formerly the top and bottom cards of the deck). "I don't want you to see the prediction just yet," you say. "I only want you to know that I actually wrote one down."

FIGURE 51

After the appropriate dramatic pause and build-up, the deck is spread (by a spectator, if you like) and the cards on either side of the prediction are noted. The prediction is then read and proves to be 100 percent correct.

TWIN SOULS

This trick can be performed at a moment's notice with any deck of cards, and though similar to Business Card Prophecy, it requires no sleight-of-hand. It was invented by Al Baker of Brooklyn, New York. Baker was an inventive genius, and developed hundreds of baffling, direct tricks. Mysterio featured Baker's "Naomi Goldfish Bowl Production" in his act for at least three seasons.

EFFECT: The magician makes two predictions, writing them on slips of paper, which are folded and left in full view of the audience. The cards are shuffled, and two are selected. "Though the cards just selected were chosen in an entirely fair and aboveboard manner, their selection was predestined." The magician's predictions are read aloud, and match the selected cards exactly!

REQUIRED: A deck of cards, two slips of paper, and a pen.

PREPARATION: None.

PERFORMANCE: Have the cards thoroughly shuffled, and sneak a glimpse at the bottom card of the deck after the cards are mixed. When the deck is returned to you, shuffle the glimpsed card to the top and then peek at the new bottom-most card of the deck.

"I require the assistance of two spectators, one man and one woman, for this experiment," you say. "What I propose is to prove the existence of destiny, of fate—something that not everyone believes in."

On the first slip of paper, write, "The gentleman will select the ten of diamonds" (or whatever the name of the top card of the deck is). Fold this billet and place it on the table in full view.

Hand the deck to your female volunteer. Tell her to think of any number, and while your back is turned, to deal that number of cards face down on the table, turn over the top card of the group dealt, memorize it, then place the balance of the deck on top. "Then cut the cards to further randomize their order."

When she finishes, take back the cards. As you look through the deck, say, "I will now fix my thoughts on the second card to be selected." Locate the former bottom card—which you are using as a key to discover the identity of the woman's selection—and cut it back to the bottom. Note the new top card of the deck. This is the woman's selection.

Now hand the cards to your male volunteer. On the second slip of paper, write, "The lady will choose the queen of hearts" (or whatever the name of the new top card is). Fold the slip of paper and put it with your other prediction.

Have the lady whisper the number she thought of to the gentleman. Turn your back and have him deal down to that number and memorize the card he stops at, just as the lady did before him. Tell him to "reassemble the deck and shuffle it thoroughly. And now," you say, "the predictions—the identities of the cards you were fated to select." Because both spectators have dealt down to the same number in the deck, the gentleman will deal to the ten of diamonds, the card you spotted on top of the deck earlier.

All that remains is for you to pick up the slips, reverse their order, and have them read!

NAME AND NUMBER

This trick derives maximum impact from a minimum of effort.

EFFECT: A card is selected, noted, and returned to the deck. Apparently forgetting this card entirely, the magician approaches a second spectator and offers the deck to him, saying, "Here…take a group of cards from the center of the deck. Grab a bunch of them as I turn my head away. When you have them, count them silently to yourself."

After the spectator has done so, the magician reassembles the entire deck. He attempts to divine the number of cards just selected, and then, when he discovers how many cards were taken, as an apparent afterthought, has the selected card appear in a position in the deck corresponding exactly to the number of cards the second spectator selected!

REQUIRED: A deck of cards.

PREPARATION: None.

PERFORMANCE: Have a card selected, noted, and returned to the deck. Then control the card to the top.

Apparently forgetting about the selection for the moment, approach a second spectator and offer the cards to him. "Here," you say, "take a group of cards from the center of the deck. Turn your head as he does so, and be certain that whatever cards he takes, the selection is not among them. Tell him to count the cards silently to himself, and then return them to the cards already in your hand. They are replaced directly on top of the first spectator's selection.

"We're going to play a game you might have heard of…something like the old carnival game in which the operator would guess your weight. But this time, instead of your weight, I'm going to try to guess, by feel alone, how many cards you removed from the deck just now."

Do exactly as you've said: Guess how many cards the second spectator removed. Make an educated guess, but do not be disappointed if you are incorrect, as most likely will be the case. What you are actually doing is setting up for the climax of the trick.

Whether you are right or wrong is immaterial; react accordingly. (Make sure you get the second spectator to reveal to you the actual number of cards he removed.) Then, as if struck by sudden inspiration, announce that you have one-upped yourself. Count down from the top of the deck the number of cards selected by the second spectator. Have the first spectator announce the name of his selection. Turn over the *next* card in the deck. It is the selected card!

REPUTATION MAKERS

These tricks have been selected because their impact is strong and the impression they make on audiences has been proven. These effects can do much to create a lasting and magical impression on your audiences.

AL BAKER'S DECK THAT CUTS ITSELF
(THE HAUNTED DECK)

Few effects excite the imagination of the lay public like the animation of an inanimate object. This effect was created by Brooklyn magician Al Baker in the 1930s, and has been a favorite of professional magicians ever since. In Mysterio's diary, an entry for December 15, 1931, states: "Al Baker flummoxed a gathering of magicians with his diabolical 'Deck That Cuts Itself.' No clue as to the method—and considering how long it has been since I was last dumbfounded, the feeling was sensational. It is moments of mystification like this one that insipire us to conjure in the first place." Those sentences are high praise indeed.

EFFECT: The magician has two spectators each select a card from the deck. These cards can be signed for later identification. After returning the cards to the deck, the magician stares intently at the cards. "Did you see what just happened?" he says. "A spirit leapt into the deck. It's taken control of the cards!" The deck is set on the performer's hand and suddenly—unexpectedly—the cards begin to move. As if guided by an astral hand, the deck cuts itself in two places, revealing the selected cards!

REQUIRED: A length of black thread, a needle, a small bead, and a dab of beeswax (or poster putty or other removable adhesive).

PREPARATION: Thread the needle with the black thread. Tie the bead to the free end of the thread and use the needle to guide the other end of the thread through your left jacket or shirt sleeve (depending on what you'll wear when performing the trick) about three inches (8 cm) below your left armpit. Unthread the needle—the end of the thread with no bead is now the free end. Stretch the thread out so it extends just beyond your left wrist. Work a small ball of the wax into the free end of the thread. (**Figure 52** shows the setup with the wax on the end of the thread, which extends from the armpit to the left wrist.) Reach inside your jacket and pull on the bead until the pellet of wax is hidden underneath your arm.

FIGURE 52

PERFORMANCE: Borrow a deck of cards, or use your own. Hand it out to a spectator for shuffling, and have her select a card once she is satisfied that the deck is well mixed. While this is going on, casually cross your arms and locate the wax pellet with your right hand. Place the pellet between the second and third finger of your left hand and uncross your arms. Have the deck handed to another spectator and ask him to select a card too.

Take back the deck and instruct both spectators to show their cards to the rest of the audience. As the cards are displayed, discreetly prepare the deck by sticking the pellet of wax to the face of the bottommost card near the edge farthest from your body. Remove the

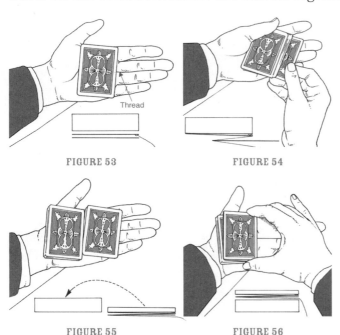

FIGURE 53

FIGURE 54

FIGURE 55

FIGURE 56

top card of the deck and place it on the bottom of the deck, sandwiching the wax between the two cards. **Figure 53** shows this arrangement. This setup should take thirty seconds or less.

Ask the first spectator to hand her card to you. Slip it onto the bottom of the deck, pressing it against the thread while doing so (see **Figure 54**), and say, "I'm going to lose this card in the deck with a simple cut."

Cut off the top two thirds of the deck and place it under the remainder of the deck. **Figures 55 and 56** show the cutting of the deck.

FIGURE 57

Return the second spectator's card to the deck's lower half, allowing it to engage the thread as you push it flush with the rest of the cards, as shown in **Figure 57.** All of the sneaky stuff is now done.

To find the selected cards with the aid of your ghostly friend, slowly and steadily extend your left arm away from your body. Ask the second spectator to name his card. As he does, the deck will slide back and forth, and reveal his selection. (**Figure 58** shows the arm extending and the deck cutting itself to reveal the selection.) Remove the card and hand it to him. Continued movement from your left arm will cause the deck to cut itself again and reveal the first spectator's card in an equally eerie fashion. When the cards have finished their gyrations and while the audience is reacting to this miracle, cut the waxed and threaded cards to the bottom of the deck, separate them, and scrape the wax off them. Hand the deck out for examination (or back to the individual who loaned it to you) and conclude your performance.

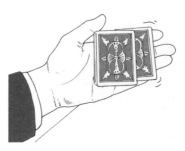

FIGURE 58

THE RISING CARDS

Since the days of the father of modern magic, Jean Eugene Robert-Houdin—in fact, even earlier, since the late eighteenth century—the Rising Cards has been a popular astonishment for conjurers from every continent. This is truly a classic, reputation-making card trick.

EFFECT: The magician has three cards selected by as many spectators. Each card is returned to the deck, which is shuffled thoroughly. The cards are then placed in a clear goblet, and a handkerchief is draped over the top of everything. Slowly and mysteriously, a shape begins to take form under the handkerchief. The magician removes the cloth from over the glass and reveals that one of the selected cards has risen from the deck! "The next card will rise visibly. I need only to snap my fingers." At the click of his fingers, another card rises from the deck, slowly and eerily. It is the wrong card—very close to the spectator's selection, but incorrect. The magician rectifies the problem magically, and then calls on the last spectator. "Don't say a word. Just *think* of the name of your card." The spectator does so, and after the appropriate dramatic pause, her card rises from the deck as well.

REQUIRED: Two identical decks of cards, a spool of fine black thread or fishing line, a wineglass large enough to accommodate a deck of cards, and an opaque silk handkerchief.

PREPARATION: Remove the following cards from one of the decks: nine of clubs, six of hearts, six of diamonds, queen of spades, and seven indifferent cards. Discard the rest of this deck, as it will not be needed.

FIGURE 59

Take one of the indifferent cards and cut a small slit in the center of one of its short edges, about ¹/₄ inch (²/₃ cm) deep. Place the end of the thread in this slit, leaving ¹/₄ inch (²/₃ cm) of thread hanging on the face of the card. Now place the nine of clubs on top of this threaded card, and on top of the end of the thread. Pull the spool of thread up behind the nine. On the nine and underneath the loose end of the thread place an indifferent card. Pull the spool over the back of this card. Now place the six of hearts on top of the thread and this indifferent card, and pull the spool up again. Continue the threading of the cards, placing the six of diamonds next, an indifferent card, the queen of spades, and finally two indifferent cards. Place the seventh indifferent card on the bottom (face) of the packet, to hide the loose end of the thread. **Figure 59** makes this arrangement clear.

A gentle yet steady pull on the thread will cause the queen of spades to rise out of the packet.

Attach the long, loose end of the thread to a convenient spot on your working surface. One option is to pin the thread to the tablecloth. Some magicians prefer to tie it to a leg of the table, near the floor. (To determine the proper length of thread to use, hold the cards about 18 inches [45 cm] above the table and about 12 inches [30 cm] in front of you. When in this position, the thread should be taut.) Place the threaded packet near the center of the table, face up. In front of the threaded packet, place the handkerchief, arranged to hide the cards from view. The wineglass should be nearby.

Complete your preparation by removing the duplicates of the seven indifferent cards from the deck you will use in performance, and place the nine of clubs, six of hearts, and queen of spades in a position that will allow you to easily force them.

PERFORMANCE: Force the three cards—nine of clubs, six of hearts, and queen of spades—on three different spectators. Be sure that you remember who took which card. After the cards are returned to the deck and shuffled, say, "This is no mere trick. This is a miracle," or something equally semi-serious. It's perfectly acceptable to occasionally play a magic trick as good as this one for gasps rather than laughs. The mood of the audience and the tenor of your performance will tell you the right attitude to assume.

As you come back to the table, set the shuffled deck on top of your secretly prepared packet, face up. Pick up the handkerchief and use it to casually clean out the glass, which incidentally shows it to be free of trickery.

Now place the deck and threaded packet (secretly added at its rear) into the glass, the thread hanging down behind it. Drape the handkerchief over everything. Move the glass forward only slightly to take up the slack in the thread. Further movement causes the queen of spades to rise. "Did you see the handkerchief move?" you ask the spectator who chose the queen of spades. "What was your card?" As she names it, remove the silk from the top of the glass, exposing the first selection. Remove it from the deck.

Have the spectator who selected the next card call its name out loud. When the six of diamonds rises and not the six of hearts, remove the diamond, place it back in the deck anywhere, and say, "It must have misunderstood you," as if the deck can understand the spectator's instructions. Then make the heart rise, as if the cards are able to correct their slight mistake.

You cannot sell the final card too strongly. Tell the last spectator to merely think of her card. "In your mind, over and over again, I want you to command the card to rise from the deck." As slowly as you can, cause the final card to rise from the deck. After you remove it, the cards can be dumped out of the glass and into your hand (or the hand of a spectator, if you are feeling bold). Because the thread is anchored at one end, it will slide out of the threaded packet as the cards exit the glass. With the exception of the card with the slit in it (which can be palmed out, if you so choose), the deck can now be examined or used for other tricks—though very few can follow the Rising Cards.

CARD IN THE ORANGE

EFFECT: A card is selected and noted by a spectator. The card is torn into several pieces, one of which is given to the spectator as a receipt. "In case you see the card again, I want you to know that you are seeing *your* card again," the magician says. "I also want you to have a souvenir of tonight's entertainment." The magician hands the spectator a ripe, round orange as a souvenir.

The torn pieces of card are then burned to a crisp. Sadly, the magician's attempts to restore the card are unsuccessful. But when the spectator's orange is cut open, the card is revealed inside, miraculously undamaged but for the torn corner!

REQUIRED: White glue, several oranges, a stack of small envelopes, two matching decks of cards, a knife, matches, an ash tray, and a hobby knife.

PREPARATION: Before your performance, take one of the oranges and carefully cut out a small plug of peel surrounding the stem. Save the plug for later use. From the duplicate deck, tear the corner off of a card (this should be approximately one eighth of the card). In this example, the card is the three of clubs. Save the corner of the card.

Roll the torn card into a compact tube and force it into the center of the orange, as shown in **Figure 60.** Replace the plug of peel, gluing it back in place so that when your preparations are finished, the orange looks ordinary.

Place the undamaged duplicate three of clubs on top of the deck (or in a convenient location from which it can be forced) and have the other props on your table. The torn corner is in a convenient pocket.

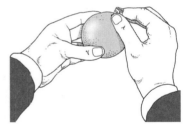

FIGURE 60

PERFORMANCE: Invite a spectator to assist you, and force the duplicate three of clubs on her from the top of the deck.

"It's okay if I see the card," you tell her. "It's not that kind of trick. This is a trick about restoring what cannot normally be restored. But before we proceed, I want you to have something—a souvenir of today's performance." Hand her the prepared orange (which, for the sake of the effect, should be in a bowl full of oranges).

As she takes the orange, secure and conceal the torn corner in your right hand. (A good way to do this is to use the finger-palm technique, described on page 128.) Take the three of clubs from the spectator and say, "Here's the broken part of the trick," as you tear the card into eight approximately even pieces (these should be about the same size as the corner already concealed in your right hand). These pieces are placed on top of the palmed fragment. As an apparent afterthought, say, "Here's another souvenir for you." Hand the spectator the torn corner from the bottom of the stack and tell her to hold on to it.

Place the torn pieces of the duplicate card into one of the envelopes and tell the audience,

FIGURE 61

"With a little help from our friend fire, the torn pieces of this card will be welded together, as good as new." Light a match and place the envelope in the ash tray. Touch the match to the envelope, which should burn merrily.

"That wasn't supposed to happen," you say. Look disappointed and then pour the ashes from the tray into another one of the envelopes. "At least you have that corner to remember this blazing failure by," you quip.

"On second thought, let's try something else." Take the orange from the spectator and cut it in half, taking care not to cut through the card concealed in the center. Separate the halves and proudly display the rolled-up three of clubs inside, as in **Figure 61.** "Whatever could it be?" you ask. Invite the spectator to pull the card free from the orange. Ask her to confirm that it is indeed her selection and then, as final and incontrovertible proof that it is the very same card that only moments before was destroyed in a fire, have the torn corner that she is holding fit back into the card, as in **Figure 62.** They prove to be a perfect fit!

FIGURE 62

OUT OF THIS WORLD

Invented by Paul Curry, this effect was reportedly performed for Winston Churchill six times by magician Harry Green. The British prime minister never discovered its secret.

EFFECT: With a deck of cards, the performer proposes an odd experiment. Indicating a specific spectator, the magician says, "You, madam, will separate the cards by color— reds from blacks—and you will do it without looking at the faces of the cards!"

The magician lays out the ground rules for the proceedings, then hands over the cards. The spectator deals the cards down into two piles, one for red, the other for black. Amazingly, when the dealing is done, she has done as the magician said she would, expertly segregating the entire deck by color, though she did not, at any time, look at the faces of the cards!

REQUIRED: A complete deck of cards (without jokers).

PREPARATION: Separate the red and black cards prior to your performance. Place the red cards on top of the blacks. Then remove three black cards from the deck and mix them with the top four red cards. Place the deck in its case.

PERFORMANCE: Introduce the effect by saying, "To separate the black cards from the red cards is easy." Remove the cards from the case and begin flipping the top cards of the deck face up onto the table. Place the cards into two piles, the left pile made up of red cards and the right made up of black cards. "I simply look at the cards and place the red cards here and the black cards there."

After you have flipped over the top seven cards of the deck, stop. Replace all but one of the red cards into the top portion of the deck (which is made up of all red cards) and all but one of the black cards into the bottom half of the deck (which is all black).

"There is no magic in separating the cards from each other in this manner. But if you were able to do it, Madam, and do it without looking, *and could do it with the entire deck*, that would be something! Something even I would like to see!"

Give the cards an overhand shuffle, running them in small batches from the right hand into the left. When you approach the center of the deck in the midst of the shuffle, run cards one at a time until you reach the middle, then continue the shuffle in the usual manner. In this way, the red cards are all brought to the bottom of the deck and the blacks to the top. (Note: To do this trick well, you'll need to practice accurately estimating where the middle of the deck is. It's easier than you may think.)

Hand the deck to your chosen spectator and instruct her as follows: "Your task is simple. There are two cards on the table, red and black. Deal the cards from the deck onto these "guide" cards, placing whichever cards you feel are black onto the black card, face down. The cards you feel are red should be dealt onto the red card, also face down.

"It sounds funny, I know, but believe me when I say that you, of all the audience members gathered here today, can do this! You have the ability and intuition to make this possible. Please begin dealing."

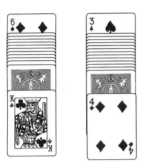

FIGURE 63

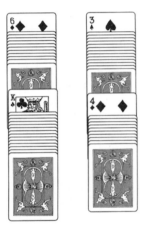

FIGURE 64

As she deals the cards, the only task you have as performer is to count the cards that she is dealing, and at the same time, to keep the procedure interesting by telling a joke or keeping the conversation going. When the spectator has dealt twenty-four cards off the deck, tell her to stop.

Retrieve the cards from her and take the top card off the remainder of the deck. It will be black. Pick another card from somewhere in the center. It will be red. Place the red card on the right-hand pile (which has, up to this point, apparently been black) and the black card on the left-hand pile, as shown in **Figure 63.** "I have changed the situation, and would like you to change your dealing appropriately," you say. "The red cards now go here (indicating the newly dealt face-up red card) and the blacks here (indicating the black card just dealt face-up)."

The spectator now deals through the balance of the deck and when she finishes, the cards are all on the table as shown in **Figure 64.** Unbeknownst to the spectators, the cards are arranged as follows: The left pile is incorrect; that is, the black guide card is beneath a pile of red cards and the red guide card is beneath a pile of black cards. The right pile is correct in every respect.

Recap what has happened—the cards were shuffled and then dealt by the spectator. You did not tamper with them. Then say, "Let's see if you delivered on my promise." Push the left pile together into a block and say, "We'll get to these cards in a minute." Begin turning over cards at the bottom of the spread on the right, saying, "these cards should be black, and they are…all of them. The rest of the cards should be red…and they are." Turn over the cards on top of the red guide card. Reveal them in an increasingly quickening pace to heighten the dramatic tension of the effect.

Now for the packet with the out-of-position guide cards. Say, "Let's check this packet." Flip the entire left-hand packet of cards over, so all but the guide cards are face up, and fan the pile out in a wide arc on the working surface. The cards will be in two groups, separated by a face-down card, as shown in **Figure 65.** "You've done it with this group, too," you say as you use your thumb

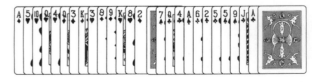

FIGURE 65

FIGURE 66

and first finger to slide the face-down guide cards (which are incorrectly positioned) out of the spread, as in **Figure 66.** With a sweep of your arm, turn the two cards over, and in that motion, use the thumb and finger to slide the cards across each other as shown in **Figure 67.**

This positions them appropriately so that when the hand completes its turn, the black card can be dropped onto the black group of cards and the red guide card onto the red card, as in **Figure 68.** Most spectators will be so flabbergasted when the final packet is spread on the table that few of them will pay attention to the guide cards at the conclusion of the trick. However, for the attentive spectators, this move should be executed flawlessly.

FIGURE 67

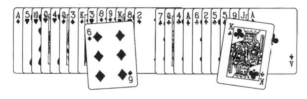

FIGURE 68

FINDING EVERYONE'S CARD

"Malini made a specialty of this sort of routine," Mysterio wrote. "Must include my own touches when writing up the routine for the book." Below is his version of a routine that is strong enough to close a show. Note that any one of the revelations described in the routine that follows can stand on its own in a series of card tricks.

EFFECT: Seven spectators select and remember cards, which are returned to the deck. The performer then produces each selection in a novel and entertaining manner. All of the cards are produced in the order they were selected.

REQUIRED: A deck of cards.

PREPARATION: Secretly place one card from the deck in your right trouser pocket, its face toward your leg.

PERFORMANCE: "It's one thing to have a card selected, then have it lost in the deck and find it again in a mysterious manner," you begin. "It is an entirely different thing to have *multiple* cards selected and lost in the deck, and then reveal them all. I assure you, ladies and gentlemen, that there is more than sleight-of-hand involved in such a feat—which I am about to present to you. The mental agility required to keep track of multiple selections is, and I am not bragging about this, considerable."

At the conclusion of this introductory speech, you approach seven spectators and have each one select a card from the deck. The cards are then returned, one on top of the other, and the block of seven cards is controlled to the top of the deck. Though bold, the overhand shuffle control (page 44) is well suited for this control, as it not only brings the selections to the top of the deck, but apparently mixes the cards in the process.

"Your cards are lost, but hope is not," you continue. "I can see that you, sir" (pointing to a gentleman in the front of your audience who did not previously select a card), "feel left out. I don't want anyone in my audience to feel as if they've missed the boat, so here, you take a card too." Offer the cards to the gentleman, but instead of allowing him to select any card from the deck, force the top card on him. Undoubtedly, he will react strangely to this—or someone else in the audience who knows the card he has selected will react. Even if no one does, *pretend* that someone has reacted in an out-of-the-ordinary manner, and call attention to this fact. "What's that? This card has already been selected? By that lady over there? I'm the one doing the tricks, sir, but thank you for finding the first card!"

"The second card I will locate by almost mundane means." You now perform a secret reversal of the top card of the deck, invented by Fred Braue, as follows. Secure a break

FIGURE 69

under the top card of the deck with the right thumb, as shown in **Figure 69.** Now, undercut the bottom half of the deck and flip it face up onto the top of the deck. Maintain the break as you do so, as in **Figure 70.** Now cut off all the cards under the break and flip them over in place, as in **Figure 71.** You have sandwiched the top card of the deck in the center, reversing it at the same time. Spread the cards between your hands, faces toward the audience, and

FIGURE 70

FIGURE 71

FIGURE 72

FIGURE 73

the reversed card will be revealed, **Figure 72.** Remove it and confirm that it was one of the selected cards.

"Two down, five to go," you continue. "The next one appears outside the deck, in my pocket, here." Reach into your pocket with an obviously empty hand and remove the card that was placed there before the show. Show its back only, and then replace the card in the pocket. "Don't believe me because I only showed you the back of the card?" As you say this, palm the top card of the deck with your right hand, as in **Figure 73.** Thrust your hand into your pocket and pull out the palmed card. "Did you pick the five of spades [or whatever the card is that you've just palmed off the top of the deck]?" Show the card to the audience and then replace it in your pocket.

"Want to see that again?" This time, remove the previously hidden card from your pocket and place it in the deck fairly and openly. "I haven't done anything yet, but the card is already back in my pocket." With an obviously empty right hand, reach back into your right trouser pocket and remove the spectator's selection for a second time.

"And now, two at once." Perform a double undercut, bringing the top card to the bottom of the deck. Now re-grip the deck in the right hand with the thumb on top and the fingers underneath, as shown in **Figure 74.** Throw the deck into the left hand, as in **Figure 75.** With pressure from the thumb and fingers, the top and bottom cards of the

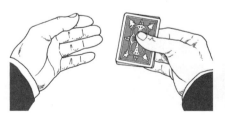

FIGURE 74

FIGURE 75

deck are held back in the right hand. As the left hand catches the deck, the right hand apparently plucks two cards from it. Both are turned toward the audience and revealed to be two of the selected cards.

Now, as if mixing the cards further, perform another double undercut, bringing the top card of the deck to the bottom. "The next one happens quickly, and takes only one hand to discover," you say. Hold the deck in your left hand, at the tips of the fingers and thumb. Reposition your thumb so that it rests underneath the cards, on the face of the bottom-most card, as in **Figure 76.** With gentle pressure from the thumb, push the bottom card out and rotate it around the long side of the deck, flipping it onto the top of the deck as quickly as you can, as shown in **Figures 77 through 79.** When performed quickly and with the left hand held well away from the body, it seems as if the card appears on top of the face-down deck. (Note: There is a certain knack to this sleight, and as you practice it you *will* drop the cards. Don't get discouraged, and rehearse over a bed to save wear and tear on your back.)

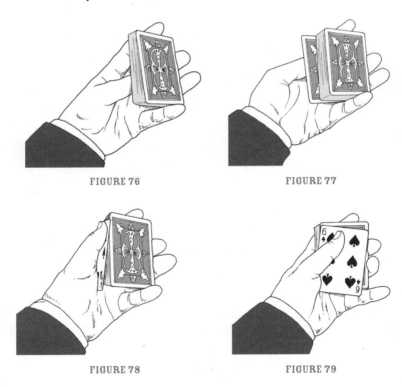

FIGURE 76   FIGURE 77

FIGURE 78   FIGURE 79

FIGURE 80

As you reveal the second-to-last card, palm the top card from the deck with your right hand.

"One card remains. Stand back!" Grip the deck of cards in the left hand, as shown in **Figure 80.** Squeeze the cards gently, applying even pressure on both short ends of the deck, and they will spring up into the air, as in **Figures 81 and 82.** Reach into the falling cards and push the palmed card to your right fingertips, as in **Figure 83.** If you cannot spray the cards into the air as described (learning to do it smoothly will take considerable practice), simply throw the cards up. As they fall, reach into their midst to produce the selected card. Turn it around to reveal it as the final selection, then take your bow at the conclusion of a spectacularly performed card routine.

FIGURE 81

FIGURE 82

FIGURE 83

MYSTERIO'S PARTING THOUGHTS: "The more you know about card magic, the more leeway you have in constructing and performing a routine as described here. The revelations described are only suggestions for creating your own magical composition. The level of difficulty each time you produce a selected card need not be high; the key to the success of any routine is to build to a climax and to keep the process of selecting and locating the cards lively and entertaining. View the different portions of what I have outlined here merely as notes and dynamic markers. Once mastered and understood, they can be used to craft your own symphony." ༄

CHAPTER III

CLOSE-UP MAGIC

SMALL MIRACLES

·~∽◦❦◦∽~·

N

O SEGMENT OF THE MAGICAL ARTS has developed more rapidly since the passing of Mr. Mysterio than close-up magic. This is not to say that there is a correlation between the two events in any way; it is merely a comment on the development of magic performed in close quarters in general.

Most spectators will agree that magic performed close-up has an immediate quality to it; the proximity of the performer to the spectator lends a different air of impossibility to magic performed in this way.

Mysterio recorded the following passage in his diary on March 3, 1924: "I have seen the undisputed master of intimate magic, and his name is Malini. This little man is so cunning, so brash, and so bold, he deserves every accolade he receives from the public and press. The magic in his stage shows is stupendous, but it is in a casual setting—perhaps at an ale house or dinner party—that he truly shines. His feats with ordinary objects are as close to real magic as I have ever witnessed."

Adulation for Malini came not only from Mysterio, but from his contemporaries as well. Nearly every great conjurer of the twentieth century who crossed Malini's path remarked at his facility with apparently impromptu close-up magic.

Mysterio went on to write, "What sets Malini's close-up magic apart is his patience. He is willing to wait for the right moment to present an effect." So, too, should you follow this sage advice. The right effect, presented at the right time, can have an electrifying impact on your audience. The right effect presented at the wrong time will be treated as nothing more than an amusing, temporary diversion.

The effects that follow in this chapter are, by and large, tricks that require little in the way of preparation or special properties. In short, they are tricks that Mysterio felt were essential to the complete education of the budding conjurer, and tricks that Malini would have loved as well.

ACROBATIC RUBBER BAND

Though this trick is almost a hundred years old, it is just as amusing today as it was when first published by British society entertainer Stanley Collins.

EFFECT: A rubber band is looped over the magician's first and middle fingers. The conjurer closes his hand into a fist. When his hand is opened out again, the band has jumped *through* his fingers, and is now circling his pinky and ring finger!

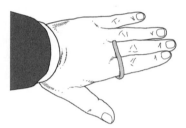

FIGURE 1

FIGURE 2

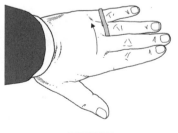

FIGURE 3

REQUIRED: A rubber band.

PREPARATION: None.

PERFORMANCE: "I've trained this rubber band to do magical acrobatics," you say. Loop the band over the first and second fingers of your left hand and let it hang down as in **Figure 1.**

Reach in to the loop of the band with your right index finger and pull back on it as you close your left hand into a fist. As your hand closes, place all four of your left fingers inside the loop your right index finger is holding open. Let go with the right finger . Your left hand should now be in the position shown in **Figure 2.**

"Watch it penetrate my fingers," you say, as you open your left hand. The jump from one hand to the other happens automatically as you open your hand. The band is now circling your ring and pinky finger, as shown in **Figure 3.**

To make the band jump back, close your left hand, again placing all four fingers into the loop of the band. Open your hand. The band has jumped back to where it started!

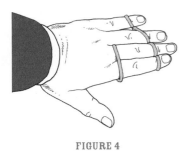

FIGURE 4

THE CONVINCER: To add another layer of deception to the Acrobatic Rubber Band, Mysterio would sometimes lock the tips of his fingers together with another band, as in **Figure 4.** Though this does nothing to impede the travel of the band from one pair of fingers to the other, it does lend an apparent level of difficulty to the trick.

Everything works exactly as described above. Place all your fingers into the loop of the band in your palm, and even with the other band apparently "locking" your fingers together, the trick still works—like magic.

TABLETOP URI GELLER

This impromptu quickie will get gasps, especially if you are dining at a fine restaurant or using the family silver.

EFFECT: With all your might, you bend a teaspoon in half. Everyone at the table sees it bend. Just as quickly, however, the spoon is restored to its ordinary, straight-as-an-arrow condition.

REQUIRED: A nickel and a teaspoon.

PREPARATION: Before performing, conceal the nickel in your right hand. There is no need to palm it. Simply hold it in your right hand and don't let anyone see it.

FIGURE 5

PERFORMANCE: Without anyone noticing, push the nickel into a position so that it can be easily clipped between the thumb and the second phalanx (the area between the first and second joints) of the index finger, as shown in **Figure 5.** "It's remarkable that an establishment as fine as this one has such cheap silverware," you comment as you pick up a spoon with your left hand.

FIGURE 6

Grasp the spoon with both hands, your right hand on top, the nickel protruding from the top of its fist. Amazingly, the coin will look very much like the end of the spoon handle. Your hands should touch each other or overlap as you grasp the handle of the spoon, as in **Figure 6.** Though it appears as if your hands are holding the handle of the spoon firmly, in actuality, only one finger, your left little finger, is gripping it, at the base of the handle.

"The cutlery is so flimsy that even a weakling—yours truly—can bend it with very little effort. It's as if I'm Uri Geller incarnate. Watch!"

Muster your abilities as an actor as you push forward and down with your hands and your body, and apparently bend the spoon. What really happens is that the right hand and most of the left hand move forward, mimicking the action of bending the spoon's handle. Because the nickel is protruding from the top of your right fist, it appears as if the spoon is being bent, as shown in **Figure 7.** Actually, the handle is levered down toward the tabletop, a fact that is concealed from the spectators by your hands.

FIGURE 7

Continue "bending" the spoon until the nickel is virtually parallel with the tabletop. Hold this bent position for a moment to allow the illusion to register with the audience, then comment, "Uri Geller never bent spoons back into their proper shapes, did he? Well, I'm a nice person, and I do." Throw the spoon out on the table for examination, and as everyone in the audience looks at it and examines it, quietly drop your hands to your lap and dispose of the nickel.

MAGNETIC FINGERTIPS

EFFECT: A pencil is rubbed on the magician's sleeve, "to generate static electricity," or so he claims. When the pencil is pressed against the palm of his open hand, it sticks there as if held fast by glue. When the magician turns his hand over, the pencil drops to the table. Everything can be examined.

REQUIRED: A pencil (or pen, or other oblong, lightweight object like a straw or ruler).

PREPARATION: None.

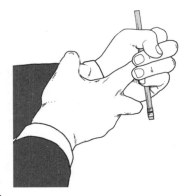

FIGURE 8

PERFORMANCE: Borrow the pencil or use your own. Rub it against your sleeve, your hair, or even a spectator's sleeve if she doesn't mind you invading her personal space. Tell her you're generating static electricity. "Very few people know that the lead inside a pencil can generate a gigantic static field if charged appropriately." This is complete bunk, but some spectators *might* take you seriously.

Next, place the pencil in your left fist, and grip your left wrist with your right hand. Make sure the back of your left hand is facing your audience, and that no one is standing behind you. Now comes the sneaky bit: Your right index finger is extended inside your left fist, where it presses down on the pencil. See **Figure 8.**

"I think the field is strong enough," you say. Slowly open the fingers of your left hand. The pencil appears to be stuck to your left hand. Wiggling your left fingers proves that they are in no way related to the working of the trick. Although this may be hard to believe, if you perform this trick with appropriate showmanship and patter no one will notice that only three fingers (and the thumb) of your right hand are wrapped around your left wrist.

Finish the trick by holding your left hand (with the pencil still "magnetized" to it) over a table or, even better (so says Mysterio), over a spectator's cupped hands. Now, several things should happen simultaneously. Say that you feel the magnetic field starting to dissipate. At the same time, turn your left hand palm up and quickly sneak your right index finger around your left wrist. The pencil will drop out of your hand and everything appears to be on the up-and-up.

HANDS-OFF VERSION: To confound a particularly astute audience, you apparently reveal the secret of the Magnetic Fingertips, and then baffle them with the very same trick! Here's how.

Note that you will need to wear a watch or a tight-fitting bracelet for this trick. Before borrowing the pencil, have a pencil of your own concealed on the palm side of your hand, stuck under your watchband, as in **Figure 9.** Now when you perform Magnetic

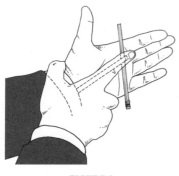

Fingertips, tuck the visible pencil underneath the one already in your watch band and place your index finger *over* the secret pencil, concealing it from view.

After executing the trick as described above, offer to explain it to your audience. As if letting them in on a big secret, turn over your left hand to expose your index finger holding the pencil in place. What the spectators do not know is that your index finger is concealing another pencil, which is doing the real dirty work.

Swing your left hand back toward your body, so that its back faces your audience. You continue gripping your left wrist with your right hand. Now say, "It turns out that you can't always rely on the method I just showed you to perform the trick. In those instances, all I do is this…" Let go of your left wrist with your right hand. The secret pencil will hold the visible one in place, and your audience will be even more confounded than before.

Finish the trick by allowing the visible pencil to drop to the table by releasing pressure on it with your left hand. As you hand this pencil out for examination, push the other pencil up your sleeve or drop it into a convenient pocket.

POSTAGE PREDICTION

This trick was devised by clever Canadian conjurer David Ben. It is an adaptation of a trick typically performed with coins.

EFFECT: The magician tells his spectators that in addition to a love of the movies, theater, and music, he is also an avid stamp collector. "I brought along a small sampling of some recently issued stamps that caught my eye," he says. A handful of stamps are dumped onto the table, and the magician offers to combine his skill with his hobby, making a prediction of future events on a small slip of paper, which is folded and left in full view of the audience. A spectator is invited to select one of the stamps in a completely random manner. After this selection is made, the magician reveals his prediction, which proves that he knew which stamp the spectator would select before even the spectator did!

REQUIRED: Thirty or forty stamps. All of them should be different (and issued by different nations), with the exception of two, which should match exactly. Assortments of stamps are available at hobby shops for a modest investment. A glassine envelope (free at most post offices and stamp shops) is also necessary, to carry the stamps.

PREPARATION: As neatly as possible, stick the two duplicate stamps together, back to back, creating a double-faced stamp. No matter which way this gimmicked stamp is dropped on the table, it will always land face up.

PERFORMANCE: Explain your interest in stamps to your audience, showing them the wide variety of stamps in the glassine envelope. Offer a demonstration of magic that directly involves your hobby. Write a prediction on a slip of paper that says, "Your journey will end in Palau [or whatever country your double-faced stamp is from]." Fold the prediction in quarters and set it on the table.

Dump the stamps from the envelope and point out that no two are alike; this also gives you an opportunity to tell stories about countries you've visited, or tell any jokes you care to about specific stamps, the images on them, or the countries that issued them.

Tell a spectator to pick up all of the stamps, shake them up between his cupped hands, and then drop them onto the table. "Whichever stamps land face down," you say, "will be eliminated. Keep mixing the stamps and drop them on to the table until we're left with only one."

Eventually, only one stamp will remain on the table—your double-facer, from Palau. You should at this point come up with some clever patter; for example: "Interesting, don't you think? Have you ever been to Palau? I haven't, but friends have told me a lot about it. It's an island nation, if I'm not mistaken. Kind of a paradise."

Even more interesting is the fact that when your prediction is revealed, it proves that you knew the spectator would select Palau before she did! As she reads the prediction, scoop up all of the stamps and place them back in the envelope.

P.S. Postage Prediction is based on an effect created by Marcello Truzzi and Johnny Thompson (the Great Tomsoni), called Heads Up. Heads Up involved the prediction of a date on a selected coin.

PSEUDO SWORD SWALLOWING

Bert Allerton was a charming magician whom Mysterio first met in the famous Pump Room at Chicago's Ambassador Hotel, where Allerton was the house magician. This cute, quick trick was an Allerton favorite.

EFFECT: The magician apparently swallows a table knife!

REQUIRED: A table knife and a healthy dose of gumption. You must be seated at a table with your feet flat on the floor to perform this trick.

PREPARATION: None.

PERFORMANCE: Your introductory patter goes something like this: "When I was young, I ran away with the circus. No, I'm not kidding! Instead of working with the animals or on the high wire, they set me up in the sideshow, doing a magic act. Of course, I wasn't always on stage, so I learned a thing or two from the other acts I worked with. Let me show you one thing I picked up from the sword swallower."

Here, you slide a butter knife toward you, so its length is parallel to the edge of the table. "I'll swallow this knife. Watch!" Grandiosely, you pick up the salt shaker and sprinkle a generous amount of the white stuff over the knife. "Looks good to me!" As you say this, look up, straight at the audience, and smile. They should look at you. As they do, you go into action, placing both hands on top of the knife, and sweeping it off of the edge of the table into your lap, as in **Figure 10.** Immediately raise your hands to your mouth, and mimic the act of swallowing the knife.

After your repast has been gulped down, tell the audience, "The only problem is, I don't know how to bring the knives back up."

Mysterio mentioned that Allerton rarely played this trick seriously, since most people will not believe you'd ever swallow a table knife. Even so, it's a good after-dinner stunt, and if you catch spectators off guard, they may (pardon the pun) swallow the ruse whole.

FIGURE 10

PAPER AND SILVER

This ancient trick was a favorite of Malini's, and remains a favorite of discerning magicians even today. It requires the mastery of one important sleight: the paddle move (see below).

EFFECT: The performer affixes three small squares of paper—pieces of a paper napkin—to each side of the blade of a knife.

REQUIRED: A butter knife and a paper napkin or facial tissue.

PREPARATION: Before your performance, attach three small squares of paper to one side of the knife's blade, as shown in **Figure 11.** Wetting the squares with saliva or the condensation from the outside of a glass of water will hold the paper in place.

FIGURE 11

PERFORMANCE: Tear three squares of paper from a napkin or tissue and affix them to the knife, using the same method you used on the prepared side. There are now six squares of paper on the knife's blade, though the audience is aware of only three.

"Whatever happens on one side of the knife happens on the other. It's like a mirror," you say. Hold the knife between your thumb and fingers, as shown in **Figure 12.** The blade of the knife points away from your body, and your hand is palm up.

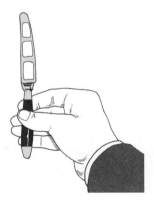

FIGURE 12

Your hand now rotates upward to display the other side of the knife blade. The spectators will be surprised to see three squares of paper there. "It's as if the mirror image of what is on one side can be seen on the other," you say. "Let's take this one step further." Return your hand to the rest position shown in **Figure 12.**

You now pretend to remove the centermost square of paper from *both* sides of the knife. Actually, you only remove it from one side. Throw this square of paper (apparently two) onto the floor and perform what magicians know as the paddle move to show that *both* sides of the knife have only two pieces of paper on them.

THE PADDLE MOVE: Rotate your hand toward your body and as you do so, use your thumb to roll the handle of the knife 180 degrees. When your hand stops turning, so does your thumb. The blade of the knife is now pointed at your chest, and the side of the knife just shown is shown yet again, making it look to the spectators that the center square of paper is missing on both sides of the knife, as shown in **Figure 13.**

FIGURE 13

"I removed two squares of paper," you say, reversing your actions. "Now I will remove another two. Again, pretend to remove two squares of paper (from the top position). Perform the paddle move again, and it will appear as if only the two squares of paper in the bottom position remain on the knife. Return your hand to the rest position and apparently remove the remaining papers, throwing them to the floor as well.

With your hand in rest position, apparently all of the papers have been removed from the knife and the blade is clean and clear. You can perform the paddle move once or twice more in the course of casual conversation to show it, but do not overdo this display.

"Here is the remarkable part of these mirrored actions," you say. "With a deft wave of the hand, I can mirror the past with the blade of this knife." Wave your hand back and forth and as you do, give the knife a half-turn, exposing the three squares of paper that have been there all along. "In the past, this knife was covered with little squares of paper, exactly as it is now!" Perform the paddle move one more time to show that the knife now has three squares of paper on each side. Then peel them off one at a time (pretending that you are peeling off pieces from both sides), and hand out the knife for examination if you wish, as you take your bow.

MORE PADDLING: "Once mastered, the paddle move can be adapted to any one of a number of effects. It can even be performed with a paper match, if the magician is adept," Mysterio wrote. Indeed, this is true. Drawings on either side of a paper match, as shown in **Figure 14,** can jump up and down the length of the match, or stickers on either side of a cigarette lighter can vanish and appear; the tricks made possible by this versatile move (which can be used to make objects or images appear, move, or vanish) are virtually endless. Try performing the paddle move with a swizzle stick, a pencil, or even a house key. Any object that is small enough to hold and can be indetectably rolled between the fingers can be turned into an object full of magic.

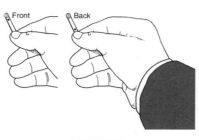

FIGURE 14

MR. FREEZE

There is a minimal amount of preparation required for this startling trick, which, in recent years, has been performed on television. Mysterio used this stunt as a quick interlude when performing in casual surroundings, like his kitchen. "Magic can be performed under any circumstances," he wrote in his diaries. "The most impressive feats are those done in an apparently impromptu situation."

EFFECT: The magician offers to demonstrate his mastery of temperature. He pours a tiny amount of water into a coffee mug. When the mug is tipped over, out comes an ice cube!

REQUIRED: A kitchen sponge, a coffee mug (or other opaque vessel), an ice cube, and a glass of water.

PREPARATION: Wedge the sponge into the coffee mug so it will not fall out when the mug is inverted. Place the ice cube on top of the sponge.

PERFORMANCE: Begin your performance of this quick trick with a brief preamble. "I've learned to control the temperature of my body to an extreme degree. In fact, with enough concentrated effort, I can cause my hands to become ice cold. Watch this."

Pour a small amount of the water from the glass into the coffee mug. If the sponge is dry, it will absorb the water. Of course, no spectators should be allowed to peek inside the mug before, during, or after your performance, lest they spot the secret sponge it holds.

Cup your hands around the mug, saying, "This is where the concerted effort comes in." After a brief dramatic pause, turn the mug over. Out drops the ice cube, apparently created by the force of your will alone.

THE CONVINCER: To convince your spectators that you are truly able to control the temperature of your body, try the following technique, which was used by master mentalist Theodore Annemann. Fill a small plastic bag with ice and seal it shut. Put the bag in your pocket. Just prior to performing the above effect, put a free hand in your pocket and grab the bag of ice. When your hand is suitably chilled, perform the effect as described. After the ice cube makes its appearance, hold your frozen hand out for examination, as "proof" of your abilities.

HANGING IN THE BALANCE

This is a quick trick, but visually arresting, and easy to do. In Mr. Mysterio's day, when smoking was a widely accepted public habit, the effect was performed with a cigarette. Chicago conjurer Arthur Trace developed the following variation, using a drinking straw.

EFFECT: The magician borrows a plastic drinking straw from a friend's beverage. Wiping it off, he makes a simple announcement: "This commonplace article will now do something that is in no way common!" So saying, he balances the straw by its very end, so that 90 percent of its length extends over the edge of a table. When the prestidigitator lets go of the straw, it remains suspended in space, hanging off of the edge of the table as if suspended by invisible thread. At the performer's command, the spell is broken; the straw is picked up and handed back to its owner. There is nothing to find.

REQUIRED: A thick nail, the head of which has been cut off, and the body of which has been trimmed to a length of approximately 1½ inches (4 cm). The ends of the nail should be blunted to prevent injury.

PREPARATION: The headless nail (hereafter, the "weight") is in a convenient pocket.

PERFORMANCE: Remove the weight from your pocket and conceal it in your right hand. There is no palming here; simply hold your hand naturally, and keep the weight concealed from your audience.

Borrow a straw, or unwrap a fresh one. In the act of unwrapping or cleaning the straw, introduce the weight into one end. "And now for a gravity-defying feat," you announce.

Balance the weighted end of the straw on the edge of a table, as in **Figure 15** (which shows the position of the straw and the weight inside it). Release your grip on the straw slowly, to show it suspended in space, and to heighten the effect. After a few moments, pick up the straw and as you do, allow the weight to slide out of it and into your hand. As the straw is handed out for examination, dispose of the weight.

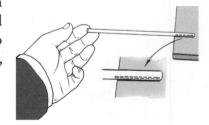

FIGURE 15

FLOATED LOAN

This quick effect, also devised by Arthur Trace, is a good follow-up to the previous suspension, and uses an entirely different method, which throws spectators off the scent.

EFFECT: The magician borrows a credit card for a quick trick. He stands the card on the back of a chair, on its edge. Amazingly, the card, as if a tightrope walker, balances on the chair back. "The clichéd line I use when performing this feat," the magician says, "has to do with 'floating a loan.' Go ahead—now that you've been amazed by the trick, you can groan at my delivery of the line." The card is then handed back to its owner, none the worse for the wear.

REQUIRED: A dab of poster putty or beeswax the size of a navy bean.

PREPARATION: Stick the putty or wax (either works well) to the button of your shirt, your belt buckle, or the back of your thumbnail.

FIGURE 16

PERFORMANCE: A credit card—or driver's license, or any other plastic card—is borrowed from a spectator. Borrowed objects like these give the quick-thinking performer plenty of opportunities to interject light humor into his performances ("But never—I repeat *never*—should you poke fun at or embarrass your audiences with your patter," Mysterio once told an eager student).

As you comment on the card you've borrowed, or while it is being produced by your volunteer, retrieve the wax from its hiding place. As you examine the card, stick the wax to one corner, so that it cannot be seen from the opposite side.

Now balance the card on the back of a chair, as in **Figure 16.** Perch it there precariously, and as you attempt to balance the card there, work the wax down against the chair, so it sticks to both the card and the chair. Finally, remove your grip on the card and show it magically balanced in space. After only a few seconds—the effect should look authentic, not hokey—grab the card as if it is about to fall and scrape the wax off of its corner as you hand it back to its rightful owner.

BOTTOMS UP

Here is Mr. Mysterio's diary entry for May 13, 1934: "I purchased a trick called Squash from Percy Abbott, in which a shot glass full of liquid vanishes from between the bare hands," he wrote. "Have discovered my own use for this marvelous gimmick." What follows is Mysterio's creation.

EFFECT: The performer's hands are unmistakably empty. He removes a handkerchief from his pocket, which is examined by spectators. "You can plainly see," he tells the audience, "that my hands conceal nothing, and the handkerchief is an ordinary pocket square, nothing more. While this is simply a restatement of the facts, I want to impress upon you the fairness of what is about to transpire." The performer drapes the handkerchief over his left hand. Suddenly, underneath it, a form pops into view. When the handkerchief is lifted from the magician's hand, on it is balanced a shot glass brimming with his favorite libation.

REQUIRED: An opaque pocket handkerchief, a shot glass nearly filled with your favorite drink, and a rubber ball. The ball must fit snugly into the opening of the glass, as in **Figure 17.** When the ball is wedged into the mouth of the glass, the liquid inside will not spill. You must wear a jacket to perform this effect.

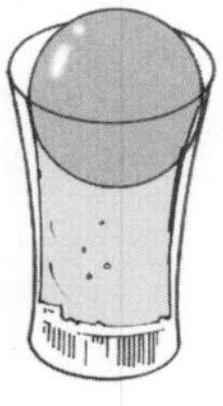

FIGURE 17

PREPARATION: Place the loaded and sealed glass in a breast pocket, along with the handkerchief.

PERFORMANCE: Show your hands to be empty, and roll back the sleeves of your jacket, if you wish. If you care to use the patter outlined above, state the obvious: Your hands are empty. When your arms again hang at your sides, your sleeves will fall down to their usual resting position—which is where they must be to perform the effect.

Reach into your inner breast pocket to remove the handkerchief. Before removing the pocket square, lift the glass (with its rubber ball stopper) from the pocket, and drop it into the sleeve of your coat. Keep your arm bent, so that the glass will not slide out of the sleeve prematurely.

Remove the handkerchief from your pocket, display it on both sides and have it examined. "You'll note I have exquisite taste," you say jokingly, as you hand it out.

When the handkerchief is returned to you, allow your right arm to drop to your side. This allows the glass to fall into your cupped, waiting right hand, as in **Figure 18.**

Cover the right hand with the hankie, so that the shape of the glass and ball is not seen underneath it. This can be accomplished by holding the hand palm down underneath the handkerchief, the fingers and thumb gripping the glass.

After the requisite dramatic pause, pop the glass up under the hankie, so its form takes shape quickly. Its appearance there will be startling. With the left hand, reach over to uncover the glass, and as you do, dislodge the ball from its mouth. Reveal the surprising production (all the more surprising considering the glass is full of a liquid!). As you do, carry the ball away under the handkerchief, which is disposed of in a convenient pocket.

FIGURE 18

CRAZY MAN'S HANDCUFFS

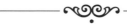

A visual tour de force, this rubber band miracle is one of the most enduring illusions of the close-up kind. Practice it with rubber bands in hand to understand its subtle secret.

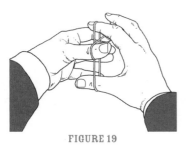

FIGURE 19

EFFECT: A rubber band is stretched between the thumb and index finger of each hand. The bands are then interlocked by the magician, as in **Figure 19.** "To someone who is not of sound mind, these flimsy, stretchy bands might be considered handcuffs of a sort," the magician says. He shows that the bands are interlocked by stretching one against the other. Then, with no suspicious moves or visible sleight-of-hand, the bands apparently melt through one another! The bands may be examined before and after the trick; they are not tampered with in any way.

REQUIRED: Two identical rubber bands. Size 19 bands work best, but virtually any thin bands will work.

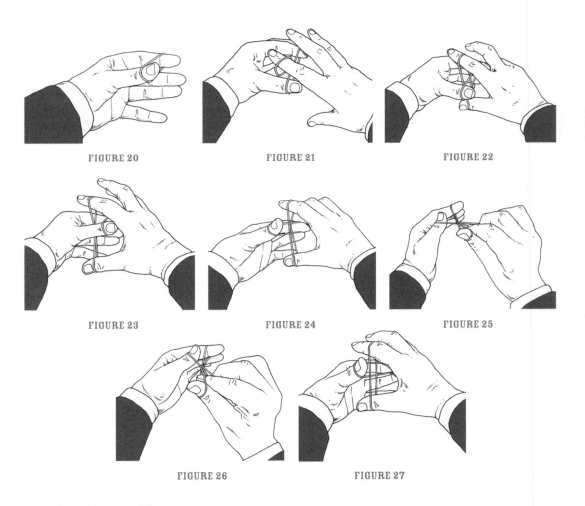

FIGURE 20   FIGURE 21   FIGURE 22

FIGURE 23   FIGURE 24   FIGURE 25

FIGURE 26   FIGURE 27

PREPARATION: None.

PERFORMANCE: Stretch a band between the thumb and index finger of your left hand, as in **Figure 20.** Hang the other band from your right index finger, then lower it into the area between the left thumb crotch and the rubber band held in that hand, as shown in **Figure 21.** Slide your right thumb into the hanging band, locking the two together as in **Figure 22.**

Without touching the bands to each other, move your hands back and forth, displaying their locked condition (see **Figures 23 and 24**).

Now for the sleight-of-hand: Maintaining your grip on the bands with your index fingers and thumbs, pull them against each other, saying something like, "Though they may be ineffective restraints in the practical sense, they are, for our purposes here today, firmly locked together. In fact, the only way to separate them is to release my grip on them, correct?" See **Figure 25.**

As you make this comment, be sure to hold fast to the end of the band hooked over each index finger with your middle fingers, so that the bands won't slip off of your fingers due to the tension on them.

As your left hand moves back, your right index finger and thumb are pinched together. As they come together, the right middle finger supports the band entirely. This allows the index finger to be inserted into the *thumb's* loop.

Everything described in the above paragraph happens in the action of pulling the bands against each other, as in **Figure 26.**

Now the hands return to the rest position, and in the process, unlink the bands. Here's how. In one smooth action, the right index finger moves away from the thumb, continuing inside the thumb's opening of the band. The right middle finger continues to grip the other end of the band.

In a continuing action, the right index finger is extended away from the thumb and the hands come back to rest. At the same time, the right middle finger releases its grip on the other end of the band.

At this point, the right hand's band is free from the left hand's band, which it was just stretched against. But the spectators don't know that. Only you do. Be sure that the square formed by the four crossing strands is an equal distance from all four fingers, as shown in **Figure 27.**

All that remains is for you to slowly—*very* slowly—separate your hands and pull the rubber bands apart, creating the illusion of one melting through the other.

VANISHING THIMBLE

In the halcyon days of vaudeville and the British music hall (the years in which Mysterio's career flourished), conjurers like Edward Victor of Great Britain made a specialty of tricks with thimbles. Today, thimbles are largely unknown to modern audiences. Even so, the thimble effects that follow teach the budding baffler an important set of skills, and should not be passed by. The moves and sleights taught here can be adapted to a wide array of common objects.

FIGURE 28

FIGURE 29

FIGURE 30

EFFECT: A thimble is placed on the magician's extended index finger. As the finger is waved up and down, the thimble vanishes.

REQUIRED: A thimble.

PREPARATION: None.

PERFORMANCE: The vanish is accomplished via a simple sleight. Place a thimble on your index finger, which is extended out from your hand. The remainder of your fingers are curled inward, as in **Figure 28.**

Bend your index finger inward, toward the crotch of the thumb. When the thimble contacts the thumb crotch, clamp down on it with the base of the first finger and the base of the thumb, which remove the thimble from the tip of the index finger, as in **Figure 29.**

Now re-extend your index finger to its initial position. The thimble should be wedged in this thumb palm position, and your index finger is bare, as in **Figure 30.**

When combined with a gentle up-and-down wave of your hand, this vanish looks like trick photography in real life. One moment, the thimble is on the tip of your finger, and the next, it's gone.

To cause the thimble to reappear, simply reverse your actions in the course of another casual wave of the hand.

AMBIDEXTROUSLY: Once you become adept at the above vanish with your dominant hand, practice it with your other hand. When both hands can perform the vanish, a thimble can be made to visibly and magically jump from one hand to the other. Use a pair of identical thimbles to accomplish the effect. Begin with one thimble thumb palmed in the left hand and the other on the tip of the right finger. By carefully timing your actions and making the right-hand thimble vanish and the left-hand thimble appear, the overall picture created is that the thimble on the right hand has magically flown to the tip of the left finger.

COMEBACK KEY

Contrary to popular belief, magicians rarely employ confederates to accomplish their tricks. This trick is one exception to that rule.

EFFECT: A key is placed underneath a handkerchief. Spectators are asked to feel the key underneath the napkin to make sure it is still in place. "I want each of you to verify that everything is on the up and up. Though you cannot see the key through the handkerchief, you can all feel it and attest to the fact that it is still here." Several spectators reach under the handkerchief and verify that the key is still in place. Despite this fact, the key vanishes! It later returns, and is handed back to its owner.

REQUIRED: An opaque handkerchief or napkin, a borrowed key, and a secret accomplice in your audience.

PREPARATION: A secret accomplice is required to perform the trick. Have a napkin or handkerchief handy. Make sure your secret assistant is sitting close to you, and is ready to act.

PERFORMANCE: Borrow a key or some other small, personal item from a member of your audience and place it under the handkerchief. "Some people believe that I've already done the sneaky stuff, and that the key has already vanished. But that's not the case. Here, why don't a few of you feel the key under the napkin and make sure it's still there?" As you say this last line, have a few spectators feel the key under the napkin. They will all agree that the key is still in place. However, the last spectator to feel for the coin is your secret assistant. Instead of simply feeling the key, your assistant takes the key out from under the napkin and holds it in her hand. Now you can dramatically cause the key to vanish from under the napkin.

To cause the key to return, drape the napkin over your hand just as if the key were there. Have a number of spectators reach underneath the napkin to feel for the key. The last spectator to feel for it, of course, is your secret assistant. She deposits the key on your hand. Now, whenever you like, the key can be caused to instantly reappear under the napkin.

Of course, any small object that can be easily held in your hand (and your assistant's) can be caused to vanish by this method. Try the trick with coins, candy, rings, or small bouncy balls.

FINGER, FINGER

Originally designed to be performed with a thimble, this effect works well with a borrowed ring. It is both quick and visual.

EFFECT: Visibly and in plain view, a ring jumps from one finger to another!

REQUIRED: A ring, which may be borrowed.

PREPARATION: None.

FIGURE 31

PERFORMANCE: Borrow a ring, or use your own if no willing volunteers exist in your audience. Place the ring on the middle finger of your right hand, and extend your index finger next to it. Your other two fingers and thumb are curled into your palm, as in **Figure 31**. Point out the ring on your middle finger by tapping the two extended fingers against the back of your left fist three times, as in **Figure 32**. On the third tap, curl your first finger inward, and at the same time, extend your ring finger, as in **Figure 33**. Though the position of the ring has not changed, because of your fancy finger work, the ring appears to visibly hop from one finger to the other. To make the ring apparently jump back to its starting position, reverse your actions. Hand back the piece of jewelry and take a bow.

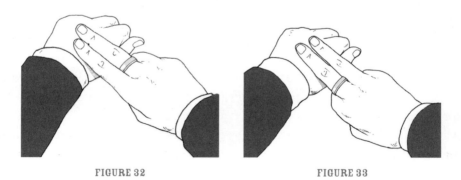

FIGURE 32   FIGURE 33

TWO IN THE HAND, ONE IN THE POCKET

This classic sleight-of-hand feat can be performed with virtually any small objects. Here, it is described with dice. Learn it and you will have an easy-to-follow, entertaining piece of magic at the ready that is guaranteed to get reactions.

EFFECT: The magician shows his audience three small white dice. "This trick has nothing to do with luck," the performer explains. "It has everything to do with mathematics." Two dice are placed in the magician's fist, and the third goes into his pocket. "How many dice are in my hand?" he asks. The question seems innocent enough. Even so, when the magician opens his fist, all three dice are seen inside! This is repeated a second and third time. Finally, the magician places the dice in his fist and asks his audience one final question: "How many dice are in my fist this time?" No matter what the spectators answer, they will be shocked to learn that instead of three, two, or even one die in the performer's hand, all three cubes have vanished without a trace!

REQUIRED: Four identical dice.

PREPARATION: Finger palm one die in your right hand (see page 128 for instructions on finger palming).

PERFORMANCE: Display three dice in your left hand, and then lay them on the table in a row. "I would now like to offer, for your consideration, a brief mathematical interlude that requires the participation of the audience." With your right hand, pick up one die from the table and drop it into the left hand, which closes around it into a fist. "That's one," you say.

Next, the right hand picks up another die from the table and drops it, along with the concealed die, into the left fist. There are now three dice there, though the audience is only aware of two. "That's two in the hand," you say.

"The last one goes in my pocket." Here, you take the die that remains on the table and pretend to place it into your pocket. Instead, you retain it in your right hand in finger palm position.

Continuing to address the audience (and not thinking about the die palmed in your right hand—remember, if you believe your hand is empty so will your audience), you say, "So, if two dice were placed in my hand, and one was taken away and put in my pocket, that leaves how many in the hand?" The spectators will inevitably answer "two."

Open your left fist to show three dice where only two should be. "I get confused myself," you say as you lay the dice on the table again. "Let's try it again." You now repeat the same actions described above, apparently putting two dice (really three) in your left fist and one in your pocket. Again your left hand is opened to reveal three dice.

"Still three in the hand," you say.

Perform the "two in the hand, one in the pocket" sequence one more time, but this time drop one die in your pocket instead of palming it as before. This leaves you with three dice in your left fist, which are counted out on the table as before. You are now set to perform the last phase of the routine.

Pick up one die with your right hand, and pretend to place it in your left fist as you count "one" out loud. Instead of placing it in your left hand, however, hold the die back in your right palm.

Pick up another die with the right hand and pretend to place it, too, into the left fist, as in **Figure 34.** If the dice held back in your right hand rattle together momentarily (this is called "talking" in the lexicon of the professional magician), do not fear. Your audience expects to hear the dice bang against each other, at least momentarily.

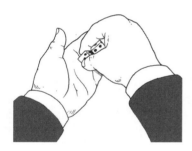

FIGURE 34

Pick up the die that remains on the table and say, "I've placed two in my hand, and this one goes into my pocket. Drop the visible die, along with the two concealed in the right hand, into your pocket. Ask a final question of your audience: "How many does that leave in my left hand?" No matter what the answer, brush your hands together deliberately and answer the question yourself: "None!"

THE CHANGE-UP: Depending on your facility with the routine outlined above, the same effect can be performed with other small objects that are easily palmed. In Mysterio's day, sugar was often served in lump form. When dining out, in the course of sweetening his coffee, Mysterio would often palm an extra lump of sugar from a bowl full of them, thus preparing himself for an impromptu version of the effect.

SUGAR TRICK

Properly built up, this effect can become the cornerstone of your impromptu magic repertoire. It is one of the most impressive close-up feats of all time, but seldom seen. In Mysterio's day, sugar cubes—the trick's essential ingredient—were commonplace.

EFFECT: "Draw a design, write your initials, or mark in some way this lump of sugar," the magician says to a volunteer. The assistant does so, scratching an image of his choosing into one side of the cube. The magician drops the sugar into a glass of water and asks the spectator to hold his hands over the dissolving confection. When the volunteer's hand is turned over, revealed on his palm is an exact duplicate of the mark he made only moments before in the lump of sugar!

REQUIRED: A pencil and a lump of sugar.

PREPARATION: None.

PERFORMANCE: Offer your spectator a plate of sugar cubes and ask him to select one. Unwrap it and begin pattering: "The effervescence of sugar—in lump form, that is—has been overlooked for ages. Let me show you what I mean."

Invite the volunteer to draw a mark on one side of the sugar cube, as shown in **Figure 35**. This can be any small picture, his initials, or a number. Make sure the spectator's impression on the cube is easily legible.

As the spectator is writing, moisten the tip of your right thumb. This can be done with saliva, or by rubbing the pad of the thumb against the condensation on the outside of a glass of water.

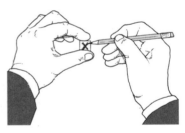

FIGURE 35

Have the cube set on the palm of your open left hand. Display the markings on the cube, then pick it up with the right finger and thumb, placing the moist pad directly on top of the drawing. Because the sugar cube is porous and the thumb is moist, an impression of the drawing will transfer from the sugar to your thumb.

"And now for that demonstration," you say. Ask the spectator to extend his hands over a glass of water, into which you drop the cube of sugar. Use your right hand to steady his hands and put them "right here." While putting his hands in position, press your right thumb into the palm of his hand as in **Figure 36,** secretly transferring the drawing to it. The transfer should take less than two seconds to make.

FIGURE 36

Allow for at least one minute to pass and for the sugar to dissolve. Say, "Though invisible to the naked eye, not all particles of sugar from the dissolving cube remain in the glass. A few crucial particulates float upward. Your hand, acting as a trap, will catch them. Give the magic of science a moment to work." After an appropriate dramatic pause, ask the spectator to turn over his hands. His mark will be revealed!

MATCHES FLY VIA GRAVITY

Though described with matches below, this trick can be easily adapted to any small object that can be held in your closed fist.

EFFECT: The magician demonstrates the properties of a commonly known physical law. "Gravity moves quickly. Though its exact properties are still in question, one thing is certain—when the force of gravity causes something to fall, it falls quickly." The magician demonstrates this with four wooden matches. One is held in each of his fists. The others are placed on top of his fists. When the performer's hands are turned over, the matches outside his fists fall to the table. "No surprises there," he says. The experiment is repeated, but this time the magician catches the matches on top of his fists before they can fall to the table. The surprise occurs when his hands are opened to reveal *three* matches in one fist, and *one* in the other.

REQUIRED: Four matches.

PREPARATION: None.

PERFORMANCE: Place one match in the palm of each hand and close your fingers around them. "Please place the other two firestarters on top of my fists. Thank you."

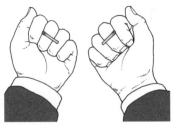

FIGURE 37

This position is shown in **Figure 37.** One match is in each hand and the others are on top of the hands. Note that the hands should be close together.

Look directly at your spectators and ask them, "There is a physical law that will pull the matches to the surface of the table when I turn my hands over. What is it?" Everyone knows the answer—gravity—but you ask the question anyway, using it as a misdirectional tool. When the spectators look at you to answer, turn your hands over. As you turn them, *catch* the match on top of your right hand, and *drop* both of the matches in your left hand. Close your left hand into a fist as soon as you release the match it contains, so that when the spectators look at the table, everything seems fair: To them, it appears as if the matches on top of your hands fell off, and nothing more.

"Gravity. That's right. Gravity moves quickly," you say. Ask the spectator to pick up the matches from the table and place them back on top of your hands. "I can move faster than gravity, if I'm lucky," you say. "Watch."

Turn your hands over again, this time catching both matches on top of them. Because of your previous deviousness, there will now be one match in your left hand and two in your right. Turn your hands palm up again, and say, slowly, "I understand how gravity works, and I understand that with practice, I can move faster than gravity and catch the matches. But what I don't understand—no matter how often it happens—is how *this* happens." Open your right hand to reveal three matches. Then open your left hand, slowly, to reveal one.

THE LAST STICK: As you reveal the matches at the conclusion of the above effect, your audience will assume the effect is over. "A relaxed audience is the performer's best friend and the magician's most powerful weapon," Mysterio wrote. A relaxed moment from an audience can be used to great advantage. In this case, at the conclusion of the match trick, one stick is your left hand and three are in your right. Drop them all to the table, then pick up the single stick with your right hand and pretend to place it in your left hand (the Fake Put described on page 148 will suffice here). Then pick up the other three matches with your right fingers and close it into a fist.

Refocus attention on your hands, as if having an afterthought about the miracle you just performed. "What's even more confusing to me," you say, "is how that last match travels from one hand to the other." Slowly open your left hand and show it empty. Then open your right hand to reveal all four matches!

TWIST AND CHANGE

Here, an old principle Mysterio used in a mind-reading effect has been adapted to a modern-day, ordinary object.

EFFECT: The magician twists the cap off a bottle of soda. "They're offering a prize in these bottles," he says to a spectator. "Let's see if I won." When the bottle cap is turned over, the magician is surprised to find that he has, indeed, won a $1000 prize! "Incredible," he says. "I thought no one ever won these games. I must be imagining things." The bottle cap is squeezed in the performer's fist and, lo and behold, when the words written under the cap are again shown to the spectator, they reveal the words "Thanks for playing, please try again!"

REQUIRED: A bottle of soda, a small pellet of wax, and a duplicate bottle cap.

PREPARATION: Cut the sides of the duplicate cap away from the top. Round the edges of the top of the cap and then, with matching material, write out (or professionally print) the message you would like to reveal in the cap of the bottle. This can be the winning message as mentioned in the description of the trick, the name of a card you will force on a spectator, or another piece of information you will reveal. Paint the back of the bottle cap the same color as the label on the bottle of soda you will perform with (or use a portion of a label from a duplicate bottle to cover the back of the gimmick you have created). This gimmicked disk is shown in **Figure 38,** next to a matching, ordinary cap.

FIGURE 38

To complete the preparation, stick the pellet of wax to the label on the bottle you will perform with. Hold the gimmicked disk in the finger-palm position (see page 128) prior to performing the effect, with the writing side closest to your palm.

PERFORMANCE: Open the bottle of soda and as you do, drop the gimmicked disk into the cap. Use your thumb to press it against the bottom of the cap, ensuring a snug fit.

At this point, you are simply drinking from the bottle, not performing a magic trick, so your audience—which may only be one spectator, since this trick is best suited to casual, situational performance moments—will not be expecting any funny business.

Pretend to notice that there is a message under the cap, of the sweepstakes variety. Turn to your spectator and say, "No one ever wins these things, do they? Let's see what it says." Keep the tone light and conversational. This is no trick, as far as anyone knows—so far.

Read the message out loud. "No way! I won?" Act surprised, and show the message to your spectator. Don't let her linger too long on the cap, so that your gimmicked disk won't be discovered. Close your hand into a fist around the cap as you say, "I'm going to hold on to this one!" Make sure that when the cap is closed in your fist, the opening is facing your palm. This allows the gimmicked disk to fall into your palm as the hand closes around the cap. See **Figure 39.**

FIGURE 39

As an afterthought, say, "You know what, here, you take this and check it again. I don't believe my eyes." Hand the cap to the spectator, and as you do, hold back the gimmicked disk in your hand, as in **Figure 40.** As you hand the cap to your spectator, pick up the bottle and, in the action of taking a drink, stick the gimmicked disk to the label, where it is camouflaged due to the fact that its back is the same color as the label.

When your spectator looks over the cap for a second time, she will be mystified. The writing on the inside of the cap has in fact changed! "I knew it was too good to be true," you say. At an opportune moment, pluck the gimmicked disk from the bottle and ditch it in your pocket.

FIGURE 40

SALTSHAKER THROUGH THE TABLE

What starts out as a gag with a borrowed coin becomes a miraculous solid-through-solid effect that will get gasps. It is perfectly suited to an after-dinner performance.

EFFECT: The magician proposes to turn a coin over without touching it. He covers the coin with a saltshaker, and then the shaker with a napkin. "With only a snap of my fingers, the coin will turn over." At the snap of his fingers, nothing happens, and the magician, though he claims to have turned the coin over, never proves this fact to his audience. "I will do it again," he says. Another snap of the fingers and the coin is shown to be heads up. Apparently the magician is joking around; nothing has happened. Then, the magic kicks in. The conjurer slams his hand down onto the paper-covered shaker. It visibly and loudly penetrates the tabletop, and is reproduced from the magician's lap!

REQUIRED: A saltshaker, paper napkin, and a coin. All objects can be borrowed.

PREPARATION: None.

PERFORMANCE: "Without touching it, I will then cause the coin to turn over, so the tail side is showing. But I don't want you to see the miracle happen, so I'm going to shield the coin from view."

Cover the coin with the saltshaker, and then say, "And just to make sure you don't peek, I'm going to cover the shaker with this napkin." Unfold the napkin and cover the shaker with it, forming it around the sides of the shaker, as shown in **Figure 41.**

Now for the gag portion of the performance. Snap your fingers over the covered coin and say, "Voilà! The coin is now tails up! Amazing, isn't it?"

Your spectators will undoubtedly want proof that the magic has happened. Without batting an eye, say, "You're unconvinced. Here, I'll do it again." Snap your fingers over the top of the covered shaker again, and say, "Look, now the coin is heads up!"

With your right hand, lift the napkin and shaker together off of the coin to reveal it to the audience. Since nothing happened, the coin *is* heads up on the table. Point to the coin and comment on its condition as you allow the saltshaker—but not the napkin— to drop into your lap, as shown in **Figures 42 and 43.** Because the napkin was wrapped around the shaker at the outset of the trick, even though it is now empty, the napkin becomes what magicians call a "shell." Outwardly, it appears as if the shaker is still inside the napkin.

FIGURE 41

FIGURE 42

FIGURE 43

Without pausing, continue your patter by saying. "Not a good trick? Here, let's try something more impressive." Place the napkin shell back over the coin, as if you are going to try the turnover of the coin one more time. Pause for a beat, and then slam your hand down on top of the napkin. To everyone's surprise, the saltshaker is gone.

With your empty left hand, reach under the table and retrieve the shaker from your lap as your hand continues its journey underneath the table. You do this to mimic what would happen if the shaker had actually penetrated the tabletop. Finally, reproduce the saltshaker from underneath the table to conclude the effect.

ALTERNATE ENDING: Some magicians prefer to vanish the saltshaker, leaving it in their laps instead of telling the spectators that it penetrated the tabletop. With careful thought and planning, the shaker can later be reproduced in an impossible location, creating a memorable, magical effect. Mysterio used a duplicate saltshaker to accomplish this feat, planting it in locations as varied as a spectator's coat pockets, in his own sock, and once (with help from a sympathetic concierge), in the hotel room of an important press agent. When the saltshaker reappeared on the agent's pillow, there was no question that Mysterio would receive complimentary coverage in the newspaper the following week.

DUAL CONTROL

The secret gimmick called Dual Control is a versatile device that can be made in under half an hour, at minimal cost. It was most likely invented by the famous British music hall artist G. W. Hunter. With the Dual Control device on your person, dozens of different effects can be performed, including several that would otherwise require sleight-of-hand ability or special and expensive props. Study the following directions and you will have one made in no time.

REQUIRED: A length of strong black elastic, available at any fabric store; a spool of monofilament (fishing line); one large and one small safety pin; and a small plastic ring, 1 inch (2 1/2 cm) in diameter or smaller. You must wear a jacket or long-sleeved shirt to use the Dual Control gimmick. Suitable plastic rings are available at craft stores and hardware stores. Metal rings can also be used.

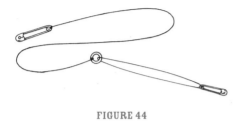

FIGURE 44

CONSTRUCTION OF THE GIMMICK: Cut a length of black elastic and tie one end to the large safety pin. Tie the other end of the elastic to the ring. To the ring, tie a loop of monofilament, onto which has been threaded a small safety pin. The entire arrangement is shown in **Figure 44.**

ATTACHING THE GIMMICK: Use the large safety pin to attach the elastic inside your coat or shirt, near your armpit, as shown in **Figure 45.** The loop end of the gimmick should hang down your sleeve. Its end should

FIGURE 45

be approximately ¹⁄₃ inch (1 cm) from the edge of your sleeve, which is where you pin the small safety pin that has been threaded onto the monofilament loop, so that when no tension is on the elastic, the entire gimmick is hidden from view just inside the cuff, as in **Figure 46.** The small safety pin is in place to make sure that the gimmick does not shoot all the way up the sleeve, which would make it difficult to put it in position in the course of a performance.

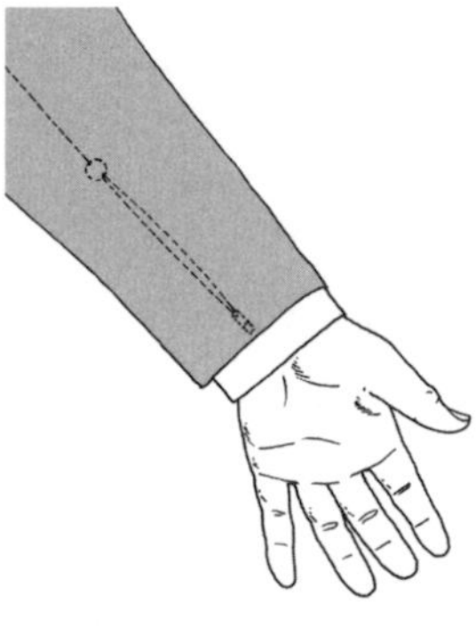

FIGURE 46

PUTTING THE GIMMICK IN POSITION: The Dual Control gimmick can be put into position—with the monofilament loop running under the magician's middle finger nail, as shown in **Figure 47**—at any time. Use the free hand to put the loop in position, and do this only when attention is directed away from your hands. If performing at a table, this

FIGURE 47

FIGURE 48

FIGURE 49

action can be concealed underneath the table. If performing while standing, put it into position under cover of turning your body, or by placing your hands behind your back.

Another way to get the gimmick ready is to start with it looped over your thumb, as shown in **Figure 48.** With some practice, the middle finger can be inserted into the loop and the nail can then engage the monofilament, as in **Figure 49.**

When you are finished with the Dual Control gimmick, you can dispense with it quickly and easily, simply by curling your middle finger in toward your palm. This will release the monofilament loop, and the gimmick will disappear back up your sleeve.

The possibilities are endless. The question is not "What will a Dual Control gimmick allow you to do?" The question is "What *won't* a Dual Control gimmick allow you to do?" There are dozens of impressive tricks that this subtle gimmick makes possible. Here are a few.

MAGNETIZED CARDS

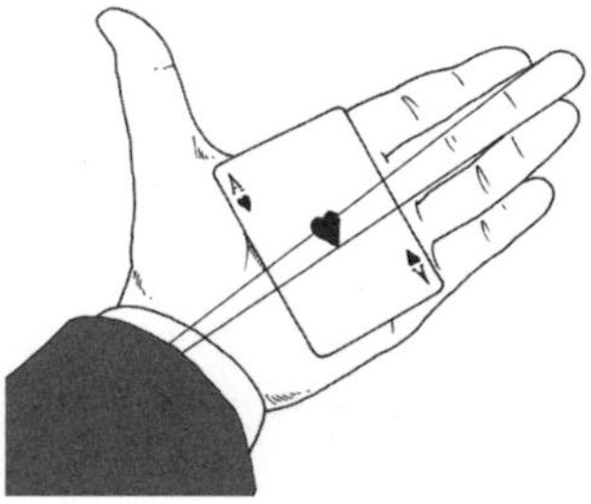

FIGURE 50

Place one card under the Dual Control gimmick as shown in **Figure 50,** then arrange a group of other cards underneath it in a fanned configuration, as shown in **Figure 51.** The cards are put in place while the hand is held palm down, against the table-top. Now, when the hand is raised, sufficient pressure against the hand by the gimmick and attached card cause the entire group to cling to the palm as if drawn to it by some secret, magnetic force.

FIGURE 51

CLINGING PENCIL

On page 94, an effect called the Magnetic Fingertips is described, along with a varia- tion. With a Dual Control gimmick, the Magnetic Fingertips trick can be performed in a very convincing, clean manner. Simply insert a pencil or pen (which may be borrowed) under the loop of the gimmick and it will cling to the hand. Because the monofilament used to construct the Dual Control gimmick is virtually invisible, the

FIGURE 52

palm of the hand can be flashed at the audience without fear of detection and the fingers can be spread wide apart, as in **Figure 52.**

With the pencil against your palm, you can cause it to rotate around your hand by flipping it into the back of the fingers (keeping it in the loop), as shown in **Figure 53.** By releasing the tension in the gimmick and moving your fingers out of the way, the pencil will quickly flip over your fingers and back into your palm, as shown in **Figure 54.**

With one pencil on the back of the hand, you can suspend another from the palm of the hand as well. This is shown in **Figure 55.**

FIGURE 53

FIGURE 54

FIGURE 55

THE DRAWER THAT WON'T CLOSE

Open a matchbox and dump the matches out onto the table. Ask a spectator to select one of the matches, and as this happens, encircle the open sleeve of the box with the loop of the Dual Control gimmick, as shown in **Figure 56.** Now slide the drawer closed. Then instruct a spectator to wave the match he selected, "the world's smallest magic wand," over the box. As you increase tension on the gimmick, and because of the monofilament's presence, the drawer of the box will open slowly and eerily, apparently of its own accord.

FIGURE 56

OTHER OBJECTS UNDER YOUR SPELL

Since the loop of the gimmick can stretch, a paper cup can be placed in it and cling to your hand, as shown in **Figure 57.** Toothpicks, toothbrushes, spoons, pretzel sticks, and similar objects can be used to produce the same effects as a pencil. Dollar bills can also stick to your hand ("You've heard of a bad penny? Well, this is a bad bill—it just won't go away!"), as can matchboxes and matchbooks.

FIGURE 57

SECRET PALMING

The Dual Control gimmick does not need to be used for an obvious, visible effect. Instead, it can act as the magician's third hand, making palming trouble-free. An object to be later produced can be placed under the loop of the gimmick and will stick to the magician's palm as long as he requires it to. Because of the gimmick's presence, the performer's fingers may be stretched apart widely while the object is concealed. As previously explained, to release the item from the palm, the magician merely curls his middle finger in toward his palm, and the gimmick shoots up his sleeve.

DUAL POSSIBILITIES

With two Dual Control gimmicks in place, objects can be moved from one hand to the other and cling to either one. ᐁ

CHAPTER IV

CUPS AND BALLS

THE OLDEST DECEPTION

·~∞~·

P ERHAPS THE OLDEST SLEIGHT-OF-HAND FEATS IN THE WORLD, versions of the Cups and Balls have been practiced and performed by prestidigitators for thousands of years. Some historians of conjuring claim that Egyptian hieroglyphs painted on the tomb walls at Beni Hasan depict this trick in midstream (though these claims continue to be a source of some controversy).

In Mysterio's notebooks, scant introductory notes preceded lengthy scribbles and comments on this venerable deception. Most notably, the great magician emphasized, with a triple underscore, the following words: "Learning the Cups and Balls is *required* for *all* serious conjurers. This is a must!!!"

Indeed, since Mysterio's passing and even during his lifetime, the Cups and Balls has stood as a sort of benchmark in all magicians' repertoires. To be a conjurer unable to perform this most elementary feat is to be a doctor with no knowledge of the human body. The trick seems simple: Little balls jump around, vanish, and appear under cups that have been placed on the table. But under this apparently easy effect lie the fundaments of all that is magic: coordination of the hands and eyes, strong misdirection, subtlety, and sleight-of-hand technique.

VERBIAGE

To understand how to work with your set of cups and balls, you'll also need to understand the vocabulary associated with the props. Here's a mini-glossary for easy reference.

TOP OF THE CUP: The mouth of the cup is generally resting against the table when the Cups and Balls is performed. Therefore, the bottom of the cup is referred to as the "top."

ATTIC: When the cups are nested together, the word "attic" denotes the space between them.

LOAD: This describes the action of secretly introducing an object into a cup, as in "to load the cup with a ball."

STEAL: The opposite of load; to covertly remove an object from a cup.

FINAL LOAD: At the conclusion of most Cups and Balls routines, large objects known as "final loads" are produced.

LIP OF THE CUP: Also known as the rim of the cup.

PROPERTIES

No SPECIAL PROPS ARE REQUIRED to perform the Cups and Balls—only a set of three opaque, stacking cups and a number of small balls. The exact configuration of your personal cups and balls will depend on your needs and performance style.

CUPS

While Mysterio favored cups made of brass, produced by Martinka & Co., the effect can be most surprising and effective when performed in an apparently impromptu situation. Max Malini, a contemporary of Mysterio's, often used coffee cups and other borrowed drinking vessels when executing the trick "off the cuff."

If money is no object and a reputable dealer in magic apparatus is at your disposal, a wide range of cups is available. Consider the following factors when selecting the tools you will use for this effect.

SIZE: Some cups are easy to carry in a pocket, and others are designed to hold large final loads. If possible, test out the cups you will use and make sure they will accommodate everything you'll need them to.

SHAPE: The late Paul Fox of Denver, Colorado, designed a set of cups with a unique shape. When final loads are produced from Fox's cups, the loads seem *larger* than the cups. While not every audience member will notice this, and it may seem a small point, small points can have gargantuan effects on an alert spectator.

Whatever cups you use, make sure they do not wobble when nested together. Finally, be sure to use cups with an indented top. The depression in the top (bottom) of each cup should ideally be deep enough to hold three balls comfortably (at a bare minimum it must hold one ball).

ATTIC SPACE: Nest your cups together. The best sets have enough room in their attics to easily accommodate three balls. Of course, using smaller balls can help you work around sets of cups with less-than-ample attic space. Most magician's cups have an outdented band around the middle to ensure that when they're stacked, the attic space is preserved.

BALLS

Traditionally, conjurers have used small balls made from cork for their Cups and Balls routines. Cork balls can be decorated in a number of ways. Mysterio found that blackening the cork balls—his were approximately 3/4 inch (2 cm) in diameter—in the flame of a candle worked well.

Modern magicians tend toward a style of ball popularized after Mysterio's passing. These, too, are often made of cork, but are covered with a tightly woven or crocheted fabric. Sets of balls in various sizes and a wide spectrum of colors are available from magic dealers worldwide.

THE WAND

A sturdy magic wand is as important to performing the Cups and Balls as are the rest of the props. Why? Because when a ball is palmed, holding a wand in the hand that hides the ball effectively conceals its presence. Giving the hand something to do while it palms a ball helps give the hand a natural appearance.

Wands can be made from just about any ordinary object: Many coat hangers have a center section made of a cardboard tube; when decorated appropriately, these work well as impromptu wands. Sturdier, more professional wands can be purchased from magic shops. A length of dowel can be cut and painted accordingly. In impromptu performances, a spear of celery or a long carrot can serve as an excellent ersatz wand.

BASIC SLEIGHTS

WHILE DOZENS OF VOLUMES have been written on the subject of the Cups and Balls (Mysterio was particularly fond of a section of Professor Hoffmann's book *Modern Magic* that was devoted to the subject), what follows is a selection of basic techniques that every budding thimble-rigger should be conversant with.

FINGER PALM

This is the most common way to conceal a ball in the hand. The ball rests at the base of the second and third fingers. The fingers should be gently and naturally curled around it. **Figure 1** shows the performer's view of this position. **Figure 2** shows it from the audience's perspective. Hold a wand between the fingers and thumb of the hand that finger palms the ball, and the concealment becomes completely natural. Note: The finger palm will work with any small object, such as a coin, a thimble, or a die.

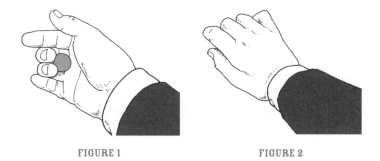

FIGURE 1   FIGURE 2

SIMPLE FALSE TRANSFER

This sleight cannot be practiced enough. Its perfect execution is essential to all Cups and Balls routines.

With a ball displayed in your right hand, pretend to place it in your open left hand. What actually happens is this: The thumb holds the ball against the base of the right fingers as the hand turns over to deposit the ball in the left hand. See **Figure 3.**

The left fingers close around the supposed ball, while the right hand moves away from the scene of the "crime." As the right hand falls out of the audience's frame of vision (all attention is focused on the left hand), the ball is held in finger palm.

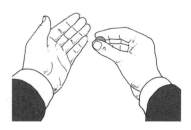

FIGURE 3

This sleight can be effectively practiced by actually placing the ball in your left hand a number of times, and then performing the sleight, which should exactly mimic the feel and look of the real action. Again, this sleight works with any small object, not just a ball.

FIGURE 4

ROLL-DOWN VANISH

Hold a ball in the right hand between the tip of the thumb and the tip of the index finger. Cup the left hand underneath the right hand, as in **Figure 4.** This false transfer is performed by allowing the ball to apparently roll down the right hand and into the left.

FIGURE 5

However, instead of allowing the ball to fall into the left hand, the right third and fourth fingers stop the ball in its tracks. See **Figure 5.** When the ball is caught, the right hand moves away (as described above) and the left fingers close into a fist, as if catching the ball. The ball can now be caused to vanish from the left fist by opening the fingers, or the ball can apparently be placed beneath a cup.

BASIC LOAD #1

This sleight allows you to secretly load a ball underneath a cup.

What happens is this: A cup is lifted from the table under some pretense (Mysterio often performed this load when showing a cup empty) and set back onto the table. In the action of setting it back down, a ball is loaded inside the empty cup.

FIGURE 6

To do this, the ball begins in right-hand finger palm. The right hand picks up a cup from the table and then, in the action of setting down the cup, performs the move. The front edge of the cup touches the table first, and at the same time, the ball, which is held against the lip of the cup at the rear as in **Figure 6**, is released from finger palm. From there, it is easily sneaked under the cup, which is lowered over it. See **Figure 7.** Due to the proximity of the ball and the lip of the cup, loading it underneath the cup from this position is easy, and can be done without suspicious-looking action from the hand.

FIGURE 7

BASIC LOAD #2

This load is even easier than Basic Load #1.

A ball is concealed in the magician's hand. As a cup is picked up with the same hand from the table, the first finger and thumb encircle its lip. The cup is tilted downward at

FIGURE 8

a 45-degree angle, its top pointed toward the table. If the magician now releases his hold on the palmed ball, gravity does the rest of the work; as shown in **Figure 8,** the ball falls directly into the cup, which is now loaded and can be set back on the table.

TIP-OVER LOAD

Begin with a ball concealed in your right hand and one ball on top of each cup. Grasp a cup with the thumb and first finger of the right hand and tip it forward, dumping the ball on top into the left palm, which is in front of it, waiting to receive the ball. This gives the right hand ample space and time to usher the concealed ball underneath the cup just before it is returned, mouth down, to the table, see **Figure 9.**

FIGURE 9

Transfer the visible ball to your right hand as you patter, where you display it casually to the audience. Then perform a false transfer, pretending to switch the visible ball to your left hand but in fact retaining it in your right. Repeat the above tipping action, loading the concealed ball into the next cup as you dump the ball off the top of it.

Repeat the false transfer and loading moves with the remaining cup and ball. Pause appropriately. Pick up the cups one at a time to show that all three balls have reappeared. This sequence will serve you well, and is an excellent opening to any Cups and Balls routine. Of course, it can also be used to load a single cup as opposed to all three.

STEAL

Use this sleight to secretly remove a ball from underneath a cup or to show a loaded cup empty. The cup is picked up with the right hand, which lifts the rear edge of the cup's lip off the table slightly before the front edge. As this happens, the right little and third fingers contact the ball, pressing it against the rear lip and then down into the hand.

Alternately, the little finger of the right hand can press the ball against the rear lip of the cup as it is lifted from the table.

THE INERTIA MOVE

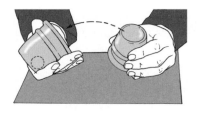

FIGURE 10

A ball is nested in the attic space between two cups, which are held in one hand, mouth up. The other hand removes the lower cup and places it mouth-down on the table, as in **Figure 10.** This is done smoothly and deliberately, but not slowly—otherwise the hidden ball will drop out of the cup. The hidden ball travels with the cup and is not seen, as inertia keeps it from falling out as the magician sets it down, as shown in **Figure 11.** Again, there's no need to hurry—place the cup deliberately on the table and the concealed ball won't fall out. The other cup is placed on the table in a similar fashion.

FIGURE 11

THE SCOOP MOVE

This is a sleight used to apparently scoop a ball underneath a cup, when in actuality it is retained in the hand. Essentially, this is a false transfer into a cup, as opposed to your hand. With a ball in your right hand at the base of the second and third fingers, tilt the front lip of the cup off the table with the left hand. The right fingertips almost enter the cup, simulating the action of shuttling the ball underneath the cup. But, because the back of the right hand is toward the audience, they will be unaware of the fact that you have held the ball back in your hand in finger palm position as shown in **Figure 12.** The thumb can assist in holding the ball back, but the less finger motion required, the better.

FIGURE 12

THE BASIC ROUTINE

Learning how to perform the Cups and Balls may seem like a lot of work to the beginning magician. And to be sure, many versions of the trick require considerable practice to master. But, even without a grasp of complicated sleight-of-hand, a novice can perform an easy-to-master Cups and Balls routine sure to win over audiences. This no-nonsense routine is laid out below.

EFFECT: The magician causes several balls to vanish and reappear from the cups in rapid succession.

REQUIRED: Three opaque cups that nest together, one on top of the other, and four balls. These can be made of crumpled dollar bills, chunks of bread rolled into shape, small pieces of cork, or even four grapes. All the balls must be similar in size and color.

PREPARATION: Place one cup on the table, mouth up. Drop in one ball. Stack the other two cups on top of the first cup and then drop in three balls.

PERFORMANCE: Roll the three balls out of the top cup and onto the table. Perform the inertia move as you unstack the cups and set them mouth down on the table. If you move at a steady, deliberate pace, the ball concealed in the lowermost cup will not drop out of it. The secreted ball travels with the cup and is not seen.

Now place one of the three visible balls on top of the loaded cup. Place a second cup on top of this loaded cup. Lift the two cups together (with one hand) to show that the ball has penetrated the cup.

Using the two stacked cups in your hand, repeat the inertia move, but cover a visible ball—the one that's already "penetrated" the cup—with the loaded cup. Stack another cup on top of this one. Repeat the penetration effect. Now two balls are underneath the lowermost cup.

The third time, use the inertia move to place the loaded cup over the two balls. Stack the other *two* cups on top of the loaded cup. Place the one visible ball in your pocket. When a spectator picks up the cups, the third ball has appeared underneath them!

Alternately, you can vanish the third ball by one of the methods described elsewhere in this chapter (using another false transfer, for example) and cause the ball to reappear underneath the cups with the other two balls.

BUSINESS ESSENTIALS

O NE OF THE ELEMENTS that will make your performance more polished and more entertaining is clever bits of stage business. Here are a few examples.

SCREWING A CUP TOGETHER

The magician patters about not having his props ready for performance. That being said, he appears to screw two halves of one of his cups together. His performance then continues as usual. There is no trick to this one; grab a cup with two hands and repeatedly twist the hands in opposite directions as if you were screwing two halves of the cup together. With an appropriate amount of acting and the right line of patter, the action will not only look realistic, but get a laugh, too.

WAND THROUGH CUP

The magician, in an effort to show the cups to be solid, raps his wand against the bottom of one of them. Unexpectedly, the wand penetrates the bottom of the cup! Even the magician is surprised at this! The bottom of the cup is then shown whole again.

Hold a cup in your left hand so that the mouth faces your right. Hold a wand in your right hand with your index finger lying along the wand.

Push the wand into the cup, tapping it against the bottom. After tapping the interior of the cup several times, pull the wand out of the cup just enough to allow it to slip behind the cup (between your left hand and the cup) as you thrust forward again. See **Figure 13.** Though the wand passes behind the cup at this point, the index finger still goes inside the cup. Don't let the image of the wand penetrating the cup linger for too long. The illusion is perfect only for a few seconds. Remove the wand from the cup and continue with your routine.

FIGURE 13

CUP THROUGH CUP

FIGURE 14

The magician drops one cup into another. As it falls, it penetrates the bottom of the cup in the magician's hand and falls to the table with an audible "clunk!"

Hold a cup mouth up in your left hand. Grasp it at the lip with your thumb and first finger. Your right hand holds a cup in a similar grip. Drop the cup from the right hand into the mouth of the cup in the left. The falling cup should dislodge the cup in the left hand and take its place as in **Figure 14.** Combined with the action of screwing together a cup, this apparent penetration always gets a chuckle.

PATTER AND MISDIRECTION

Your patter for the Cups and Balls—as well as other effects you perform—is as important as the trick itself. Appropriate phrasing combined with careful use of eye contact during your patter can direct the attention of your audience where *you* want it to be—keeping the spectators from "burning" your every move.

Take, for example, the false transfer of a ball from hand to hand. When executing the move, try to perform it this way: Pick up a ball in the right hand. Look at it with interest. Say, "The amazing thing about these little red balls is…" Now look directly at your audience as you place the ball in the left hand and make the false transfer. As you execute the sleight, *focus on your words, not your actions.* Continue, "…how small they become when you squeeze them." At this point, the ball has been retained in your right hand, but the audience thinks that it is in your left. Squeeze your closed left fist tightly. Return your attention to it, and the audience will follow your lead. Say, "In fact, if you squeeze hard enough, they're impossible to see." Open your left hand to show that the ball is gone.

This is only one example of how an audience's attention can be focused where you want it with the appropriate combination of actions and words. As you study the Cups and Balls, consider how your words, together with your movements, can combine to hold, shape, and direct (or misdirect) the gaze of your audience.

IMPROMPTU CUPS AND BALLS ROUTINE

Inspired by the work of Dai Vernon, the following routine was developed with the Cups and Balls. Study the instructions carefully; the final sequence is one of the most important, impressive, and essential in all of magic.

EFFECT: The magician displays a bewildering sequence of vanishes, appearances, and translocations with three small balls and three opaque cups. Balls jump from cup to cup, vanish from the magician's hands, and penetrate the solid cups. At the conclusion of the routine, three new objects appear from underneath the cups!

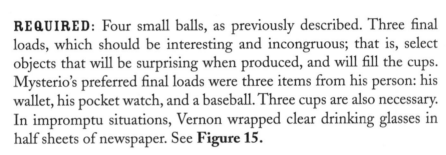

FIGURE 15

REQUIRED: Four small balls, as previously described. Three final loads, which should be interesting and incongruous; that is, select objects that will be surprising when produced, and will fill the cups. Mysterio's preferred final loads were three items from his person: his wallet, his pocket watch, and a baseball. Three cups are also necessary. In impromptu situations, Vernon wrapped clear drinking glasses in half sheets of newspaper. See **Figure 15**.

PREPARATION: The four balls begin in your right trouser or jacket pocket. The final loads begin in the left rear trouser pocket (in a pinch, the left coat pocket can be used).

PHASE ONE—GONE AND BACK AGAIN

The cups are placed in a row on the table, mouth down. Reach into your pocket and remove all four balls. Toss three of them into your left hand, using finger palm to secretly hold back one ball. Gently toss two balls back from the left to the right. This maneuver, known as the shuttle pass, casually displays the hands as empty, while you are in fact concealing an extra ball. End with three visible balls in your left hand, and one concealed in finger palm in your right. Drop the visible balls on the table and use your left hand to place one under each cup.

"This looks like the old three shell game," you say, as you lift the rightmost cup with your left hand and transfer it to your right hand. Pick up the exposed ball with your left hand and set the cup back down, loading the concealed ball underneath as you do. See **Figure 16.**

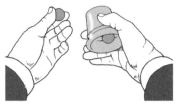

Using one of the false transfers already described, vanish the visible ball. It ends up concealed in your right hand.

Repeat this sequence of loading and vanishing with the center cup, and then the leftmost cup. "They're gone, but not far," you say. Lift the cups to show that all three vanished balls have returned, concluding the first phase of the routine.

PHASE TWO — INVISIBLE FLIGHT

Cover the left and right balls with cups. As you do so, load the ball hidden in your right hand underneath the right cup. Cover the center ball with the center cup.

"I will now—invisibly—pluck a ball from beneath the center cup with the end of the wand," you say, pantomiming this action, "and will pass it into the cup at the right."

Show that the center ball has vanished by picking up the cup that covers it with your right hand. As you do so, your middle finger maintains contact with the table. Unobserved by the audience, you tip the cup slightly to the left as your little finger slides underneath and presses the ball against the inside of the cup. With your other hand, wave the wand underneath the apparently empty cup, "proving" that it holds nothing. Set the cup back down, this time on the *right* side of the table, making it the rightmost cup.

Raise the centermost cup to show two balls underneath, and then set the cup down to their left. The rightmost cup (which was, just a moment ago, shown empty) is now tilted slightly toward the audience so that the two visible balls can be swept underneath it. Three balls are now under this cup, but the audience is only aware of two.

"For the nonbelievers, we'll perform this invisible migration one more time." Mime the action of invisibly plucking a ball through the leftmost cup and passing it into the rightmost cup. Show the left cup empty, as described above, by clipping the ball inside and passing the wand underneath. Set the left cup down between the other two, making it the new center cup. Announce, "The invisible journey is complete!" Lift the rightmost cup to reveal three balls. Set the cup mouth down, keeping it to the right of the other two.

At this point, the center cup conceals one ball, and the cups on either side are empty.

A ball is placed in front of each cup. Picking up the leftmost ball in your right hand, say, "And now, a different type of migration—no wand required. I will first place one ball under each cup." Execute a false transfer into your left hand. Pretend to place the ball under the leftmost cup, tilting it up with your right hand and apparently pushing the ball underneath with your left hand. In reality you are finger palming the ball in your right hand, and the leftmost cup is still empty.

Use your right hand to pick up the centermost ball. Place it and the palmed ball under the center cup (which, you will remember, already conceals a ball). Be careful not to expose the ball already hidden under it. The center cup now conceals three balls, though the audience is aware of only one.

Pretend to place the rightmost ball underneath the right cup, again using a false transfer to your left hand and palming the ball with your right hand, as described above. It appears as if you have placed one ball under each cup. Actually, there are three under the center cup and one concealed in your right hand.

Ask a spectator to choose one of the cups. Most of the time, he will select the center cup. If he does, your job is simple: Lift the two outer cups, showing them unmistakably empty. Set them back down to the right of the loaded cup. Lift this cup with your right hand to show three balls.

If the spectator names one of the other two cups, use the equivoque technique—a technique in which the magician frames his questions in such a way that the spectator is maneuvered into arriving at the conclusion the magician desires—to force him to select the center cup anyway. In this instance, equivoque works as follows: Ask him to select a second cup. If he chooses the cup on the other end of the table, say, "That leaves us with the center cup. Watch!" Then proceed as described in the previous paragraph, showing the balls gathered together under the center cup.

If, instead, he selects an end cup first and the center cup second, ask another question, namely: "Now name one of these two." If he selects the center cup, go with it, and reveal the balls underneath. If he selects the other cup, say, "We'll eliminate this one," and push it lightly out of the way. No matter what decisions the spectator makes, at no time should he be told *why* he is selecting a cup. Only announce whether a cup will be eliminated or selected *after* the spectator has made a decision. Regardless of the choices he makes, he always ends up with the center cup.

At this point in the routine, three balls are on the table, and one is concealed in your right hand. Place one ball under each cup. "This trick may be overly complicated," you say, "so I will eliminate two of the balls."

With your right hand, pick up the cup on your left. Load the palmed ball inside it as you do. A ball will now be visible on the table. Pick it up with your left hand and set the loaded cup back on the table.

Use a false transfer to pretend to place the ball in your left hand, and then apparently in your left rear trousers pocket—the pocket that contains the final loads.

Repeat the above steps, this time with the rightmost cup: Pick it up and load the concealed ball into it. Again, use a false transfer to apparently place the visible ball in your left rear pocket. As you do this, retrieve one of the final loads from that pocket.

As you pull the load from your pocket, pick up the center cup with your right hand and say, "This looks like the shell game again, doesn't it? Three cups and one ball…"

While delivering the above line, the *right* hand loads its concealed ball under the center cup. All attention is focused on the ball on the table as you talk. It is at this moment that the left hand emerges from the pocket and hangs loosely at your side. No special attempt is made to hide the load that the left hand conceals, as no attention is given to the left hand, which is curled in a natural position.

As the center cup is set down over the visible ball, you immediately lift the right cup with the right hand, and say, "The only problem is, I'm using more than one ball." The right hand carries the cup toward the left. Say, "You see, I cheat by using more than one ball." Stare at the ball that was just revealed as you say this, and as you look at it, the right and left hands meet near the left pocket. At this moment, the large final load—which you totally ignore with your body language and eyes—is introduced into the cup. In a continuing action, the left hand takes the cup from the right.

The loaded cup is transferred back into the right hand, which holds the final load in place by means of a secretly extended little finger across the opening of the cup. Set the cup down in front of the newly exposed ball. "Let me explain how that happened—how I sneaked the ball under the cup," you say.

"I never put the ball in my pocket," you explain, as you perform a clumsy and exposed false transfer. Show the left hand empty and continue your patter: "The ball never made it into my pocket." Here, your left hand is placed into your pocket where it secures the second final load. At the same moment, you expose the ball in your right hand completely, drawing all attention to it.

"With a ball hidden in my right hand, it was easy enough to sneak it under the cup," you continue. Pretend to load the ball in the right hand under the left cup—but don't. Simply lift the cup and display the ball already there. Gently nudge the ball with the rear rim of the cup, rolling it forward, toward the edge of the table. As the ball rolls forward, load the cup with the second large object. As you grab the rolling ball, place the loaded cup on the table.

"Now that you know how the trick works, I'm going to try to fool you. Be on the lookout for anything suspicious." With your left hand, openly and fairly place the just-revealed ball in your left pocket. Palm the remaining final load as you put the ball away. Look directly at a nearby spectator and ask him, "How many balls are under the middle cup?" No matter how he responds, you react with the same actions every time: Lift the center cup with your right hand, dropping the palmed ball as you do, adding it to the two already underneath it. Three balls have apparently appeared under the centermost cup.

Your audience will undoubtedly react strongly at this moment. The balls were apparently removed from play, yet all three have reappeared. Taking advantage of this moment of surprise, load the final cup and set it down behind the three balls on the table. Pick the balls up and say, "I'll give you one more chance, and this time, no funny business." Fairly and openly, place all three balls into your left pocket. Finally, ask, "Where do you think the three little balls are now?" After they answer, lift the center cup. Pause for only a moment as they react, and then raise the outer two cups simultaneously to produce the loads they contain.

TWO BUILDING BLOCKS

WHAT FOLLOWS ARE TWO SEQUENCES that can be added to any Cups and Balls performance, like building blocks, to create a routine unique to the individual.

CUPS RUNNETH OVER

Sleight of Hand, a classic conjuring text by Edwin Sachs, was one of the treatises on conjuring from which Mysterio learned elementary trade secrets. Today, more than a hundred years after its first publication, Sachs's book remains an excellent introduction to the magical arts. It is particularly descriptive of feats requiring digital dexterity, including the Cups and Balls. The following paragraph, gleaned from *Sleight of Hand*, describes a method whereby it appears as if the conjurer is able to produce an endless number of balls from the cups.

"This is very easily managed by first covering each of the three balls with a cup openly. Take up cup No. 1 and set it down a few inches off with the (extra) ball concealed beneath it. Pick up ball No. 1 and pretend to put it in your pocket, but conceal it in the fingers; take up cup No. 2, and replace it, with concealed ball underneath it, and affect to put ball No. 2 into the pocket, but conceal it as before. Repeat operation with cup and ball No. 3, and then recommence with cup No. 1. This phase can be prolonged at will. A number of balls can be carried in the pocket, and afterwards exhibited as the ones you have manufactured; but this is by no means necessary to the success of the trick."

This never-ending production of balls from the cups should be made to appear as startling and unexpected to the performer as it is to the spectators. As the balls are produced, they should be placed in the magician's pocket (Mysterio pretended to place them in a small opaque vase behind his table).

STACKED APPEARANCE

These maneuvers make balls vanish one at a time and then reappear *between* two nested cups.

The sequence begins with two cups on the table, mouth downward, nested together, with a ball concealed in the attic space between them. Use a false transfer to vanish a ball. As you reveal the ball between the nested cups, load the concealed (vanished) ball inside the upper cup of the stack. Leave the visible ball on top of the lower cup as you re-nest the pair. Vanish another ball, and cause it to reappear between the cups as before. To conclude the sequence, load the upper cup one last time as you show that the second ball has joined the first. The third ball follows the same path, vanishing and reappearing with the other two between the tabled cups, through the same actions outlined above. ❧

CHAPTER V

MONEY MAGIC

CONJURING WITH CURRENCY

⋅∿⤜⥲∿⋅

M AGIC WITH MONEY excites immediate interest in an audience. What is more natural than a trick with an everyday object, something that nearly everyone, in every country on the planet, carries on his person every day? Many excellent tricks with currency can be performed on the spur of the moment, with articles—coins and bills—borrowed from spectators. These sorts of "organic" feats can secure your reputation as a mystifier ready to work his unique brand of miracles at any moment. After all, if your powers were real, wouldn't you be able to put them to work at a moment's notice?

Before introducing you to various tricks with coins and bills, it should be noted that the coin best suited for the purposes of manipulation and sleight-of-hand is the U.S. half dollar. Similarly sized coins exist in nearly all countries; for years, the English penny was of a diameter nearly identical to that of the half dollar. Nowadays, the Canadian "Twonie" (two-dollar coin) works well, as do various foreign coins. For the sake of consistency, Mr. Mysterio selected tricks using half dollars for inclusion in this *Encyclopedia*. In his day, the coin was circulated as frequently as nearly any other denomination, and was made of real silver. Also common were silver dollars. From the stage, Mysterio manipulated "Morgan" dollar coins, named after the designer that engraved them for the U.S. Mint.

Though many of the effects described in this chapter can be performed with quarters and other pocket change, if you don't have access to five or ten half dollars, go to your bank and request them. You'll be glad you did.

Thomas Nelson Downs was the first magician to specialize in tricks with coins, and it was he who inspired Mr. Mysterio's love of conjuring with currency. In fact, the Miser's Dream, described in the following pages, was as much a part of Downs's professional repertoire (it was, in fact, his feature trick and the one that catapulted him to stardom on the world's leading stages) as it was Mysterio's. The trick is one of the finest in all of conjuring.

When the sun set on vaudeville and the music-hall era of Mysterio and his contemporaries, so did a chapter in magic's development. Coin tricks, like other genres of magic, became more intimate and personal. Developments were made by close-up performers. Techniques created for larger, showier circumstances were adapted for use at close quarters.

Based on Mysterio's experience, the successes of his contemporaries, and more modern developments, the pages that follow include techniques, tips, tricks, and tactics that will give the aspiring wizard a solid foundation in one of the most fascinating branches of the arcane arts.

COIN SLEIGHTS: PALMING, SWITCHING, AND VANISHING

THE MOST BASIC OF ALL CONCEALMENTS IS PALMING. You have likely heard this term in casual conversation and can probably infer its meaning. To palm an item (here, a coin) is to conceal it naturally in your hand. Switching refers to the act of substituting one coin (or similar small item) for another. Vanishing is what the name implies—causing a coin to disappear, seemingly into thin air.

To practice palming techniques, some performers—Mysterio among them—advocate palming a coin while running errands, taking a walk, or performing everyday tasks. Mastery is said to be attained when the magician has forgotten the presence of the coin entirely. There are dozens of ways to palm a coin. Here are several important, useful palms, as well as a switch that will serve you well with only a little practice.

THE CLASSIC PALM

This technique allows the fingers of the hand that does the dirty work to remain open and free. While the coin is concealed, the fingers can still grasp, drop and pick up other small objects.

Place a half dollar in your palm-up right hand, slightly off center. One edge of the coin should lie on the ball of your thumb, and the opposite edge close to the large crease (line) running through the center of your hand. See **Figure 1** for this position.

FIGURE 1

Clamp down on the coin by curling your middle and ring fingers inward. Squash the coin into the flesh of your hand.

Now gently squeeze your hand together, pressing the ball of your thumb and the pinky side of your hand toward each other. The coin should be held between the center line of your hand and the ball of your thumb, as in **Figure 2.** When your hand is viewed from the back, it appears naturally open and free, with the fingers curled slightly inward.

FIGURE 2

Exert as little pressure as possible on the coin to maintain as natural a look as possible. Avoid a cramped, clawlike look. Your thumb should not stick straight out from the hand, but rather be held loosely and naturally.

In performance the opportunities to place a coin in classic palm using your free hand are unlikely to occur. To classic palm a coin with one hand, the coin must first be set on the tips of the middle and ring fingers. Make a fist.

As the fingers curl in toward the palm, the coin will contact the center of the hand, at which point the coin can be easily classic palmed. It should be noted that more than one coin can be concealed in classic palm at a time.

FINGER PALM

This palm is described on page 128, in the chapter on Cups and Balls. The technique is the same for any small object.

THUMB PALM

FIGURE 3

For this technique, the coin is pinched in the crotch of the thumb, between the base of the first finger and the thumb. **Figure 3** shows this position.

Like the classic palm, the thumb palm allows the fingers to move freely. However, the thumb is somewhat restricted due to the position of the concealed coin. It is advisable to hide a coin in the thumb palm for only a short period of time, especially if spectators are "burning" (closely watching) your hands.

PURSE PALM

This palm was used by British magician Charles Morritt, a brilliant illusionist and mind reader. Among other tricks, Morritt invented the Disappearing Donkey illusion (the secret of which led Mysterio to profess profound awe—an emotion he did not often admit to).

A coin is held at the base of the middle finger. The thumb presses the coin down, as the index and ring fingers are extended toward the palm slightly, and then pressed back down, against the edges of the coin.

The end result of these exertions is that the coin is gripped between the flesh of the index and ring fingers, but is concealed behind the middle finger. See **Figure 4.**

FIGURE 4

DOWNS PALM

Thomas Nelson Downs billed himself as the King of Koins, and built his entire career around a specialty vaudeville turn focused on one magic trick: the Miser's Dream. In this sleight Downs apparently produced hundreds of silver coins from thin air. He headlined the leading theaters of the world, rubbed shoulders with royalty, and retired at an early age. This palming technique was a favorite of his, and bears his name.

The Downs palm is accomplished by clipping a coin between the tips of the index and middle finger, as in **Figure 5.** The fingers then curl inward, to the crotch of the thumb, keeping the coin perpendicular to the hand. Once there, the coin can be re-gripped by the inside of the thumb and the base of the first finger, as shown in **Figure 6.**

With a coin in Downs palm, the palm of the hand can be plainly shown to the audience, so long as the thumb blocks the audience's view of the coin. **Figure 7** shows the palm of the hand with a coin concealed in Downs palm.

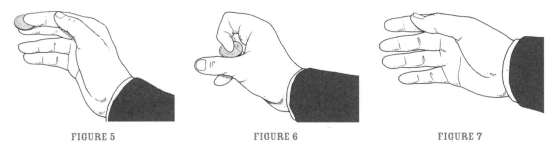

FIGURE 5   FIGURE 6   FIGURE 7

THE BOBO SWITCH

This method of switching one coin for another is perhaps the most popular of its type. It was invented by J. B. Bobo, a professional magician from Texarkana, Texas. The sleight takes place as the magician toys with a coin, casually throwing it from one hand to the other.

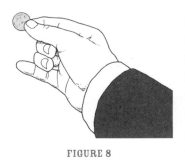

FIGURE 8

A coin—in this example, a penny—is concealed in the right-hand finger palm position. Another coin—a quarter—is held at the right fingertips, as in **Figure 8.** Toss the quarter into the left hand and close the fingers around it. Open the left hand, pick up the quarter with the first two fingers and thumb of the right hand and toss it back into the left hand, which closes around it for a second time. Open the left hand and pick up the coin again.

On the third throw (or whenever you're ready to make the switch), use the first finger and thumb to pull the quarter back into the hand, and at the same time, release your finger-palm grip on the penny (**Figure 9**),

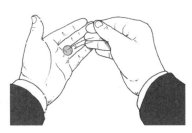

FIGURE 9

allowing inertia to carry it into the left hand, which closes around it tightly. It takes very little motion from the right hand to launch the concealed penny out of it.

As with most sleights, it is important not to rush the Bobo switch. Cover it with an appropriate remark and mask the move by performing it casually, as if merely tossing the coin into your left hand to keep your hands occupied.

COIN VANISHES

Causing a coin or another small object to vanish is such an intrinsic part of magic that conjurers have made the word *vanish* into a noun. Mysterio used various coin vanishes over the years in thousands of impromptu situations. The tricks that follow employ several, including some methods that rely on sleight-of-hand and others that do not.

FAKE PUT

EFFECT: A coin vanishes from the magician's clenched fist.

REQUIRED: A coin.

PREPARATION: None.

PERFORMANCE: The magician borrows a coin and places it in his palm-up right hand. The coin is displayed at the base of the middle and ring fingers.

"Even if you're not a magician, it's easy to make money disappear, isn't it?" he asks his audience. Heads nod in assent.

Cupping his left hand, the magician apparently drops the coin into it, and the hand closes into a loose fist. When the hand is opened again, the coin has vanished. What actually happens is this: As the right hand turns palm down to deposit the coin into the cupped left hand, the right thumb presses down lightly on the coin, preventing it from falling into the left hand, as in **Figures 10 and 11.**

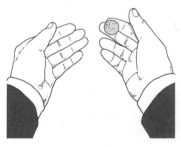

FIGURE 10

FIGURE 11

The right hand then drops to the magician's side, where the coin is concealed in finger palm.

As the coin is apparently transferred from one hand to the other, the left hand closes into a loose fist as if it actually contained the coin. See **Figure 12.**

This is the most important part of the trick. More than the mechanics of holding on to the coin with the right thumb, your conviction—a belief that the coin is *actually* in your closed left fist—will sell this vanish to an audience better than any fancy sleight-of-hand technique.

To effect the vanish, slowly (take advantage of this moment—the work is already done) open your left hand to reveal that the coin is gone!

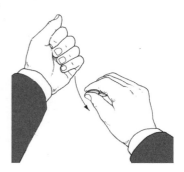

FIGURE 12

LAPPED

The mechanics of this vanish are simple. Acting and conviction, as just described in the Fake Put, above, remain tantamount to this sleight's successful execution.

EFFECT: A coin is picked up off the table. It vanishes completely from the magician's hands.

REQUIRED: A coin.

PREPARATION: None.

PERFORMANCE: A coin lies on the table in front of you. As you talk, set both feet flat on the floor. If there is a cloth on the table, drape it over your lap.

With your right hand, cover the coin completely (your fingers are held together, so the coin cannot be seen from any angle), and drag it off the edge of the table. Instead of actually picking up the coin, however, it is allowed to drop off the tabletop and into your lap. See **Figures 13 through 15,** which show the coin being swept off the table and apparently taken by your hand.

Don't end the illusion here! Instead of simply showing that the coin has vanished from your right hand, deliver an Academy Award–worthy performance; pretend to place the coin in your open left hand, which closes around it. Pause. Savor the moment. Then, when the time is right, gradually open your left hand to show that the coin is gone.

FIGURE 13

FIGURE 14

FIGURE 15

THE FRENCH DROP

This is one of the most frequently mangled sleight-of-hand moves of all time. With only a small amount of careful study, it can be made into an effective coin vanish.

EFFECT: A coin vanishes from the magician's bare hands.

REQUIRED: A coin.

PREPARATION: None.

PERFORMANCE: Hold a coin in your left hand, by its edges. Your thumb is on top, and your index, middle, and ring fingers are underneath it. The coin is held near the fingertips. See **Figure 16.**

FIGURE 16

The right hand now approaches the left, as if to take the coin. But the coin is *not* taken by the right hand. Instead, as the right fingers screen the coin from view, as in **Figure 17,** the coin is dropped into the waiting left fingers. The coin drops into the left hand, nearly into finger palm position at the base of the middle and ring fingers as the right hand gently curls into a fist. To complete the mechanics of the vanish, the right hand moves away, and all attention is focused on it. The left hand, concealing the coin, drops to

FIGURE 17

the magician's side, and is essentially forgotten about. Now, at the magician's discretion, the right hand can be slowly opened to reveal that the coin has vanished.

The keys to executing the French Drop effectively are, as previously described, conviction and naturalness. You must convince the audience and yourself that the coin really is in your right hand. You must also act natural when making the apparent transfer of the coin from one hand to the other. Your movements should exactly mimic the action of the right hand actually taking the coin from the left. In fact, an excellent way to practice the mechanics of the French Drop is to actually take the coin in the right hand ten or twenty times. Once you understand the rhythm of the real action, you can transfer this muscle memory (as Mysterio dubbed it) to the mechanics of the French Drop. You can fool your spectators only if the fake actions you execute appear to be real.

RETENTION OF VISION VANISH

EFFECT: A coin vanishes from the magician's closed left fist.

FIGURE 18

REQUIRED: A coin.

PREPARATION: None.

PERFORMANCE: Grip a coin between your right thumb and middle finger, as shown in **Figure 18.** Hold your left hand palm up and touch the center of the palm with the

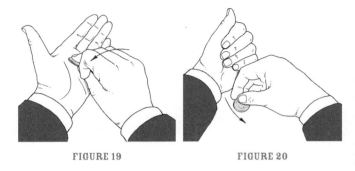

FIGURE 19   FIGURE 20

edge of the coin, as shown in **Figure 19.** As you do this, begin to close your left fingers around the coin. At the last possible moment, and without letting go with the right hand, rotate your right hand backward *very* slightly, toward your body, as in **Figure 20.** This small action will secretly remove the coin from your still-closing left hand. Move your left arm forward, all attention focused on it, as if it concealed the coin. Your right hand, and the coin it still holds, are dropped to your side. Open your left hand to show that the coin has vanished.

PINCH VANISH

This vanish is most effective when a spectator is looking down into your hands.

FIGURE 21

EFFECT: A coin is dropped into the magician's hand, from which it vanishes.

REQUIRED: A coin.

PREPARATION: None.

PERFORMANCE: Grip a coin at its opposite edges, between your right thumb and first finger, as shown in **Figure 21.** Cup your left hand underneath the coin. Squeeze your right thumb and first finger together as the coin is apparently dropped into the waiting left hand.

Instead of letting go of the coin, in the act of pinching your thumb and finger together, the first finger slides rapidly along the flat surface of the coin. See **Figure 22.** The end

FIGURE 22

result of this quick pinching action not only gives the vanish its name, but also allows you to grip one edge of the coin between your thumb and first finger, which are now held together, concealing the coin from view. The right hand falls out of the spectator's frame of vision, and the left hand, apparently holding the coin, becomes the center of attention. When the left fist is opened, the coin has vanished.

FOILED VANISH

While the other vanishes taught in this chapter require sleight-of-hand, the method offered here is extremely easy to do, and entirely novel.

EFFECT: A coin is placed in the performer's hand. When the magician rubs his fingers together, the coin vanishes completely. It is *not* in his other hand, or even in his pocket. It really is gone!

REQUIRED: A square of tinfoil, a half dollar, and a pen.

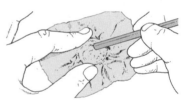

FIGURE 23

PREPARATION: Place an ordinary U.S. half dollar coin on a hard surface, and on top of it, lay a small square of tinfoil. With the edge of a pen or pencil, gently rub the tinfoil over the coin, as in **Figure 23.** This will create an impression of the coin in the foil. When the excess foil is trimmed away from the rubbed image, the foil appears to be the genuine article—a U.S. half dollar. Finger palm the tinfoil coin in your left hand and place the pen in your right pocket. Handle the tinfoil coin with care—it is fragile!

PERFORMANCE: Display the real half dollar in your right hand, saying, "At one time, these coins were minted from pure silver. But not since the 1960s has the government produced them that way. Now, they use a metal that's much more malleable—less durable, that is—and wears much more rapidly. Let me show you what I mean."

Pretend to place the half dollar into your left hand, but execute the mechanics of the Fake Put (described on page 148) instead. The spectators now see the tinfoil coin in your left hand, which they assume to be the real coin.

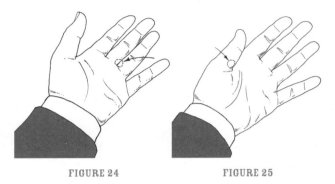

Remove the pen from your pocket and at the same time, leave behind the real half dollar. Close your left fingers around the tinfoil coin and squeeze it into a tiny ball. Wave the pen over your closed left fist. After the tinfoil has been squeezed into a tiny ball, work it into the gap between your middle and ring fingers. Put the pen in your pocket, then open your left fist to reveal that the coin is gone (even though the tinfoil ball is concealed), as in **Figure 24.** The ball of tinfoil can also be concealed in the crotch of the thumb, as in **Figure 25.** As your spectators react to the vanish—but not until they look away from your left hand—discreetly drop the foil on the ground to eliminate all evidence of the coin.

FIGURE 24   FIGURE 25

FIRST THE PENCIL, THEN THE COIN

This effect starts out like a gag, but ends up a mystifying vanish of a coin.

EFFECT: The magician taps a coin in his hand with a pencil three times. On the third tap, the pencil vanishes. "I was just kidding around," the magician says. He then reveals the pencil behind his ear. Starting the trick again, he says, "This time, no funny business." He waves the pencil over the coin, which vanishes completely from his tightly clenched fist!

REQUIRED: A pencil and a coin. Both can be borrowed.

PREPARATION: None.

PERFORMANCE: Display the coin (its denomination is immaterial) in your palm-up left hand. Hold the pencil in your right hand and say, "Watch what happens to the coin on the count of three." Close your left hand into a loose fist and tap it twice with the end of the pencil, swinging your right hand up toward your face after each tap. After the second tap, leave the pencil behind your right ear. Bring your hand down to complete the third tap, only to discover that the pencil is gone. Since your attention (and everyone else's) is focused on the coin in your hand, no one will see you place the pencil behind your ear.

After the vanish of the pencil has registered, tell your spectators, "I'll let you in on a little secret. The pencil's behind my ear." Turn the right side of your body toward the spectators, and point to the pencil with your right index finger. As you remove the pencil from behind your ear, drop the coin, which is still in your left hand, into a convenient pocket. See **Figures 26 and 27.**

Turn your left side back toward the audience and keep your left hand closed, so no one but you knows that the coin is not in your left hand. Wave the pencil over your left hand. Slowly open the fingers. The coin is gone—completely!

FIGURE 26

FIGURE 27

BORROWED, THEN GONE

For a spur-of-the-moment miracle, this coin vanish cannot be topped.

EFFECT: The magician picks a coin up off a pile of change in a spectator's hand. Placing the coin in his free hand, the magician causes the coin to vanish completely!

REQUIRED: A willing spectator with a pocket full of change.

PREPARATION: None.

PERFORMANCE: Under casual circumstances, when pressed to perform a quick trick, ask your spectators if any of them have a pocketful of change. When someone offers you a handful of coins, look it over and say, "I'm looking for a nickel…an older one."

Reach over to the pile of coins in your volunteer's hand, pretending to spot exactly the coin you need. With your right hand, *pretend* to pick up the coin from her hand. In fact, you take nothing. Since her cupped hand holds a quantity of coins, the fact that you have removed nothing from her hands will go unnoticed. Instruct her to "put the rest of the coins away. We won't need them."

Take advantage of the situation, but don't overact. Summoning every ounce of your inner Sir Laurence Olivier, pretend to place the coin in your free hand, and close your fingers around it. Pause. Then say, "The reason I needed an older nickel is because they evaporate the fastest. It has something to do with the silver content."

As you utter this last line (or one you find considerably less corny), slowly open your hand, one finger at a time. The coin (which was never there to begin with) is gone!

MORE COIN SLEIGHTS: PRODUCTIONS

MYSTERIO FEATURED A COIN PRODUCTION ROUTINE called the Aerial Treasury in his drawing-room performances. As he noted, few basic tricks excite the imagination more than the magical materialization of coins from the ether. ("The minds of all laymen are naturally excited by the free and unlimited coinage of silver," wrote Mysterio.) The following techniques were used in that routine.

FROM FINGER PALM

Finger palm a coin (a half dollar will be more visible than other coins, though any denomination can be used). With your hand containing the palmed coin resting naturally at your side, pretend to spot an invisible cache of change floating in the ether. Bring your hand up to shoulder height, continuing to hold the fingers in a naturally curled position.

With the tip of your thumb, slide the coin up, out of finger palm (as in **Figure 28**), into view (as in **Figure 29**), and pretend to pluck it from the air. Pocket the coin.

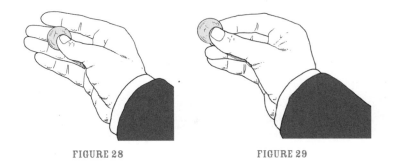

FIGURE 28   FIGURE 29

FROM DOWNS PALM

This coin production is done with the spectators looking into an apparently empty palm. Mysterio was fond of the maxim "Guilty hands make for suspicious spectators." In this case, though your audience is looking into your hand, a coin is concealed in

FIGURE 30

Downs palm. To borrow a more common phrase, "Don't run if no one is chasing you." Remain confident.

Conceal a half dollar using Downs palm (see page 146). With this palm, your hands can be shown relatively freely, front and back, without fear of exposing the coin. Turn your body to the right, so your left side faces the audience. The palm of your right hand should be staring them in the face.

Now pretend to see a coin floating in the ether. When you have zeroed in on it, curl your middle and index finger in toward the coin and nip its edge with the fingertips—see **Figure 30.** Carry the coin out of Downs palm, behind your thumb. When your fingers are nearly straight, the coin will be just behind the tip of the thumb. Press down gently on the coin with the tip of the thumb, at the same time releasing the index finger's hold on the coin. The coin will "snap" into view at your fingertips. See **Figure 31** for this position.

FIGURE 31

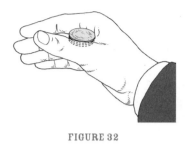

FIGURE 32

STACK IT UP: More than one coin can be concealed in Downs palm. (See **Figure 32,** which shows a stack of four coins in Downs palm). As such, more than one coin can be produced from Downs palm in a row. The mechanics of the production are the same as those described above. Each coin is pulled from the bottom of the concealed stack by the middle finger, which guides it toward the index finger. The coin is then snapped into view. **Figure 33** shows one coin being produced, while three remain palmed.

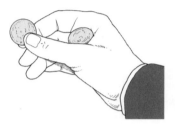

FIGURE 33

Care must be taken to keep the palmed stack of coins from "talking"—that is, clinking together in your hand. If coins "talk," the fact that they are hidden from view may be revealed, and spoil the effect.

KEEPING UP THE CHARADE

Using both productions described above in concert with the Fake Put, you can create a short routine (like Mysterio's Aerial Treasury, also mentioned above).

Begin by producing a coin from the air. Use whichever method of production you prefer. Pretend to place the coin in your left hand with the Fake Put, then take this supposed coin and place it in your left trouser pocket.

As the coin is apparently being placed in your pocket, act as if you've seen another one in the air. Produce it, too. Again, pretend to place this coin in your left hand, which transfers it (apparently) to your left pocket. This continuous production of coins (varied to keep it interesting by producing coins from various parts of your clothing or unobjectionable parts of a spectator's body) can be kept up until either (a) someone applauds or (b) the spectators ask you to stop. Though Mysterio kept no notes on the subject, it is reasonable to assume he would have preferred quitting while ahead, and possibly making the last coin vanish from his hands to give the sequence a fitting denouement.

A further layer of deception can be added to the continuous production of coins by adding a duplicate piece of change to the mix. If the coin you pluck from the air over and over is a half dollar, to increase the Mysterio-factor you'll need another half dollar.

Start with one coin in each trouser pocket. At an opportune moment, finger palm one coin in each hand. Produce the coin from the right hand, and in the action of placing it in the left hand, expose the coin in the left hand (which has been there all along). This technique is known to magicians as the shuttle pass.

In other words, as your right hand turns over to apparently deposit its coin into the waiting left hand, as in **Figure 34,** the left hand turns up to reveal the coin it has concealed all along. The right hand's coin is retained, while the left hand's coin is revealed. See **Figure 35.** Coordinating the two hands so they work together to create the perfect illusion is challenging, but the end result will be worth it.

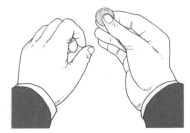

FIGURE 34

Once the shuttle pass has been executed and the left hand's coin is visible, pretend to place it in the left trouser pocket but retain it in finger palm.

Produce the right hand's coin again, and repeat the above sequence: shuttle pass, apparently place the coin in the left trouser pocket, retain it in finger palm, and so on. When you want to end the production of the endless stream of coins, leave the left hand's coin in the pocket, and cause the coin still in your right hand to vanish. Voilà!

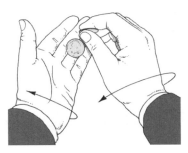

FIGURE 35

CUT IN HALF (THE COIN FOLD)

Sleight-of-hand seems impossible when you perform this startling vanish.

FIGURE 36

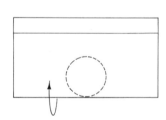

FIGURE 37

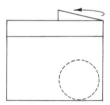

FIGURE 38

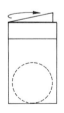

FIGURE 39

EFFECT: The magician folds a small slip of paper around a half dollar. The coin is clinked against the rim of a glass to prove it is still inside the paper bundle. The magician then demonstrates an apparent feat of super-strength by cutting through the paper with a pair of scissors. "This is no Samson-like display," he declares. "The coin is gone." The remaining bits of paper are torn to shreds. The coin *is* gone!

REQUIRED: A half dollar (though any coin will do), a piece of fairly stiff paper approximately 5 inches (13 cm) square, and a pair of scissors.

PREPARATION: Place the scissors in a convenient pocket.

PERFORMANCE: The coin is placed on the paper, just below the center point, as in **Figure 36.** The bottom half of the paper is now folded up to within ½ inch (1 cm) of the top of the sheet, as in **Figure 37.** The right side of the paper is folded away from the magician, and the left side is folded away from him as well, creating a small packet. These last two folds should *not* be snug against the coin. See **Figures 38 and 39.** Finally, the upper "lip" of paper is folded down and away from the performer, apparently sealing the coin inside. There is, however, still a chute through which the coin can slide out, if the paper is turned 180 degrees.

But first, to prove the coin is still within the paper's folds, the magician clinks it against the rim of a glass, or knocks it on the tabletop. Only then, after audible proof of its presence is given, does the magician turn the paper around and allow the coin to slide out into his waiting hand.

This same hand, concealing the coin, reaches for the scissors, ditching the coin in the pocket as it does so. "I've spent hours in the weight room perfecting this Herculean feat," you say, as you apparently cut through the coin with considerable effort. "Actually, that's not entirely true. I've spent hours in front of a mirror practicing magic. And even though you saw the coin go into the paper and you heard it inside, it's gone." So saying, you cut or tear up the remaining pieces of paper, or simply let them flutter to the table where they can be examined. The money has vanished!

THE FOUR COIN ROLL-DOWN

This flourish (not exactly a trick) instantly proves to an audience of laymen that you know how to handle yourself when sleight-of-hand is concerned. Considerable practice will be required to master it.

EFFECT: The magician rolls four coins out between his fingers, a fabulous feat of digital dexterity.

REQUIRED: Four half dollars or other coins, all of the same size.

PREPARATION: None.

PERFORMANCE: Hold all four coins in an even stack between the tip of your right thumb and index finger, as in **Figure 40.** With your middle finger, reach under the stack so that the side of your middle finger touches your thumb pad and the two outermost coins of the stack—the coins farthest from your palm. See **Figure 41.**

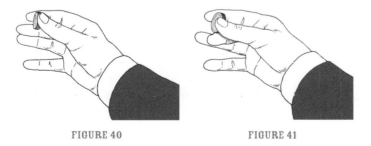

FIGURE 40   FIGURE 41

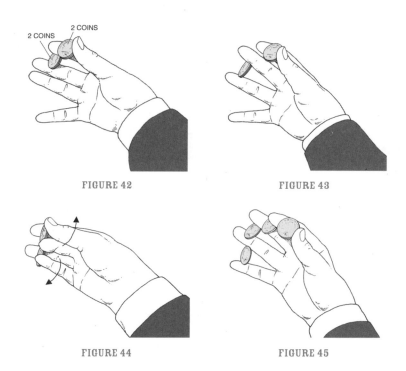

FIGURE 42

FIGURE 43

FIGURE 44

FIGURE 45

The middle finger and thumb now swivel in opposite directions, rolling the outermost two coins between the index and middle finger, as in **Figure 42.**

Keeping a tight grip on the coins between the index finger and thumb, the other two coins are next rolled between the middle and ring finger, as in **Figure 43.** Then roll them once again, so that they end up between the ring and little fingers.

Now for the hard part. Lower the coins to the position shown in **Figure 44,** and use the middle finger as a lever to roll the outermost coin of each pair up and into the final position shown in **Figure 45** (one coin between each pair of fingers).

Mastering the Roll-Down will be difficult. At least two weeks of steady practice are required to master it at the most basic level. To practice, start by rolling one coin back and forth from between your thumb and index finger to between your ring and little finger. This will give you the confidence and dexterity to attempt the more complicated flourish.

MYSTERIO'S ADVICE ON COIN SLEIGHTS: "When practicing difficult coin sleights, be sure your hands are held over a soft surface, like your bed. You *will* drop the coins. Therefore, I advise the dedicated student to save himself the tyranny of a sore back by adopting this contrivance while rehearsing."

THE FIVE COIN PIROUETTE—A CHALLENGE

Once you have trained your hands to roll four coins—and if you are interested in a challenge—add a fifth coin to the mix for an impressive and extra-difficult flourish.

EFFECT: The conjurer rolls five coins into a glittering circle between his fingers.

REQUIRED: Five half dollars or other coins, all of the same size.

PREPARATION: None.

PERFORMANCE: Begin with five coins held between the index finger and thumb as shown in the Four Coin Roll-Down. Roll *two* of the coins down to the position be-

2 COINS

FIGURE 46

tween your ring and little fingers, and then roll two more coins, individually, to positions between your ring and middle finger and middle and index fingers, respectively. The spaces between your fingers and thumb are now all occupied by coins, and the space between your little finger and ring finger contains two coins, as in **Figure 46.**

Maintaining a firm grip on all the coins, swing your thumb toward your little finger. Contact the outermost coin of the pair held there nearest your ring finger, as shown in **Figure 47.** Roll the coin down and away from your ring finger, using your little finger as a pivot point, until your hand holds all five coins in a circle (or pirouette) as shown

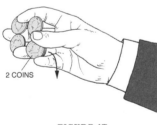

2 COINS

FIGURE 47

in **Figure 48.** To return the coins to rest position between your thumb and index finger, begin by rolling the coin between your thumb and little finger back, and then return the others to the starting position one at a time.

FIGURE 48

This advanced flourish will take considerable practice to master. But if you have conquered the Four Coin Roll-Down, it will be much easier to add a fifth coin than you might expect.

THE COIN ROLL

This pretty flourish is well known by laymen, and is considered to be almost a required part of the repertoire of any conjurer worth his salt.

FIGURE 49

EFFECT: A coin dances across the magician's knuckles.

REQUIRED: A half dollar or similar-sized coin.

PREPARATION: None.

PERFORMANCE: Begin with the coin clipped between the pad of your right thumb and the left side of the base of your index finger, as shown in **Figure 49.** Use the thumb to push the coin onto the first phalanx of your index finger (the part between your knuckle and the first finger joint). Once there, use the side of the middle finger to press down gently on the rightmost edge of the coin, as in **Figure 50.** This levers the coin up and onto the first phalanx of the middle finger. The weight of the coin does some of the work, and gentle pressure from your fingers does the rest.

In a continuing action, the coin is levered up and onto the ring finger, as in **Figure 51.** Finally, the side of the little finger levers the coin over and into the space between it and the ring finger, as in **Figure 52.**

To complete the flourish, the thumb moves underneath the fingers and the coin is allowed to fall through the gap between the little and ring fingers onto the thumb, which slides the coin underneath the hand and back to the starting position. The flourish can now be repeated ad infinitum, the coin traveling around and around in an ever-more-dizzying pattern.

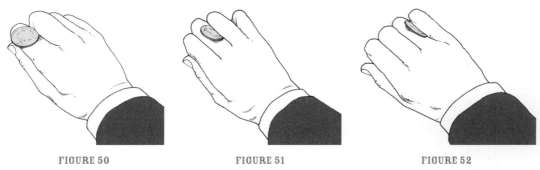

FIGURE 50   FIGURE 51   FIGURE 52

BALLPOINT MAGIC WAND

Fountain pens were common in Mysterio's day, but not everyone the great wizard encountered owned one. Nowadays ballpoint pens with caps are everywhere, making this effect a natural for impromptu performances.

EFFECT: The magician vanishes a coin from his hand by waving his impromptu magic wand (a ballpoint pen) over it. The coin is then reproduced not with a wave of the pen, but from *inside* the pen cap, the coin being visibly ejected from what appears to be the top of an entirely ordinary writing instrument.

REQUIRED: A coin and a ballpoint pen with a cap. Both can be borrowed.

PREPARATION: None.

PERFORMANCE: Set the pen on the table. "Since I'm light on props today," you say, "we're going to have to improvise. This pen will serve as the stand-in magic wand."

Pretend to place the coin in your left fist. With the coin concealed in the right hand in Downs palm (see page 146), pick the pen up off of the table and wave it over the left hand. "I realize this is a poor substitute for the real thing," you say, indicating the pen, "but it still has the desired effect. Watch!" Slowly open your left fingers to reveal that the coin is gone.

"It hasn't gone far," you say, as you use your left fingers to pull the cap off of the pen. Set the pen down and grasp the pen cap with the tip of your thumb and first finger. Because the coin is concealed in Downs palm, even from the front, it will be hidden from view. See **Figure 53.** As you utter the next line, "I think it's in there," referring to

FIGURE 53

the pen cap, swing your right hand down sharply, and release your grip on the coin (while maintaining your hold on the pen cap). Because the larger action of your moving hand and wrist covers the smaller action of the coin falling from its secret hiding place, to a spectator, it appears as if the coin has fallen out of the pen cap.

THE POROUS PAW

The title of this trick was coined (pardon the pun) by one of the finest sleight-of-hand magicians of the twentieth century, Ross Bertram. Though known among the fraternity for his work with coins, Bertram was an all-around virtuoso magician who worked close-up and on stage.

EFFECT: The magician places a coin in his left hand, which closes around it tightly. "A momentary massage from the right hand is all that's required for the magic to happen," the performer says. Rubbing the back of his hand, the magician causes the coin to penetrate his flesh and appear on the back of his left hand!

REQUIRED: A coin (preferably a half dollar).

PREPARATION: None.

FIGURE 55

PERFORMANCE: Examine the coin and then place it on your open left palm, at the base of the first finger, as in **Figure 54.** Turn the left hand over and close the fingers into a fist. As the hand turns and closes, the left thumb clips the coin to the hand.

As the left hand turns over, use your thumb to push the coin out of the fist, toward the body, so that when the turn of the hand is completed, approximately half of the coin (or more) is outside of the hand, as shown in **Figure 55.** To the audience, it should appear as if you have done nothing more than turned your left hand over and closed it into a fist. Be sure that your spectators are positioned at an angle at which the coin will not be seen.

"The molecules of the coin will now dematerialize," you announce. "It takes nothing more than slight agitation from my right hand to make the miracle happen."

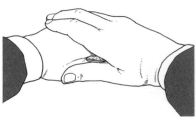

FIGURE 56

Begin rubbing the back of your left hand with your right fingertips. As you do, steal the coin by clipping it between the base of the right index finger and thumb, as in **Figure 56.** As you continue massaging the back of your left hand, deposit the coin in its center. Continue rubbing, then gradually reveal the coin on the back of the left hand to complete the penetration effect.

THROUGH A RING

"There are few tricks finer for after-dinner entertainment than this one," Mysterio wrote in the margins of his copy of *The Art of Magic*. Traditionally, the trick has been performed with a specially machined coin. The method described here, however, requires no special props or preparation.

EFFECT: A coin is placed in the center of a handkerchief. The corners of the fabric are then threaded through the center of a ring, trapping the coin inside the cloth. Showing his hands empty, the performer grasps the coin through the hankie, and with a gentle tug, pulls it directly through the fabric! Everything can now be examined.

FIGURE 57

REQUIRED: A handkerchief, a ring, and a half dollar. Everything may be borrowed from the audience. It is best to use a plain, solid ring like a wedding band (as opposed to an ornamented ring) for this effect.

PREPARATION: None.

PERFORMANCE: "The properties I'll use for this experiment are entirely ordinary," you say, to introduce the trick. "The tricks they will do, however, are anything but ordinary." Center the coin (which is held in your left hand) under the handkerchief. With your left thumb at the rear, grip not only the coin, but also a pinch of extra fabric, as shown in **Figure 57.**

"Because I am an adept practitioner of legerdemain, skilled in sleight-of-hand, you may not believe that the coin is actually underneath the handkerchief at this point," you

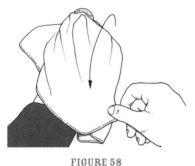

FIGURE 58

say. "Let me give you another look." Lift up the front end of the handkerchief and flip it over, exposing the coin, as in **Figure 58.** "There it is."

Maintaining your thumb's grip on the extra fold of fabric, you now re-cover the coin—apparently. In fact, instead of flipping the front end of the cloth back over the coin, you have tossed the *entire* handkerchief over it, as in **Figure 59.** To the audience it appears as if the coin is still in the center of the fabric. In reality, though, it is only covered by a small portion at the front.

Twist the handkerchief around the coin, "locking it in place" as you do so. The coin should be held in the folds of the fabric, as shown in **Figure 60.**

"We will now secure the coin even further. May I have the ring, please?" Thread all four ends of the handkerchief through the ring, then invite two spectators to assist by each holding two corners of the handkerchief, as shown in **Figure 61.**

"And now, those anything-but-ordinary tricks I promised." Push down gently on the ring, and work the coin out of the impromptu pocket concealing it in the handkerchief. Slowly work it free, as if the coin is passing through the fabric slowly, and not without some effort. The coin has apparently penetrated the cloth! When it has, the ring will pop up and off the handkerchief—nothing is holding it in place any longer—and onto its surface. It can now be returned to its owner.

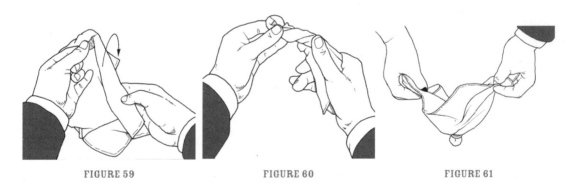

FIGURE 59   FIGURE 60   FIGURE 61

SILVER EXTRACTION

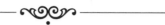

EFFECT: A half dollar is held tightly in the magician's fist. "Please, sir, heat the elements of the coin," says the conjurer. "The result will be startling, I promise." The open flame of a match is waved beneath the performer's hand. When the magician opens his fist, what is revealed is not the half dollar, but a small lump of metal and a clear disk—the elements that apparently make up the coin!

REQUIRED: A half dollar, a glass disk approximately the size of the coin (the lens of a flashlight works well), and a ball of tinfoil.

PREPARATION: Clip the ball of foil between the middle and ring fingers of your left hand. Finger palm the glass disk in your right hand. The half dollar is held in the fingertips of your right hand. The matches are in your right pocket.

PERFORMANCE: Display the coin at the tips of your right fingers and say, "Half dollars are a rarity these days. While they're still manufactured by the U.S. Mint, they're not commonly used. Here's why."

Perform the Bobo switch, substituting the glass disk for the coin as you appear to toss the coin into your left hand. Be sure that you keep the ball of tinfoil in the left hand concealed as you catch the glass.

Reach into your pocket with your right hand to secure the matches, at the same time leaving behind the palmed half dollar. Hand the matches to a spectator and ask him to light one and wave it in a circle around your clenched left fist. "We're going to use the heat from my hand, combined with the heat from the match, to break the coin down into its two basic elements. Don't believe me? Watch!"

Open your hand and roll the ball of foil onto the table, along with the glass disk, which can both be examined!

ANOTHER LUMP: A possibly more convincing illusion can be carried out if you are able to obtain a melted lump of shiny metal and can substitute it for the ball of foil. Finding a source for this may be difficult, but it will enhance the illusion.

SILVER FROM PAPER

This effect is easy to do, and provides the perfect interlude between a series of tricks with bills and a series with coins. The trick was invented by Milton Kort, a deft finger-flinger from Detroit.

EFFECT: The conjurer shows a dollar bill, front and back. "The old, clichéd line is that 'You can't get money for nothing.' The other clichéd line, which I like a whole lot more, is 'You have to spend money to make money.' Let me show you what I mean." The bill is rolled into a flattened tube. When tipped up over a spectator's hand, a genuine half dollar spills out of it!

REQUIRED: A half dollar and a dollar bill. The bill can be borrowed.

PREPARATION: Finger palm the coin in your left hand.

FIGURE 62

FIGURE 63

PERFORMANCE: Ask a spectator for the loan of a bill. When he finally digs one out of his wallet and hands it to you, take it with your right hand. Your left hand, with the finger-palmed coin, rests at your side. Lay the bill on your left palm, timing it so as to conceal the half dollar under the bill. Make sure the bill lies across your palm, its length perpendicular to your fingers.

To show both sides of the bill while still hiding the coin on your left fingers, pull the end of the note closest to your index finger down and between your middle and index finger, as in **Figure 62**. Now reach under your left hand, pull the bill up, and curl it back around your left index finger, as in **Figure 63**. Keep pulling the end of the bill until it has been turned over entirely and run completely through the gap between your fingers. This is apparently nothing more than a fancy way to display the bill on both sides, and while it certainly is this, it also allows you to conceal the coin in the process.

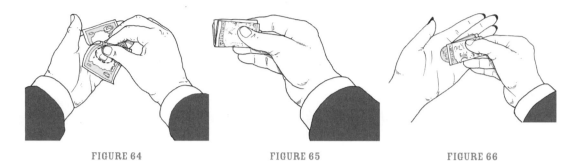

| FIGURE 64 | FIGURE 65 | FIGURE 66 |

Display the bill in the same manner one more time. Then, through the bill, grip the coin with your right fingers and fold the bill around it, as in **Figures 64 and 65.** This need not be a precise fold; you simply shape the bill into a loose, flat tube around the coin. To produce the half dollar, ask a spectator to hold out her hand, palm up. "Here's the 'spending money to make money' part of the trick," you say, as the coin slides slowly out of the end of the bill and into her hand, as in **Figure 66.**

THE SYMPATHETIC COINS

This coin trick is one of the best—yet least-performed—pieces of close-up magic extant. It was first published in 1909 in Thomas Nelson Downs's famous book *The Art of Magic*, where it was credited to Yank Hoe, a vaudeville magician. Since the trick incorporates playing cards and coins, it offers a perfect segue between a series of card and coin tricks in a longer routine.

EFFECT: The magician lays a handkerchief on the table and places four coins on top of it—one near each corner. He covers two of the coins with playing cards. "And now, a miraculous penetration of one solid through another," he says. A visible coin is picked up and placed under the handkerchief. Amazingly, it is pushed up through the fabric and joins a coin underneath one of the cards. This is repeated, a second coin passing through the fabric. "The last coin will not penetrate the fabric, but rather, travel invisibly," says the performer. Upon his command, a third coin—the other covered coin, untouched by the magician—vanishes from under its card and joins the others across the table.

REQUIRED: Four coins (half dollars or quarters), a handkerchief, and two playing cards.

PREPARATION: None.

PERFORMANCE: Arrange the four coins, which may be borrowed, at the corners of the spread handkerchief, as in **Figure 67**. In the action of showing that only two coins can be covered at any one time ("It's only logical, since there are only two cards!" you explain), perform the following secret steal of one coin.

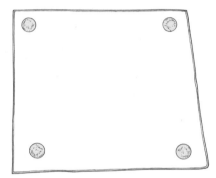

FIGURE 67

Hold a card in each hand with thumbs underneath and fingers on top. Use the cards to cover the two coins closest to you, as in **Figure 68**. Next, in an apparent effort to demonstrate that only one coin can be covered by one card, move the card in your left hand toward the lower right corner of the handkerchief, to cover the coin there. At the moment it reaches the lower right corner of the handkerchief, use your right thumb to clip the coin its card is already covering, and move the coin and card forward together, to the upper left corner of the handkerchief. Lay the card in your left hand in place in the lower right corner, apparently covering a coin. In the upper left corner, lay the right hand's card (and the coin concealed under it) over the coin already in that position.

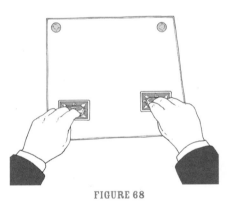

FIGURE 68

These actions, though lengthy in description, should take no more than two seconds to execute, and should be performed in a casual, offhand manner. The steal should not be rushed.

At this point, two coins in the upper right and lower left corners of the handkerchief should be visible. The upper left corner contains a card covering two coins, and the lower right corner contains a card that is apparently covering a coin, but is in fact covering nothing.

"And now, I will defy the laws of physics by passing one solid object through another." Pick up the coin on the upper right corner of the handkerchief with your right hand. With your left hand, raise the rear edge of the handkerchief slightly. As your right hand

FIGURE 69

passes under the handkerchief to apparently push its coin up through the cloth, allow the coin to fall in to the left hand, as in **Figure 69.**

Pretend you're pushing the coin through the cloth underneath the card on the upper left corner of the hankie. Remove your right hand, now empty, from underneath the hankie and use it to remove the card in the upper left corner. Two coins are seen underneath it.

As your spectators react to this magical moment, transfer the card in your right hand to your left hand (which is holding a concealed coin) as shown in **Figure 70.** Lay the card and coin on top of the two coins already on the upper left corner of the handkerchief. There are now three coins there, but your spectators are aware of only two.

Repeat the same penetration effect described above with the remaining visible coin. Again, cover the concealed coin in the left hand with the card, and then load this concealed coin onto the three coins already in the upper left corner of the handkerchief.

FIGURE 70

"The last coin will join the others by more magical means," you say. With the appropriate dramatic flair, lift the card in the lower right corner of the handkerchief. The coin is gone. A spectator can now lift the card in the upper left corner to reveal four coins, and bring the effect to a close.

MORE SYMPATHY: Instead of using playing cards, other small objects can be used as covers for the coins. In a bar, cardboard drink coasters work well. In a professional setting, business cards can be used (though, as they're smaller, greater care must be taken when executing the various sleights involved).

COIN IN THE BALL OF WOOL

While remarkable in effect and perfect for the closing spot on a program, this trick requires an engaging presentation to put it across. Variations of it have been featured by dozens of famous conjurers including Mysterio's mentor, the enigmatic M. Charlier.

EFFECT: A coin is marked with a grease pencil by a spectator. It is wrapped in a handkerchief and handed to an audience volunteer for safekeeping. Next, the magician introduces a paper bag, which has been on his table in full view throughout the performance. "I'm almost ashamed to admit this," he says. "My hobby—believe it or not—is knitting." The magician removes a ball of yarn from the bag, and places it in a glass bowl, which he hands to another spectator. The coin then vanishes from the handkerchief, and the ball of yarn is unraveled by a spectator. At its center, a matchbox is discovered. Inside the matchbox, which the performer does not touch, is found the borrowed, marked coin!

REQUIRED: A ball of yarn, a matchbox, several rubber bands, a grease pencil, a glass bowl to hold the yarn, a paper bag, a coin-vanishing handkerchief and a coin slide

(these items are described below). The yarn should be of fairly thick material, so that when wound into a ball around the matchbox, it will gain bulk quickly.

PREPARATION: A coin slide can be made from a long, skinny strip of metal or plastic. When finished, it should be 6 to 8 inches (15 to 22 cm) long, and be wide enough for a quarter to slide through easily, but not much larger. This is shown in **Figure 71.** A coin slide can be constructed from a flat strip of metal cut and bent into shape for a relatively modest investment. As an alternative to metal, a sturdy cardboard tube could be constructed.

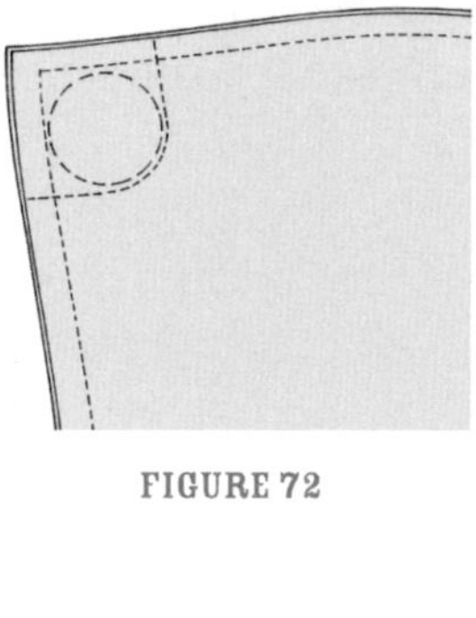

FIGURE 71

The coin-vanishing handkerchief is constructed from two identical handkerchiefs sewn together on all hems, with a coin sewn into one corner, as in **Figure 72.**

Before performing, the coin slide is placed in the matchbox, which is closed around it and secured with rubber bands. The yarn is then wrapped around the matchbox and slide, as in **Figure 73.** The entire arrangement is placed in the paper bag,

FIGURE 72

FIGURE 73   FIGURE 74

with the slide end first. Push the slide through the bag near the bottom, so its opening juts from the bottom of the bag slightly, as in **Figure 74.**

PERFORMANCE: "Would someone in the audience be so kind as to loan me a quarter?" Once your request has been complied with, have the date on the quarter noted, and if possible, have the coin marked with the grease pencil—use a spectator's initials or have him draw an identifying mark on the coin.

"Thank you for the loan, sir. Now that the coin has been marked, there is no other in the world exactly like it. Is that correct?" Saying this, you place the coin under the coin-vanishing handkerchief and, in that action, conceal the coin in your palm and bring the coin sewn into the corner of the fabric to the center of the handkerchief. As you hand the handkerchief to a spectator to guard, ask him, "Do you feel the coin under the cloth?" His answer will be affirmative, as he feels the sewn-in coin where the marked one should be.

"Please don't let go of the coin, whatever you do." Leave the handkerchief with the spectator and return to your table. Pick up the bag with your right hand (which conceals the marked coin) near the slide, which is projecting from it near the bottom, at the back. Continue chattering at your audience. "Knitting is both entertaining and educational. I've ingratiated myself to many friends by making scarves, hats, and mittens for them. Don't laugh! Handmade gifts are always treasured! And now, I'd like to blend my passion for magic with my fascination for arts and crafts. Don't groan—this will be far more interesting than it sounds. I promise."

As you talk, reach into the bag with your left hand to remove the ball of yarn. Drop the coin into the slide from the outside of the bag with your right hand. You can now pull the ball of yarn free from the slide with your left hand, concealing the operation inside the bag. The mechanics of the trick are now complete. Dispose of the bag.

The rest of the effect is merely presentation and build-up. Cause the coin to "vanish" from the folds of the handkerchief shaking it out. Set the ball of yarn in the glass bowl, then have a spectator begin unraveling the yarn. (Placing the ball in a glass bowl maintains visual interest in it as it unravels, and makes the appearance of the matchbox more visual when the yarn has been unwound.) Invite the spectator who lent you the coin to join you on stage, open the matchbox, remove its contents, and verify that it is the same coin that vanished only moments before—date, identifying mark, and all!

THE MISER'S DREAM

In Mysterio's program, this effect was billed as the Aerial Treasury. It has been a staple in the repertoires of virtually every well-known professional magician in the history of the art, most likely because its theme is universal: the endless production of money from thin air.

EFFECT: The magician shows that his hands are empty. Reaching into the air, he produces a shining silver coin from it, and drops it into a paper bag. "The coins develop, sort of like film," he says, reaching for another invisible coin, catching it, and then displaying it—visible and quite real—to the audience. In rapid succession, the prestidigitator produces ten more coins, each of which is dropped into the bag, where it is heard to rattle about with the others. After dropping the last coin into the bag, the magician tears it open to reveal that the entire effect was nothing more than a figment of his imagination—the coins have vanished without a trace!

REQUIRED: Between twelve and twenty U.S. half dollars or other coins, all of the same size (the bigger the coin, the more visible it will be to the audience), two paper bags, and a handkerchief.

PREPARATION: Use the two paper bags to construct a double-walled bag as described in Silken Lunch (page 292). Place one coin in your right trouser pocket. The remaining coins begin in the left trouser or jacket pocket. The handkerchief starts in the breast pocket of your coat, or any other conspicuous location on your person. Set the bag on the table.

PERFORMANCE: "It is the dream of every man," you say, "to make money materialize from thin air." Continue pattering along these lines, and as you do, without calling attention to the fact, gesture with your hands, fingers spread wide apart, showing them to be empty, both front and back.

FIGURE 75

As your opening address continues, your right hand naturally falls to your side, and eventually into your pocket, where it palms the coin stored there. Use your right hand to pick up the paper bag from your table and show it empty, and as you are doing so, turn the right side of your body toward your audience. At the same moment, use your left hand to steal the stack of coins in the left pocket, holding them as shown in **Figure 75.** Make every effort to keep the coins from "talking" as you remove them from the left pocket.

Transfer the bag to your left hand, and insert your left fingers into the secret pocket in the bag. The left thumb on the outside of the bag clamps down on the stack of coins, keeping them quiet. This is done openly, as if you are simply transferring your grip on the bag from one hand to the other.

Your patter continues: "Tonight, I will make that dream come true." Produce the palmed coin from your right hand in the most convincing manner you know how. Several methods have been described already in this chapter, and any one of them will suffice.

Now pretend to drop the coin into the bag. Instead, however, as your right hand enters the bag, your left hand releases one (and only one!) of the coins from its stack. Remove your right hand from the bag with its coin still palmed. Properly timed, it appears to the audience that the coin in your right hand was produced and then dropped into the bag.

Now repeat the production of the coin from your right hand, this time plucking the coin from another "pocket of the ether." Drop it into the bag (apparently) as before.

The third and fourth coins should be produced from different parts of your body—your lapel, the bottom of your shoe, or even your mouth. Varying the location of each production keeps the trick entertaining and novel. Each time you drop a coin into the bag, release one more coin from the stack controlled by your left hand.

The fifth and sixth coins can be produced from the air, and subsequent coins can be found about the persons of spectators. Mysterio often involved a child from the audience in his performance of the effect, bringing the youngster up on stage and producing coins from his nose, elbow, and ears, much to the delight of the crowd. Seek out new and un-usual (but not obscene) locations from which to produce the coins, and your audience will both marvel at your skill and laugh at the situation, a winning combination.

When the supply of coins in your left hand is exhausted, produce the palmed coin one final time from your right hand, and then, very openly, drop it into the secret pocket of the bag. Remove the handkerchief from your breast pocket and wipe your brow, as if exhausted by the effort you just put in. For a laugh, if working with an audience volunteer, wipe his brow, too. Then stuff the handkerchief into the secret pocket of the bag, on top of the coins.

Close up the bag, blow it up, and twist up its neck to keep the air inside. "As real as the money seemed to be," you say, "the fact is, its appearance was nothing more than an illusion, a figment of my imagination, made real only temporarily." Pop the bag and tear it open to show that the coins and handkerchief have disappeared entirely. It was a dream, after all.

SLOW-MOTION BILL TRANSPOSITION

The method of this miraculous transposition effect is elegant in its simplicity. Don't discount it for that reason. As a close-up effect, it's hard to beat.

EFFECT: The magician folds a five-dollar bill and a one-dollar bill into quarters. "Watch me closely," the performer says. "I'm about to demonstrate an age-old swindle that's so clever, it's impossible to spot. This technique has been used to defraud millions of suckers out of millions of dollars." The bills are placed in a spectator's hand, which is closed tightly around them. The magician removes the dollar bill from the volunteer's hand and places it in his own. "It seems as if I've taken the one from your hand, doesn't it?" Miraculously, when the magician opens his hand, he is holding the *five*-dollar bill. The spectator opens his fist to discover the one-dollar bill!

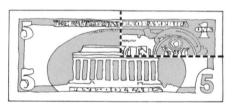

FIGURE 76

REQUIRED: A five-dollar bill, a one-dollar bill, a pair of scissors, and rubber cement.

PREPARATION: Cut a corner off the one-dollar bill and paste it, back-out, to the back of the five-dollar bill, as shown in **Figure 76**. Place this prepared bill in your wallet.

PERFORMANCE: Remove the prepared bill from your wallet. Then borrow a one-dollar bill from a willing volunteer. "This swindle is as old as paper money, and it happens very slowly. Watch me closely."

Fold both bills into quarters, making sure that the prepared side of your five is (a) hidden from the spectators in the process, and (b) ends up on the outside of the bill after the folding is complete. Place the five on top of the one.

"Sir, please hold out your hand, palm down." He does so, and you place both bills under his hand. As you do so, turn the packet upside down. "Now close your hand into a fist around the money." He does this.

"Now for the swindle. Let me get my thumb and finger into your fist and remove one bill." Here, you remove the *lower* bill of the two. As it is removed, the duplicate corner, which you prepared in advance, will show. Outwardly, this makes the bill look like a one. In actuality, it's a five.

"This is how the con man swindles an innocent, decent man like yourself out of his hard-earned cash. Watch the one-dollar bill." Place the five (which appears to be a one) in your fist. Turn your hand over and open it to reveal the transformation; now that the bill has been turned over, it has turned into a five. Unfold the bill to show its full face— a five—and turn it over (while concealing the prepared corner with your right fingers) to casually flash the back of the bill.

"Open your hand." When the spectator does, he unfolds the bill inside and finds that it is a one.

NOTES ON THE BANKNOTES: The utterly fair (what Mysterio called "clean") handling of this effect is what makes it work. Every action can be performed smoothly and openly. The effect was invented by U. F. Grant of Pittsfield, Massachusetts, whose reputation was built by inventing countless simple, practical, and baffling effects.

RIP-IT

Jack Chanin of Philadelphia was famous for his boldness. "Last night I saw Chanin, an expert at sleeving, shuttle an empty bottle of Coca-Cola up his sleeve," Mysterio wrote in his diary on July 21, 1935. It was from Chanin's mind that the following mystery evolved.

EFFECT: The magician tears a small section out of a dollar bill and eats it. As quickly as he can snap the bill open again, it is restored!

REQUIRED: A dollar bill.

PREPARATION: None.

FIGURE 77

PERFORMANCE: "This could be the most disgusting trick I do," you say as you introduce the bill. "They don't call it 'filthy lucre' for nothing." Fold the bill in half, as in **Figure 77**. Now, tear down the center of the bill, through the portrait of George Washington,

FIGURE 78

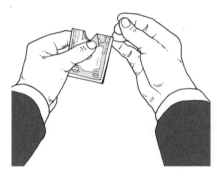

FIGURE 79

approximately ³/₄ inch (2 cm), as in **Figure 78.** Plainly display this tear to the audience. It is real.

Now *mimic* the action of tearing out this portion of the bill entirely. What actually happens is that the torn section of the bill is folded down and under the larger portion of it, thus concealing it from view, as in **Figure 79.** As you complete the apparent tear, hold the fingers of your tearing hand closed, with the thumb behind them, as if you were holding a small piece of the bill. Pretend to place this piece into your mouth, then mime the actions of chewing and swallowing it.

"It's surprisingly light and refreshing," you say after apparently swallowing the paper. To conclude the feat, re-grip the bill with both hands, as in **Figure 80,** at the corners. The bill is still folded, but you are prepared to snap it open. When you do, the currency is visibly and instantly restored, and appears to be good as new, as in **Figure 81.** Immediately place the bill back in your wallet so that the tear in it—concealed even at a short distance by the busy pattern printed on it—will not be noticed and cannot be inspected by your befuddled audience.

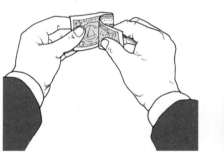

FIGURE 80

FIGURE 81

ROLL-OVER

Reading through this trick with the required props in hand will make learning it and understanding its diabolical secret much easier.

EFFECT: "Big bills always rise to the top. Let me demonstrate exactly what I mean." Two banknotes, a one-dollar bill and a fifty-dollar bill, are rolled into a tight tube on the table. The fifty is clearly underneath the one. A spectator holds the corners of the bills. Even so, when unrolled, the fifty has magically penetrated the other, and is now uppermost.

REQUIRED: Two bills of significantly different denominations.

PREPARATION: None.

FIGURE 82

FIGURE 83

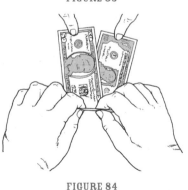

FIGURE 84

PERFORMANCE: Place the one-dollar bill on top of the fifty in a *V* shape, as shown in **Figure 82.** The *V* formation of the bills is very important. Begin rolling the bills into a tight tube, as shown in **Figure 83.** When the bills are nearly entirely rolled, look directly at your spectator and ask the following question: "The fifty is clearly underneath the one, is it not?" As he looks up to answer you, continue rolling the bills forward. Due to the angle at which they were set, you will feel the end of one bill make a 180-degree rotation underneath your hand. When this has taken place, the secret stuff of the trick is done. Remove your hands from the bills to show the corners still on the table. "Put one finger on each corner, please. And remember, the fifty is under the one. But not for long."

Slowly unroll the bills back toward you, as in **Figure 84.** The fifty will now be on top of the one!

FOREIGN ROLL-OVER: To further emphasize the illusion, the trick can be performed with two bills from different countries, and of different colors. Note, though, that they must be roughly the same size.

CUTTING MONEY

Mysterio learned the secret of this effect from the Chicago-based escape artist Joseph J. Kolar, who dubbed the trick Kolar's Magic Shears. "Kolar had a clever tag line which he used to advertise his appearances as an escapist (though he was no Houdini)," Mysterio wrote on April 30, 1921. "He signed his letters, 'Give my regards to the chief of police.'"

EFFECT: Two one-dollar bills are shown, front and back. Cleanly and openly, the money is then cut in half with a pair of scissors. There is no question they've been cut. In fact, a spectator can snip the bills in half. Even so, the magician instantly and visibly restores the bills.

FIGURE 85

REQUIRED: Two new one-dollar bills, rubber cement, and talcum powder. Since the destruction of U.S. currency is against the law, we recommend that you use play money for this effect; otherwise, proceed at your own risk.

PREPARATION: On the backs of the bills, spread a layer of rubber cement in a wide strip over the "N" in the word "ONE." The strip of cement should be in the same location on both bills. Sprinkle the cement-coated portions of the bills with a thin layer of talcum powder, as shown in **Figure 85.** This will keep them from sticking together before you want them to.

PERFORMANCE: Show the bills front and back and then place them together back to back. Be sure that the bills are precisely squared up and both right side up. Then, with the scissors, cut entirely through the center of the bills. Really cut through the

FIGURE 86

bills! You will want to cut through the exact center of both bills, or as close as you can. Try to cut through the letter "O" in the word "Dollar" and George Washington's eye. These two objects will act as your guides. The pressure of the scissors will cause the two bills to stick together along the glue strip.

Separate the cut pieces, taking one in your left hand and one in your right. (At this point, each "cut piece" is actually two half bills glued together at one edge.) Let go of one end of the pieces in each hand and perform an unfolding motion, as in **Figure 86.** It looks just like the bills have been restored! Fold the bills up and put them in your pocket so no one can examine them. Later on, if you want to spend the bills, tape the cut pieces back together permanently.

THE FRUGAL MAGICIAN'S VERSION: Kolar's Magic Shears was originally performed with a strip of newspaper, and is popularly known (at least among Mysterio's professional comrades) as Clippo. The same preparation of talcum powder and rubber cement is applied to one side of a column-wide strip of newspaper, which, when folded back on itself, can then be cut in half and restored in the same fashion as described above. If performing the trick with newspaper, cutting the paper at an angle, as in **Figure 87,** will yield interesting results when it is again unfolded. The paper "restores" at an angle, as shown in **Figure 88.** ❧

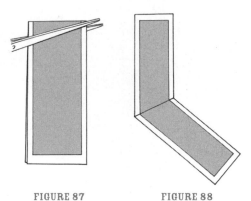

FIGURE 87   FIGURE 88

CHAPTER VI

ROPE MAGIC

CONJURING WITH CORDAGE

·•~𝕖~•·

 NE OF THE MOST INNOCENT "ordinary" items in the conjurer's bag of tricks is a coil of rope.

The first book in the English language to explain magic tricks, Reginald Scot's *Discoverie of Witchcraft*, was published in 1584 in England. It included a description of the best-known, most-performed rope trick of all time, the Cut and Restored Rope. The method described in Scot's book is also explained in this one, for, as Mr. Mysterio wrote, "Often times, the oldest secrets and the oldest effects remain the best. Classics are classic for good reason."

Professor Hoffmann, author of *Modern Magic*, wrote very little on the subject of rope tricks. "I learned many great feats from Hoffmann's classic book," Mysterio wrote, "but rope tricks in his work were few and far between. If that great volume were sparsely populated in any branch of the art, it would have been in the rope trick department."

In the years since the publication of Scot's book, and even since the release of *Modern Magic* in 1876, rope magic has advanced considerably. In Mysterio's day, Harlan Tarbell, a magician, writer, and lecturer from Chicago, developed a number of revolutionary methods for cutting and restoring a rope. Stewart James and Martin Gardner also explored the genre, inventing dozens of fascinating puzzles and tricks with cord.

Represented in this chapter is a mélange of magic with rope, including both ancient and recent effects. Regardless of their age, all of the tricks explained have one common thread (if you will excuse the pun): All of them will, properly presented, mystify and entertain an audience.

MAGICIAN'S ROPE

Not all cordage is created equal. Common clothesline is readily available at most hardware and home supply stores. Even the most inexpensive rope—as long as it is made of soft cotton—is acceptable for magical purposes. In most cases, conjurers should avoid hard, synthetic rope when performing the effects outlined below.

CORING A ROPE

Most commercially available rope is made in two parts: an outer sheath (shell), and an inner core, as illustrated in **Figure 1.** Some rope tricks require that the rope used be extra flexible. To make your rope extra flexible, you'll need to remove its core prior to performance. Cut the appropriate length of rope from a spool or hank, as needed. Nip the end of the core with the tips of your fingers and work it free from the rope sheath. You will likely have to bunch up the rope sheath and slide it down and away from the core several times. Discard the core when it is finally free of the outer rope shell. You are left with an ordinary-looking length of rope that is much more pliable and easier to compress and handle than an ordinary strand containing a core.

Core

FIGURE 1

THE ENDS

If you plan on working with any length of rope for an extended period, you will need to keep its ends from fraying. There are several ways to do this:

1. Dip each end of the rope into a small amount of white glue. Let it dry thoroughly.
2. Surgical or masking tape can also be used to bind the ends of the rope. Wrap the frayed ends in one or two layers of tape for a long-lasting, clean-looking piece of rope.
3. Wrap the ends with a length of white thread.
4. Treat the ends of the rope with soft (melted) wax. After it has hardened, the ends will be pliable but will not fray with repeated use.

CUT AND RESTORED ROPE

This is one of the most popular magic tricks of all time, and the method described here is *the* classic. Though this modus operandi has been in constant use for over five hundred years, it is still remarkably deceptive.

EFFECT: A rope is cut in the center and the two pieces are tied together. "As if mended by magic, I will now restore the rope to its original condition." Saying so, the magician makes a pass, and as promised, the rope is restored into a single, solid piece, which can be examined by the audience.

REQUIRED: A length of soft cotton rope approximately 5 feet (1 1/2 m) long, and a pair of scissors.

PREPARATION: None.

PERFORMANCE: "This is a trick that has baffled audiences for ages, perhaps because of its simplicity," you say. "I use only two objects: a length of rope and a pair of scissors. Watch this."

Hold the ends of the rope in your left hand, between your fingertips and thumb, allowing the ends to hang over your fingertips, as in **Figure 2**. Reach down with your right hand and stick your right thumb and forefinger through the loop at the center of the rope, as in **Figure 3**.

Raise the center of the rope toward your left hand. As the hands meet, grab the length of rope just below your left thumb and first finger with your *right* thumb and first finger, as shown in **Figure 4**. Pull up on this portion of the rope, which, from the front, appears to be its center. The real center of the rope slides off your right fingers and into your left hand, as in **Figure 5**.

From the audience's point of view (shown in **Figure 6**), it appears as if the center of the rope has been gathered up in your left hand. As you know, it has not. You have visibly exchanged the center for a portion of the rope close to one end, though the spectators are unaware of it. When performed smoothly, this switch is impossible to detect.

Cut through (or have a spectator cut through) the loop of rope now extending above your left fist, as in **Figure 7**.

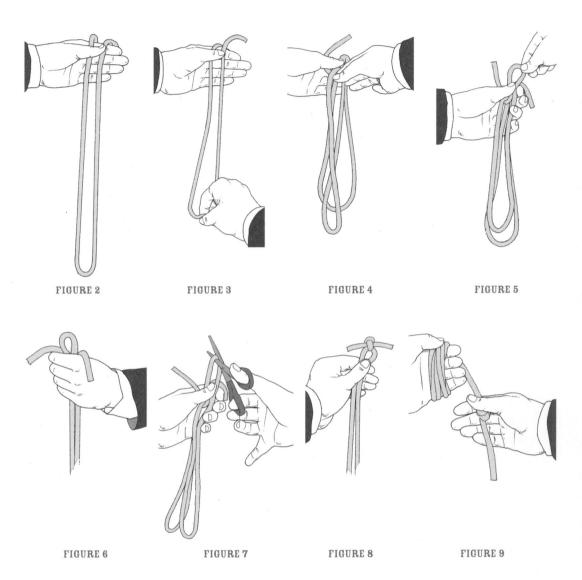

FIGURE 2   FIGURE 3   FIGURE 4   FIGURE 5

FIGURE 6   FIGURE 7   FIGURE 8   FIGURE 9

Put the scissors in your right pocket. Release the long ends of the rope from your left hand and tie the cut ends together, around the rope, into a single knot. Don't tie it too tightly. From the perspective of your audience, the rope has been cut into two pieces and these pieces have been tied together in a knot. See **Figure 8.**

Hold the end of the rope in your left hand and begin winding the rope around the left fingers. When the right hand comes into contact with the knot, allow the knot to slide along the length of the rope, and then off it, into the right hand as in **Figure 9.**

Retrieve the scissors with your right hand, at the same time, leaving the knot behind in your pocket. "This is the sharpest magic wand I've ever waved," you comment, as you wiggle the scissors over the rope. "It sounds funny, but it works. Watch!" As you slowly unwind the rope from around your left hand, it is shown to be restored.

ALTERNATIVE RESTORATIONS: For a more surprising finish, instead of ditching the knot, simply slide it off of the rope in full view of the audience as you say, "I have to confess something: This knot's not a knot."

The knot can also be trimmed away from the rope in full view of the audience, one snip at a time, with the scissors. First cut off the ends of the knot, and then the center, allowing the small pieces to fall on the floor. Clamp your hand over the apparently severed sections of rope just before the last bit of the knot is cut away. Rub your hand along the length of the rope to effect the magical restoration.

FLASH RESTORATION: Perhaps the most visually arresting way of restoring a length of cord that has been cut as described above is as follows.

When the long ends have been dropped from your hand, you apparently hold two pieces of rope, as in **Figure 10.**

Grab hold of one of the long ends of the rope with your right hand, near its base. Swing the right hand up toward the left, where the opposite side of your right hand grasps the end of one of the short pieces of rope, as in **Figure 11.** This happens very quickly.

When the right hand has a firm hold on both ends of the rope as pictured, the left hand releases everything it holds. The rope is restored in a flash.

When properly performed, it should look as if you pick up one end of the rope, touch it to one of the others, and the rope restores itself.

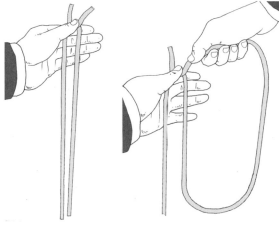

FIGURE 10   FIGURE 11

SCISSORCUT

EFFECT: A pair of scissors is looped onto a length of rope and a spectator is asked to hold tight to both ends of the rope. The magician covers the scissors with a handkerchief and says, "Now for the magic. I will separate the scissors from the rope without using the ends." A distinct snip is heard, and the scissors are indeed separated from the rope, which is revealed, when the cloth is removed from over it, to be tied together. "Not much of a trick, you say?" The magician then restores the tied-together rope into one piece.

REQUIRED: A length of rope at least 40 inches (1 cm) long, a second section of rope 6 inches (15 cm) long, an opaque handkerchief, and a sturdy pair of scissors.

PREPARATION: Place the short length of rope in your pocket, along with the scissors and the handkerchief.

PERFORMANCE: Thread the ends of the rope through the scissors, as shown in **Figures 12 through 14.** First thread it through the left handle, then down and around the blade, through the right handle, back around the blade and finally back out of the right handle, as illustrated.

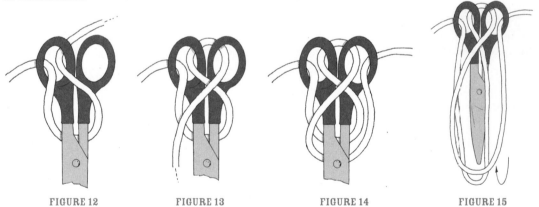

| FIGURE 12 | FIGURE 13 | FIGURE 14 | FIGURE 15 |

Invite a spectator to assist and instruct him as follows: "Sir, please hold both ends of the rope in front of you." He does so, and you then drape the handkerchief over the scissors, removing the short length of rope from your pocket along with the hankie, and keeping this short piece concealed from the audience.

After the scissors have been covered, draw one of the two loops running over the blades down and over them. Then pull the other loop down and over the blades. These actions and loops are shown in **Figure 15.** The scissors are now free of the rope. Keep the scissors under the handkerchief with the aid of one finger, while you tie the short piece of rope around the center of the longer rope. When finished, make a loud snipping noise with the scissors, as if you were cutting the rope in half. Pretend to tie the pieces of rope together and, finally, remove the hankie and reveal the scissors to be free of the rope.

The audience will groan, thinking that you simply cut through the center of the rope to free the scissors and keep your promise. "It seems as if I took the easy way out, didn't I?" you say. "Well, I promise you I didn't."

Use the scissors to trim away the knot from the rope, one small piece at a time, until it is gone entirely and the rope has been apparently restored to one solid piece!

THREE THERE, THREE GONE

This mystery is based on the work of New York magician Milbourne Christopher, who toured European nightclubs (where Mysterio saw him) with a fifteen-minute vaudeville-style act made up entirely of rope magic. The effect makes for an excellent opening to a series of rope tricks.

EFFECT: The magician displays a length of rope between his hands. With a shake, three knots appear in it, one in the center and another near each end. The first knot vanishes from the end of the rope. The second knot is untied, "to prove that it is real." The last knot of the trio is slid off of the rope and thrown to an audience member as a souvenir.

REQUIRED: A length of rope 5 feet (1½ m) long and a length of rope 6 inches (15 cm) long.

PREPARATION: Tie a slip knot near the left end of the longer rope (as described in the Dissolving Knot, page 276). Near the right end of the rope, tie the shorter length into a false knot; in other words, tie the shorter length into a knot around the long piece of

FIGURE 16

rope, and trim the ends down. This false knot and the setup are shown in **Figure 16.**

PERFORMANCE: Approach the audience with the rope held as shown in **Figure 17,** concealing the false knots in the rope. The end in your left hand points back toward your body and the end in your right hand points away from it.

As your hands come together, clip the right end with the left fingers and the left end with the right fingers, as shown in **Figure 18.** As your hands separate (briskly!) a knot is tied instantaneously in the rope, as shown in **Figure 19.** Three knots have apparently been tied in the rope with one movement.

"As quickly as they appear, so do they vanish," you say. Slide one of your hands over the dissolving knot at the left end of the rope and cause it to vanish.

"Some of you may think that these knots are not what they appear to be," you continue. "They are genuine, I assure you." Untie the center knot in the rope slowly and deliberately, proving it to be real.

"The last knot is handled in an entirely different manner," you say. In plain view of the entire audience, slide the false knot off of the rope and toss it into the audience. "That's yours to keep," you say. Now proceed with a series of rope tricks (such as the Cut and Restored Rope, page 187), since the cord in your hands is unprepared and free from trickery.

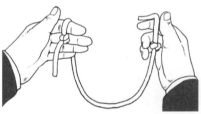

FIGURE 17

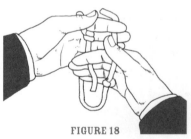

FIGURE 18

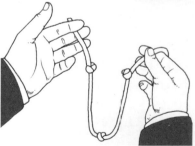

FIGURE 19

RELEASE THE RING

The category of tricks with rings and ropes is a relatively recent phenomenon in the world of magic. The effect described here, however, is quite old, and quite good.

EFFECT: A metal ring is threaded onto a length of rope and locked into place. Despite being secured to the rope, the ring is then visibly plucked off the cord.

REQUIRED: A metal or sturdy plastic ring around 3 inches (8 cm) in diameter (a bracelet will work as long as it is rigid, not flexible) and a length of rope approximately 5 feet (1½ m) long (experiment with what works best for you).

PREPARATION: None.

PERFORMANCE: Loop both ends of the rope through the center of the ring and both ends of the rope back through its own center, as shown in **Figures 20 and 21.** Now slide the two loops of the rope away from each other, so each loop sits opposite the other, as shown in **Figure 22.**

To release the ring from the rope, continue pushing the loops away from the point at which they started. The ring will eventually pop off of the rope!

RINGING—REVERSED: Under cover of a handkerchief, a ring can be threaded onto a rope by reversing the actions detailed above.

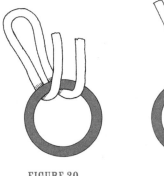

FIGURE 20

FIGURE 21

FIGURE 22

MILLER'S MIRACLE MOVE

In vaudeville, Mr. Mysterio saw "Professor" Jack Miller manipulate giant playing cards as if they were from an ordinary deck. "He was as skilled with the oversized pasteboards as most magicians are with a poker-sized pack," Mysterio noted. The rope effect described below was created by Miller after his retirement from the vaudeville stage.

EFFECT: The magician holds a ring and a length of rope in his hand. The ends of the rope are tied together and the ring then magically penetrates the unbroken loop and is shown linked to the cord!

FIGURE 23

FIGURE 24

REQUIRED: A solid ring and a piece of rope approximately 3 feet (90 cm) long.

PREPARATION: None.

PERFORMANCE: Thread the rope through the ring, as in **Figure 23.** "Seems simple, doesn't it? The ring goes on the rope." Move the ring up and down the rope, finally bringing it up to within 6 inches (15 cm) of the end of the rope. Then, with your right fingers, make a loop in the rope, as shown in **Figure 24.** The ring is now flipped over onto the right arm, *apparently* removing it from the rope in the following manner.

Raise the ring to the position shown in **Figure 25,** then flip it over the right hand as shown in **Figure 26.** Throughout these actions, the right fingers and thumb do not release the end of the rope or the loop, which is now concealed from the audience behind the right hand and wrist.

"The ring comes off the rope just as easily," you say. Grab the rope at the point indicated by the X in **Figure 26** and pull it "out" of the ring, apparently separating the rope and ring from each other. The actual situation at this point, from the performer's view, is shown in **Figure 27.** From the view of the audience, things look like **Figure 28.** It seems obvious to your spectators that the ring and rope are separate from each other (they are not, but only you know that).

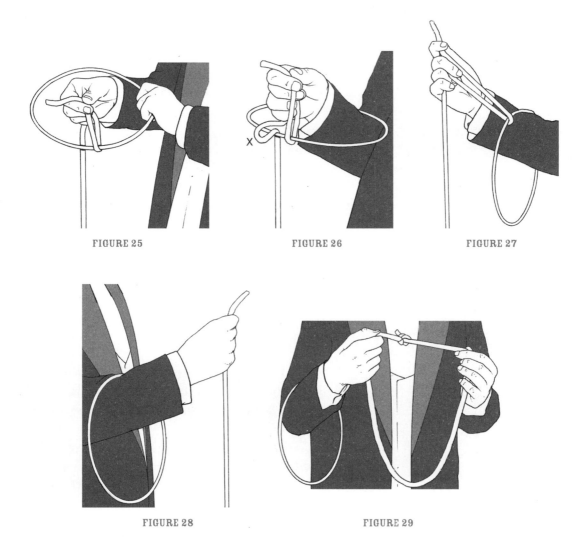

FIGURE 25   FIGURE 26   FIGURE 27

FIGURE 28   FIGURE 29

"I'm going to magician-proof the rope," you say as you tie the ends of the rope together. Move the ring toward your elbow, which increases the size of the loop concealed behind your right hand and wrist, but reinforces the idea that the ring and rope are separate. The audience sees the situation as shown in **Figure 29.** Now for the magical moment: The ring will be threaded on the rope, even though the rope's ends have been securely tied. This can be done by throwing the ring and rope into the air together, or by dropping them to the table and then lifting the rope, which must now be untied to remove the ring!

TIGHT-ROPE WALKING IN MINIATURE

⎯⎯⎯⎯⎯⎯⎯⎯⎯⎯ ✦ ⎯⎯⎯⎯⎯⎯⎯⎯⎯⎯

This effect is more of a shortcut to a virtually impossible skill than a magic trick. But regardless of how one classifies it, it's always impressive.

EFFECT: The magician offers a demonstration of impossible skill. With some effort, he balances a small rubber ball on a short length of rope. The ball skitters back and forth along the length of rope, "like an ant running for its nest," says the performer. No matter how impossible the feat of balancing seems, the ball is under the complete control of the magician.

REQUIRED: A length of soft cotton rope 12 to 20 inches (30 to 50 cm) long, a lightweight rubber ball approximately 2 inches (5 cm) in diameter, and a spool of thread approximately the same color as the rope.

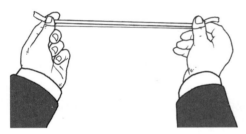

FIGURE 30

PREPARATION: Tie the thread securely to the rope approximately 1 inch (2 ½ cm) from each end. There should be some slack in the thread—enough to allow your thumbs to comfortably rest between the thread and rope. See **Figure 30.**

PERFORMANCE: In your best sideshow bally-voice, announce your spectacular feat of jugglery. Show the ball and the rope to your audience. As the rope hangs from your left hand, insert your left thumb between the thread and the rope. Set the ball "on" the rope as you stretch it out between your hands, making the thread taut by inserting your right thumb in place as you do so. Now allow the ball to balance—pretend great difficulty here, as there's "nothing impressive about skill made to look simple," according to Mysterio's note-book—first at one end of the rope, and then let it roll down to the opposite end as slowly as you can. See **Figure 31.** When you've received a suitable round of applause, launch the ball into the air, let go of the rope with one hand, catch the ball, and take a bow.

FIGURE 31

STIFF ROPE

The legendary Hindu Rope Trick (which is just that—a legend, never actually witnessed) can be re-created (in part) with the cleverly gaffed piece of rope described here.

EFFECT: The magician ties a piece of invisible thread to each end of a length of cotton rope. "It may look as if I'm doing absolutely nothing," he says, "but in fact, I'm in complete control of my faculties. And in complete control of this rope, by means of the invisible thread I'm using. I'll show you. Watch." So saying, the performer mimes the action of lifting up one end of thread toward the sky. As the imaginary thread moves, so does the end of the rope, which stands straight up, stiff as a board. When the magician lets go of the thread, the rope falls.

FIGURE 32

REQUIRED: Approximately 20 inches (50 cm) of cotton rope with its core removed and two plastic drinking straws.

PREPARATION: Insert a straw into each end of the cored rope; 5 to 6 inches (12 to 15 cm) of rope should be between the ends of the straws. Tie off the ends of the rope so the straws cannot be seen and will not fall out of the rope. See **Figure 32**.

PERFORMANCE: The center of the rope hangs from your left fingers, apparently unprepared and limp. "Allow me to demonstrate the properties of a new invisible thread I recently discovered," you say, as you mime the action of tying a length of invisible thread to the ends of the rope. You may want to set the rope on a table as you apparently tie the thread to its loose ends. "If I hadn't explained my actions before I did this," you continue, "you all might think me mad. But that's not the case at all."

With the rope hanging down from your left hand, use your left thumb to press the end of one straw against your index finger through the rope. As you mimic pulling upward on the "invisible thread" with your right hand, the left thumb and finger help raise the magically

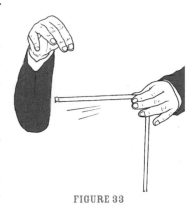

FIGURE 33

stiffened rope, until the rope is now pointing straight out, as in **Figure 33.** Pretend to let go of the invisible thread. At the same time, let the rope fall, limp and lifeless, back into your left hand.

"To conclude the demonstration," you say, "I will use both pieces of thread at the same time, and an invisible skyhook as well." Pretend to tie one end of the invisible thread to an "invisible skyhook," which makes the rope stand straight out to your right. Bring your right hand back so that you're holding the center portion of the rope with both hands, and adjust your grip so that your right thumb and forefinger hold the straw through the rope. Then, mime the action of lifting the dangling end of the rope with the other piece of invisible thread (perhaps with your mouth, since your hands are busy). This time, of course, your left hand does the dirty work with the concealed straw, and the entire length of rope appears stiff as a board, suspended horizontally in front of you as shown in **Figure 34.**

FIGURE 34

Finish the trick by apparently unhooking the rope from the skyhook and allowing it to dangle from your left hand. To convince the audience that nothing is concealed inside the rope, wrap it tightly around your fist. The straws will bend with the rope and yet, when the rope is uncoiled later on, will spring back into shape.

CHEFALO'S VANISHING KNOT

Once the workings of this ingenious knot are learned, like the skill of riding a bicycle while juggling three spinning Indian clubs, it will not be forgotten. It can then be worked at a moment's notice—with borrowed rope, string, or even a handkerchief. The knot bears the name of its inventor, an Italian illusionist called Chefalo, who was a contemporary of Mr. Mysterio.

EFFECT: The magician ties two knots in a length of rope, and then, "like a cloud fading in the summer breeze," as the ends of the cord are pulled upon, the knot melts away.

REQUIRED: A piece of rope 2 feet (60 cm) long.

PREPARATION: None.

PERFORMANCE: A double knot is tied, and one end of the rope is threaded back and forth first through one and then the other of the loops thus formed. The ends of the rope are pulled and the knots dissolve.

The illustrations explain the method of tying the knot. Be sure to follow the various steps exactly as pictured in **Figures 35 through 38.** When the final tie has been made, pull *gently* (this is important) on the ends of the rope, and the knot will dissolve. What appeared to be a perfectly genuine knot will prove to be as intangible as a wisp of smoke.

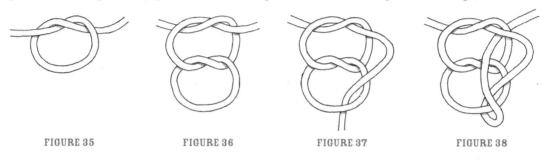

FIGURE 35   FIGURE 36   FIGURE 37   FIGURE 38

ROPE THROUGH NECK

"The great Japanese magician Tenkai Ishida made a feature of this deceptive rope illusion," wrote Mysterio. "Though his sleight-of-hand with cards and cigarettes was superlative, this was the effect in his repertoire I enjoyed the most."

EFFECT: A rope is passed twice around the magician's neck. "No, this is not a new method of checking the blood pressure at the jugular," the conjurer says. "It's far more dangerous. In fact, one slip-up and my air supply could be cut off." With that he gives a sharp tug on the ends of the rope. It apparently penetrates the neck—but the performer is left unharmed!

REQUIRED: A piece of rope approximately 4 feet (120 cm) long.

PREPARATION: None.

FIGURE 39   FIGURE 40   FIGURE 41

FIGURE 42

PERFORMANCE: Drape the rope unevenly over your neck, as shown in **Figure 39.** Though you are aware that end B is slightly longer than A, your spectators will not notice this fact.

Figure 40 shows how you reach across your body and grasp the short end of the rope (end A) with your right hand. Now reach across end A and grasp end B with your left hand.

When the loop held in the right hand is about halfway around the neck, the left hand begins wrapping the short piece around the neck too, following the same path as the right hand, as in **Figure 41.** The right hand stops when halfway behind the neck and goes no further, but the left hand goes all the way around. This allows you to create a bight (a loop) in the rope behind your neck, though it appears as if you have wrapped it around your neck twice. This is shown in **Figure 42.**

To your audience, everything looks copacetic. Your patter continues: "No medical professional will condone what I've just done." **Figure 43** shows a view from the front. Because you began the trick by hanging the ropes over your neck unevenly (remember, B was longer at the start), the ends now hang evenly.

To finish the effect in a quick, startling way, tug sharply on the ends of the rope. It will apparently penetrate your neck!

FIGURE 43

LINKED

— ❧ —

Paul Curry invented what is arguably the greatest card trick of the twentieth century, called Out of This World (see page 82). This rope trick, also a brainchild of Curry's, is another winner, and requires no preparation.

EFFECT: Two lengths of rope are shown. The ropes are doubled and one is thrown over each of the performer's shoulders. The loops hang down in front, about a foot below each shoulder. The ends are behind him.

The performer turns his back on the spectators. "I know this isn't polite," he says, "but believe me when I say that the impropriety of this action is worth the spectacular feat you are about to witness." Holding a loop in either hand, he slowly raises the ropes above his head. The two loops of rope are now linked together, though the ends have never left the sight of the spectators!

REQUIRED: Two pieces of rope, each approximately 5 feet (1½ m) long. If possible, they should be of contrasting colors, say white and red.

PREPARATION: None.

PERFORMANCE: The method behind Linked is simple and effective. (Much to the chagrin of budding magicians, great magic tricks have simple methods.) The strong point is that the spectators are led to believe that the ropes are linked together before they actually are.

Fold the ropes in half and throw one over each shoulder, as in **Figure 44.** Turn your back on the spectators, as in **Figure 45,** and patter about how "impolite" it is to do so. Bring both hands up and insert one loop through the other, as in **Figure 46.**

Fold loop A back on itself, as shown in **Figure 47.** Note the linked effect that results. Use both hands to grasp the ropes on either side of this link, as shown in **Figure 48.** Note that a second link is created.

Lift both of your arms so that the first link is at eye level. "The miracle happens right about here," you say as you lift up the ropes. The link at B is just underneath your chin and still out of the view of the spectators (since your back is turned). See **Figure 49.**

"Keep your eyes glued to the center of the ropes as I lift them over my head," you say. Raise your arms. Use your chin as a third hand of sorts, stopping the B link as the

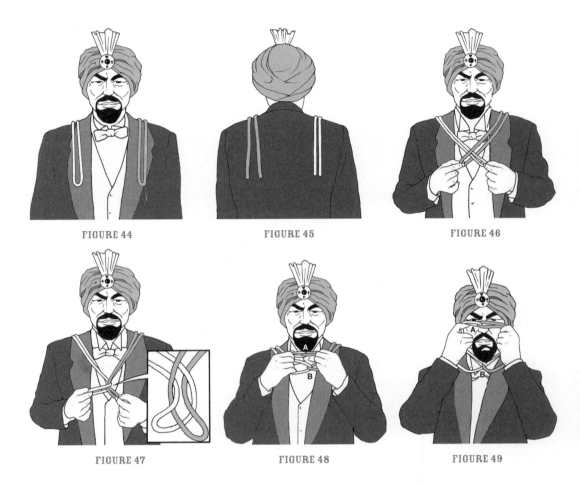

FIGURE 44

FIGURE 45

FIGURE 46

FIGURE 47

FIGURE 48

FIGURE 49

ropes are lifted and making them slide through each other. Once your arms have been completely extended, the ropes at B should be clear of each other. If they are not, slide the hands away from each other to complete the linking of the ropes.

It's important to remember that these twists and links of rope, as well as the secret linking of the two loops are completely covered by the performer's back. See **Figure 50.** The puzzling effect of seeing the two loops apparently linked together at the start is what fools laymen (and many magicians unfamiliar with the effect). The ropes are actually being linked as the hands are raised—thanks to what happens underneath the magician's chin.

FIGURE 50

SEFALALJIA

The term *Sefalaljia* is, at present, most commonly associated with the baffling rope trick—which was originally part of a larger Spirit Cabinet routine that involved a small, curtained box—described below.

EFFECT: The performer introduces a length of rope, a small ring, a safety pin, and a handkerchief. These objects are entirely ordinary and free of preparation—they can be examined before and after the performance. The rope is doubled and pinned together, and laid on the table or floor along with a spectator's ring. Everything is then covered with a handkerchief. The ends of the rope extend out from under the handkerchief. "This will take but a moment," the magician says. He reaches under the hankie for a moment, and then removes his hands. A volunteer comes forward, grasps one end of the rope and draws it out from under its covering. The borrowed ring is now threaded on the middle of the rope and locked in place by the pin. The ring, still on the rope, is returned to the owner and the volunteer can examine all properties to his heart's content.

REQUIRED: A piece of white cotton rope 40 inches (1 m) long, with its core removed, an opaque handkerchief, a ring (yours or borrowed), and a safety pin.

PREPARATION: None.

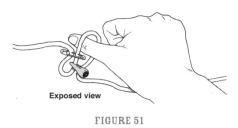

Exposed view

FIGURE 51

PERFORMANCE: Double the rope and use the safety pin to pin it together near its midpoint. Lay it on the table, set the ring beside it, and cover both with the hankie. After the rope, pin, and ring are placed under the handkerchief, several things happen in rapid (but not rushed) succession. First, the safety pin is removed and placed on the table. Next, the midpoint of the rope is looped and tucked through the ring. Then place the pin through the left side of the loop thus formed, and the half of the rope extending from under the left side of the hank. Finally, to completely link the ring onto the rope, enlarge the loop and hook it over your thumb, as shown in **Figure 51.** These steps should take no more than thirty seconds to perform, and with practice can be executed very rapidly.

To complete the trick, have a volunteer pull the left end (from the performer's perspective) of the rope. As it is pulled, the ring is automatically threaded upon the rope and found to be pinned in the center!

GENUINE DISSOLVING KNOT

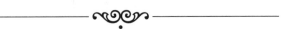

Mysterio wrote: "Most scouts and campers will be familiar with this knot, but few are aware of its magical properties." Indeed, this ordinary, sturdy knot can be applied to a wide variety of tricks.

EFFECT: The magician firmly ties the ends of a piece of rope together. He pulls on it to tighten it. The knot is placed in his fist and, when removed from it a moment later, has dissolved into nothingness.

REQUIRED: A length of rope.

PREPARATION: None.

PERFORMANCE: Tie a knot in the rope as illustrated in **Figures 52 through 54.** This is known as a square knot, and is a very sturdy, reliable knot...unless you know its weakness, which allows it to dissolve entirely.

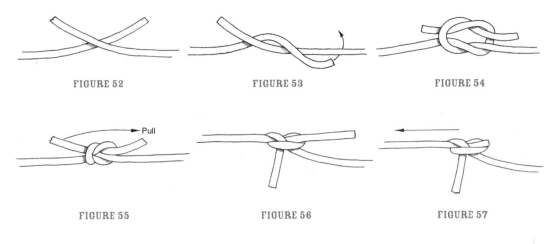

FIGURE 52   FIGURE 53   FIGURE 54

FIGURE 55   FIGURE 56   FIGURE 57

To cause the knot to vanish, grip one of the ends and pull on it smartly, as shown in **Figure 55.** This upsets the knot, as shown in **Figure 56.** Now the end just pulled is easily worked out of the knot itself, as indicated by the arrow in **Figure 57.** In other words, when both ends of the knot are pulled in unison, it holds together tightly, as it should. However, when only one end is pulled, a square knot can be dissolved by simply pulling one end free from the other, as illustrated.

To present this as a trick, tie the square knot (which many remember by silently chanting the phrase "right over left, left over right," to indicate which ends of the rope cross each other) and have a spectator tighten it, or tighten it yourself. Then say, "It couldn't be clearer, could it? This is a solid knot. I'll give it one last pull, just so we're all certain." As you say this, pull on one end of the rope, upsetting the knot, and then place the knot into your clenched fist. Now, if you pull the appropriate end of the rope out of your fist, the knot will dissolve entirely, even though it is held in your fist.

ANOTHER DISSOLVING KNOT: Read the description of the Dissolving Knot on page 276 in the chapter on handkerchief magic. The false knot described there (a slip knot) can be tied in a piece of rope.

NO ESCAPE (VEST TURNING)

Rarely seen today, in Mr. Mysterio's heyday on the vaudeville circuits, several acts performed versions of this feat. It packs a double punch, in that at first blush it appears as if the magician is unable to accomplish what he set out to do. The surprising finish, however, is astounding and apparently impossible.

EFFECT: The magician's wrists are tied together by a spectator. "And now, a feat not attempted since the days of Houdini," the performer announces. "I will escape from these bonds—so securely tied by a member of our audience—in less than one minute!" The magician steps behind a screen as lively music plays. When he steps from behind the screen again, he has not escaped from the rope. Instead, his vest has been turned inside out on his body even though he is wearing a coat!

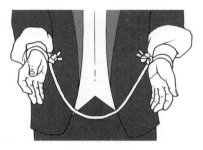

FIGURE 58

REQUIRED: A piece of rope approximately 30 inches (75 cm) long. You must be wearing a vest, preferably one that has a lining that contrasts with its exterior nicely.

PREPARATION: None.

PERFORMANCE: Introduce the feat as an escape, "an unparalleled feat, an impossible extrication." Have the ends of the rope tied around your wrists by a spectator, as in **Figure 58**. "Tie tight knots, knots that will be nearly impossible to loosen. I say 'nearly' because I will need to loosen them somehow in order to escape. But I will do so without the aid of special tools, scissors, or other apparatus. And I will do this in less than one minute—a world record."

As you step behind a screen, a door, or a cloth held by an assistant, you reverse your vest. The basic secret is much simpler than it might appear on first read-through. Remove your coat and allow it to hang down from your arms. Unbutton your vest and turn it inside out through its own armholes, which must pass over the coat. Put the vest back on in its reversed state, and then your coat. If possible, re-button the vest in this inverted position.

Step out from behind the screen and admit defeat. Then, as if thinking of it for the first time, look down at your vest and say: "Though no records have been broken and no escape was made—and for that, I hang my head in shame—I have somehow managed another impossible feat." Reveal that your vest has turned inside out!

POP OFF KNOT

This quick trick is easy to do and surprising. It is the perfect lead-in to a longer routine of rope tricks, or can be added to another effect using cord as a magical aside of sorts.

EFFECT: The magician ties a knot in the center of a length of rope. When he tugs on the ends of the rope, the knot flies off it!

REQUIRED: Two pieces of rope, one 4 inches (10 cm) long, the other 5 feet (1½ m) long.

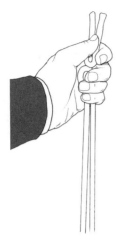

FIGURE 59

PREPARATION: Double both pieces of rope and hold the short piece next to the long one, together in your left fist. From the front, it appears that your left hand is holding two pieces of rope of the same length. **Figure 59** shows the performer's perspective.

PERFORMANCE: Display the "two pieces" of rope (in reality the two ends of the longer piece) and tie them together with a knot using both hands. To do this, loop the center of the long piece over the center of the short one, as shown in **Figure 60.** The index finger of either the right or left hand (practice will tell you which one makes the job easier) performs this action under cover of the two hands. Now the short piece of rope is knotted around this loop (called a bight). To the audience, it seems as if the two ropes have been tied together.

To make the knot jump off the rope, simply pull on both ends of the long rope smartly. The bight will tighten and finally disappear, sending the knot flying.

MYSTERIO'S COMMENT: "Though I have seen this effect used as a quick interlude in a longer rope routine, I have always thought it best suited to a flashy restoration of a cut rope. Work out a routine with this idea."

FIGURE 60

PROFESSOR'S NIGHTMARE

Along with the Cut and Restored Rope, the Professor's Nightmare is one of the most popular rope tricks of all time—and with good reason. It is visual, requires no special props, and can be seen close-up or when performed on the stage. The effect was invented in the 1950s—too late for Mysterio to include it in his programs—by Bob Carver.

EFFECT: Three different lengths of rope are shown. The magician gathers all the ends together in his hands. Visibly and magically, the ropes all become the same length! He says, "It seems as if the ropes are made of elastic, doesn't it? They're entirely ordinary, I assure you. Here, I'll show you." With a deft tug on the ends of the ropes, all three return to their original sizes and can be handed out for examination.

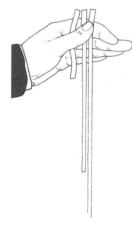

FIGURE 61

REQUIRED: Three pieces of rope: one short (4 inches/10 cm), one medium (18 inches/45 cm), and one long (36 inches/90 cm). Note that, unlike in many of the tricks described in this chapter, reasonably precise measurements *are* important here.

PREPARATION: None.

PERFORMANCE: Display the three pieces of rope and comment on their sizes. "Short, medium, and long. So far, so good."

Hold the pieces of rope in your left hand. Approximately 1 inch (2 $^1/_2$ cm) of each rope should extend over the top of your fist. The short piece is held in the crotch of the thumb, the medium rope is in the middle, and the long rope is closest to and held by the fingertips. See **Figure 61.**

The next step is to bring the hanging ends of the ropes up into the fingers of the left hand. The short rope comes up first, followed by the medium rope, and the long rope last. **Figure 62** shows this.

Now hold both ends of the short piece and the leftmost end of the medium piece with your left hand. Grab the other ends with your right hand and give the ropes a gentle and slow pull. "Watch closely," you say. "This happens right out in the open." As you pull, visibly, all three ropes become the same length! See **Figure 63.** The interconnections that make this possible are screened by the left hand (what makes this work is the fact that the long piece is doubled over the short piece).

Now count the ropes to show that all three are the same length and that you are apparently not hiding anything in your hand. Start by pulling the medium piece out of your left hand, counting "One," as you do so. See **Figure 64.**

Next, use your right hand (which holds the medium rope), to grab both ropes that remain in your left hand at the same time, and exchange the single, medium piece for the ropes already in your left hand. Pull the two ropes into your right hand, counting "Two" out loud as you do so. See **Figure 65.**

To complete the count/display, count "Three" as you pull the single rope out of your left hand and into your right. See **Figure 66.**

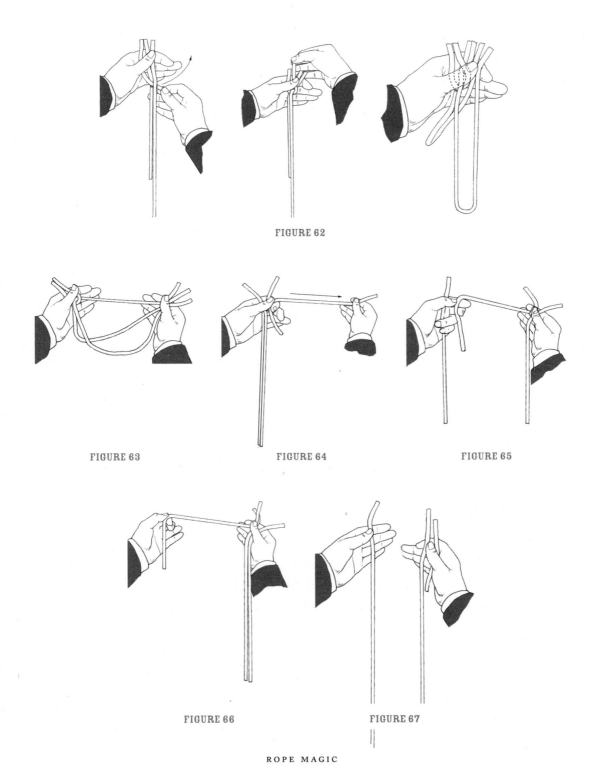

FIGURE 62

FIGURE 63   FIGURE 64   FIGURE 65

FIGURE 66   FIGURE 67

For the big finish, transfer the ropes back to your left hand. Pull on the separate ends that project above your left hand one at a time, and in rapid succession. The apparently equal lengths will quickly and magically return to the condition in which they began the performance: three unequal pieces of rope! See **Figure 67.** Everything can now be examined, if your audience so desires.

CLIFTON'S RING MOVE

This clever and deceptive sleight replaces a need for special props and handkerchiefs that, in Mysterio's day, were often used to effect the vanish of a ring. It is easy to learn—and easy to perform.

FIGURE 68

EFFECT: A ring, borrowed from a spectator, is threaded onto a length of rope, which is then wrapped around the magician's fist. The ring is hidden from view inside the magician's hand. When the magician opens his fist, the ring has vanished!

REQUIRED: A piece of rope 24 inches (60 cm) long, and a ring (which should be borrowed).

PREPARATION: None.

PERFORMANCE: Borrow a ring and thread it onto the midpoint of the rope. Place the ring on the palm of your left hand, with the ends of the rope dangling down on each side of the palm, as in **Figure 68.** "I don't want to lose your ring," you say, "so I'll wrap the rope around my fist to make sure it can't go anywhere."

With your left hand, make a *loose* fist around the ring, then turn your hand over as shown in **Figure 69.** Using your right hand, grab the end of the rope that is hanging over your left thumb and pull this end of the rope up and over the left hand. **Figure 70** shows this.

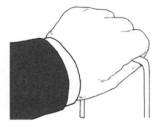

FIGURE 69

In the action of reaching across your body and grabbing the rope hanging down on the left side of your left hand, your right hand should come very close to the heel (the palm on the pinky finger side) of your left hand. In that instant, relax your left hand's grip on the ring and let it fall into your right hand, as in **Figure 71.**

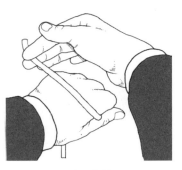

FIGURE 70

The right hand travels down toward the end of the rope, finally grasping it near the end, and, just as you did with the other end, brings the cord up and over the back of the left fist.

The ring slides along the rope as you perform this movement, and eventually slides off the end as your right hand finishes wrapping the rope around your fist. **Figure 72** shows this. Drop the right hand naturally to your side to conceal the ring. Focus all attention on your left fist.

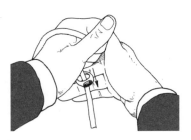

FIGURE 71

Now you must dispose of the ring. The obvious way to ditch it is by reaching into your pocket under the pretense of picking up another object, like a magic wand, a pencil, or anything else you "need" to cause the magic to happen.

Suitably armed with your magic device, say the appropriate incantation, wave the appropriate magic utensil, then open your hand. The ring has vanished!

It's now up to you to cause it to reappear. You could simply produce the ring from your pocket, but that wouldn't be particularly deceptive or entertaining. Experiment with places to have the ring reappear. A nest of boxes would work well. So might a sealed envelope (a

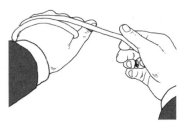

FIGURE 72

self-sealing envelope, already in your pocket, would be a good way to accomplish this). Some magic dealers even sell specially made brass ring boxes that are easy to load with a borrowed, vanished ring (like the one now in your pocket), but are hard to open (because they are locked, or their caps are threaded on, for example). This feature makes the spectators wonder not only how the ring vanished, but also how it ever made it inside a tightly sealed container.

In the end, however, the reappearance of the ring is up to you. Just be sure to give it back!

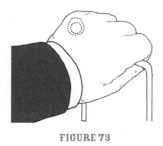

FIGURE 73

CONSIDER THIS: To make the move easier to perform, you may wish to have the ring situated near the heel of your palm (see **Figure 73**) before you make a fist and turn your left hand over.

Perform the move slowly and casually. Speeding up your patter at the exact moment you steal the ring off of the rope is a dead giveaway that something sneaky has just happened.

THE HUNTER KNOT

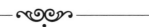

Devised by Britisher G. W. Hunter, this tricky knot is more a challenging brain-teaser than an out-and-out trick.

EFFECT: The magician ties a knot in the center of a length of rope—without letting go of either end!

REQUIRED: A length of rope at least 36 inches (90 cm) long.

PREPARATION: None.

PERFORMANCE: To begin, hold one end of the rope between the index finger and thumb of each hand. The other fingers are curled in toward your palm.

Cross the portion of rope in your right hand over the left arm, as shown in **Figure 74**. Then swoop your right hand back down to the position shown in **Figure 75**. Now feed the right-hand end of the rope through the loop in the rope and back to the right again, so that it travels the path indicated by the arrow in **Figure 76**. Separate your hands, and you will be in the position shown in **Figure 77**.

FIGURE 74

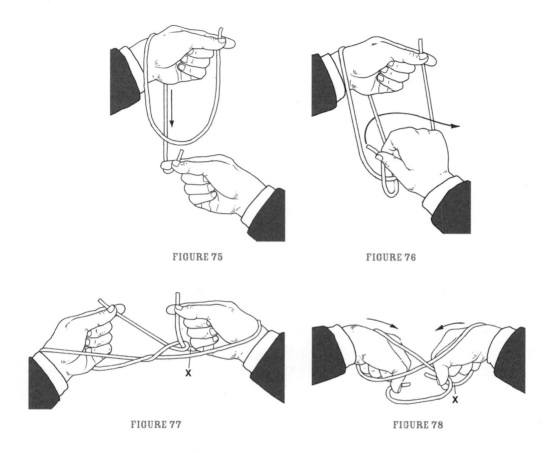

FIGURE 75

FIGURE 76

FIGURE 77

FIGURE 78

In order to complete the knot, you must now transfer the grip of the right hand from the end of the rope to the portion that is marked with an *X* in **Figure 77.** To do this secretly, turn your hands down to shake the ropes from your wrists, changing your grip as you do so. A genuine knot will form in the rope!

The key to making the Hunter Knot deceptive is to make the transfer of the right hand's grip from the end of the rope to position X a secret. You can do this effectively by directing all attention to your left hand, which moves away from your body, ostensibly to throw the rope off the left wrist. If you maintain your grip on the rope as you move your left hand forward, you will find that position X comes very close to the right hand, as shown in **Figure 78.** This makes the transfer (done under the cover of the left wrist throwing off its loop of rope) very easy to accomplish.

STRETCHING A ROPE

This is a visual trick that's easy to do. It can be performed in pantomime, or with a quick and witty line of patter.

EFFECT: "I'd like to show you a rope trick," the magician says, "but I don't have enough rope to do so." He displays a short piece of white rope in his hands. "I need at least six feet." The problem comes to a satisfactory conclusion by means of magic. As the magician tugs on both ends of the rope, it visibly stretches to the required length and can now be used for the magician's next effect!

REQUIRED: A piece of rope approximately 6 feet (1³/₄ m) long, and a wristwatch. In addition, you must be wearing a jacket to perform this effect.

PREPARATION: Double the rope and tuck the looped mid-point into the inside breast pocket of your jacket. Now run the ends down your sleeve and tuck them under the band of your watch. Approximately 1 foot (30 cm) of rope should be visible to your audience, six inches (15 cm) extending from either end of your hand. **Figure 79** shows the setup.

FIGURE 79

PERFORMANCE: Approach your audience with the set-up rope in your hand. "This will never do," you say. "For my first trick, I need much more rope than what we have here."

Tie the ends of the rope together into a square knot (see page 204). Then grasp the rope near the knot and begin pulling on it with your left hand, pretending to exert considerable force on it. "If you massage the molecules in a piece of cotton rope in just the right way, you can solve a problem of this nature," you continue.

Slowly pull the rope down through your sleeve. As you do, the circle of rope in your hand will begin to grow in size, which will eventually register with your audience. Give a final swift tug on the rope to free it from your pocket (and then watchband) and proudly display the stretched piece between your hands. You can now cause the square knot holding the ends together to magically dissolve (as explained in the Genuine Dissolving Knot on page 204) and proceed with your next rope trick.

IMPOSSIBLE KNOT

For the thinking spectator, this feat is especially puzzling. Like many good tricks, the secret is simple.

EFFECT: "Please tie my wrists together," the magician begins, "so that I can show you something impossible." A spectator complies with the performer's request, and the magician continues by saying, "I will now tie a knot in the center of this rope—without untying my hands." The magician turns his back to the audience for five seconds. When he faces the crowd again, a genuine knot has, indeed, appeared in the center of the rope!

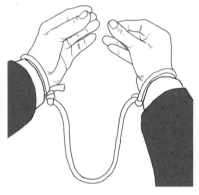

FIGURE 80

FIGURE 81

REQUIRED: A piece of rope 36 inches (90 cm) long.

PREPARATION: None.

PERFORMANCE: Have your wrists tied with rope as shown in **Figure 80.** Make sure that the rope around each wrist is not too tightly tied. If you would like to add an element of challenge to the effect, you can invite a spectator to seal the knots with tape. That way, you cannot tamper with them.

Turn your back on the spectators and feed a loop of rope under the rope circling your left wrist, as in **Figure 81.** Then twist this portion of the rope clockwise, forming a loop as in **Figure 82.** Keeping this loop intact, pull it up and over your left hand as in **Figure 83.** The loop is then fed down the back of your hand and under the rope that circles your wrist, as in **Figure 84.** The center of this loop is brought back over the rope circling your wrist, and then over your fingers, as shown in **Figure 85.** This forms a knot in the rope. Center the knot on the rope that runs between your hands, and then turn around and face the audience. A knot has, impossibly, appeared in the center of the rope!

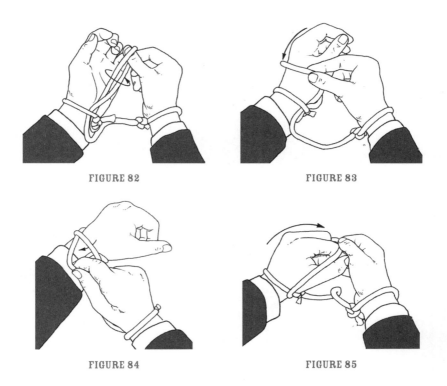

FIGURE 82   FIGURE 83

FIGURE 84   FIGURE 85

Though the effect is described as taking place in five seconds, actual time of performance may vary. As with most skills, the speed at which you can tie the knot will increase with practice.

KELLAR'S ROPE TIE

This method, devised by Harry Kellar ("He was appointed Dean when I first joined the Society of American Magicians," Mysterio wrote), was used for years in America's leading theaters for a séance effect.

EFFECT: A piece of rope is used to bind each of the magician's wrists, and then the ropes are tied together behind the performer's back. "This is how, in the first half of the twentieth century, spiritualist mediums were secured by sitters in séances," the magician explains. A hat, wristwatch, glass of water, and necklace are placed on the table in front of the tied-up magician. The lights are turned out and a rustling noise is heard. When the lights are again turned on, the magician is wearing the necklace, watch, and hat, and the glass is now empty!

REQUIRED: A piece of rope 36 inches (90 cm) long, and the articles of clothing or props you will use in the performance. Note: It's best to choose items that do not require two hands to put on; for example, don't use a necklace that must be secured with a clasp.

PREPARATION: None.

PERFORMANCE: Have your left wrist tied as shown in **Figure 86,** with the center of the rope looped over it and secured with a tight knot on the back of the wrist. Turn your hand palm down so that the rope falls as shown in **Figure 87.** Clip one end of the rope between your fingers as shown in **Figure 88,** then raise your hand as shown in **Figure 89.**

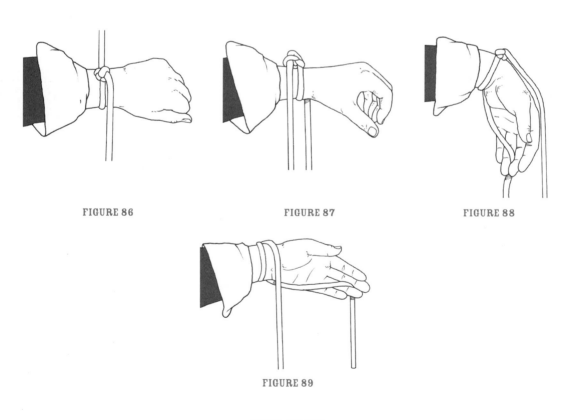

FIGURE 86   FIGURE 87   FIGURE 88

FIGURE 89

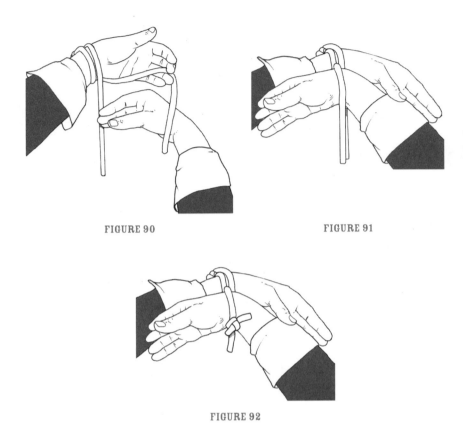

FIGURE 90

FIGURE 91

FIGURE 92

Explain how your wrists are about to be tied together, precluding the possibility that you are involved in the manifestations that are about to occur. Loop your right hand under the length of rope clipped between your left fingers as shown in **Figure 90.** Now bring your wrists together as shown in **Figure 91** and have a spectator tie the loose ends of the rope together snugly, as shown in **Figure 92.**

Instruct a spectator to stand near a light switch that controls all overhead lights in the room. "When I give the signal, please extinguish the lights for ten seconds—no more, no less. Count to ten in your head, and when you reach ten, turn the lights back on."

When the lights go out, it is a simple matter to release yourself from the rope by shifting the left hand toward the right and the right hand toward the left, as shown in **Figure 93.** The right hand now slips free of the loop in the rope, which the left hand holds open, as shown in **Figure 94.** Releasing the right hand should take no more than two seconds. With practice, it will take even less and can be done in the dark—something you will take advantage of when the lights are turned out.

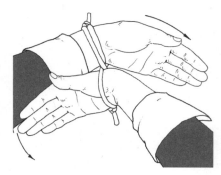

FIGURE 93

FIGURE 94

As soon as they are shut off, release your right hand, lay the loop down, still open, on your lap and drink the glass of water (which should only be half full). Then use your right hand to put the necklace around your neck, the hat on your head and the watch on your wrist (or in a pocket, if that is easier). Set the glass back on the table, and return your right wrist to the rope and "secure" yourself again before the lights are turned on.

When the spectators see the altered positions of the various objects and that the glass of water has been consumed, your performance of this pseudo-spiritualistic demonstration is concluded. Have a spectator untie you and accept a hearty round of applause. ᎧᎳ

CHAPTER VII

MAGIC
OF THE MIND

MENTAL MARVELS

·~◦~·

16	1	12	7
11	8	15	2
5	10	3	18
4	17	6	9

NO BRANCH OF CONJURING strikes a
more realistic chord with the public than magic
of the mind. When presented with care, feats of
apparent mind reading can cement the reputation
of the performer in ways that no others can. Mysterio's notebook contains a telling entry about mental magic:

"This afternoon, in a drawing room on Sudbury St., I was invited to entertain after
a luncheon of the Northern Explorers Club. Though I presented my best material, the
effect that had the most profound effect on the assemblage—the one that kept them
chattering endlessly—was the minor mind-reading stunt I performed, the number
prediction. I'm still surprised and pleased that such a simple trick can have such a
strong effect on a crowd of obviously educated personages. One gentleman (a banker)
approached me after the show to ask if my 'powers' could be used to help determine the
best course of action for an upcoming business transaction he was considering. Of
course, I told him I would not be able to help him, and this only after he offered me a
large sum of money to do so."

A number of factors contribute to this phenomenon. Most mental tricks involve little
by way of exotic props. Pads of paper, pens, envelopes, pencils, and playing cards are seen
as, for the most part, ordinary and everyday; they seem above suspicion. Additionally, when
carefully presented, mind-reading feats can take on a much more personal and meaningful
bent than, say, a card trick. When a magician divines the birthday of a spectator, or her
mother's maiden name, the spectator will often take acute interest in the outcome of the
effect; certainly more than, say, whether or not the magician is able to reproduce the
queen of hearts with a fancy flourish after the cards have been shuffled.

It is the often personal nature of mental magic that can lead audiences to believe
that the performer has supernatural powers. And while deception is the goal of every
upstanding conjurer, that deception should only be on a theatrical level. To pretend to

supernatural abilities like the capacity to steal a spectator's thoughts is to commit a fraudulent act. Offering your performance, rather, as a demonstration of "unique, underdeveloped techniques" or as "examples of psychological abilities not commonly known" provides enough of a disclaimer. In less than plain language, you are saying, "What I am presenting here is entertaining trickery. Please enjoy it."

GRAY ELEPHANTS IN DENMARK

The method behind this impromptu mental miracle has been known to magicians for centuries. This presentation can be performed in virtually any situation—even over the telephone.

EFFECT: A spectator makes a number of entirely free choices—of a number, of a country, and of an animal. With unerring accuracy, the mind reader reaches into the participant's head and divines the name of the animal and the country that has been merely thought of!

REQUIRED: Loose memorization of the script that follows.

PREPARATION: None.

PERFORMANCE: Ask a spectator to follow your instructions closely. If they veer off course in the initial steps of the effect, all will be lost.

Begin by asking your volunteer to select a number between one and ten, and to multiply it by nine.

Assume she selects five: $5 \times 9 = 45$. "You've arrived at a new number," you say. "If it's a two-digit number, add the digits of that number together to make an entirely new number. If it's a one-digit number, we'll skip to the next step." In this example, forty-five breaks down into four and five: $4 + 5 = 9$.

"Now you've arrived at a completely random number. Subtract five from that number." In our example, $9 - 5 = 4$.

"Let's stop the math there. Now I want you associate the letters of the alphabet with numbers. A equals one, B equals two, C equals three, and so on. Whatever number you're thinking of, please associate it with its corresponding letter of the alphabet." In our example, 4 = D, so the letter they will think of will be *D*. In fact, no matter what number the spectator selects initially, they will always arrive at the number four, and hence the letter *D*.

"Taking things a few steps further, I want you to think of a country in Europe that begins with the random letter now in your mind. Think of a country in Europe." There are very few countries whose name begins with the letter *D*. Denmark is the obvious choice.

"Now you're thinking of a country. Good. I want you to think of one more thing. Let's make it an animal. Whatever the *second* letter in the name of your selected country is, use it. Think of an animal with a name that begins with that letter. Picture it walking through the forest, and think of the color of that animal." Because there are very few animals with names that begin with the letter *E* (the second letter in Denmark), virtually all spectators will think of an elephant. Through a simple procedure, you have forced your volunteer to unknowingly select two seemingly random things: a country (Denmark) and an animal (an elephant).

"Picture that animal and its color. Picture that animal in the country you arrived at. Imagine yourself riding that animal—if that's possible—in the country you randomly selected. I find that scenarios like this, no matter how strange, are easy to pick up on. In fact, this one is very easy to pick up on," you say, "because it's so out-of-the-ordinary."

Now you deliver the final line of the routine: "You're picturing yourself riding a large, gray elephant…in Denmark, aren't you?" Voilà!

MASS MATHEMATICAL MENTALISM

In this effect, a little-known mathematical fact is transformed into a trick that can be performed on your entire audience.

EFFECT: The performer invites everyone in his audience to perform two quick mathematical computations. He then correctly announces the total of each and every equation!

REQUIRED: Nothing.

PREPARATION: None.

PERFORMANCE: "Please think of a three-digit number. Any number will do, as long as all the digits are different. Once you have it set in your mind, reverse the digits, creating a new three-digit number." For example, if someone is thinking of 527, they then reverse the digits to create a new number, in this case 725. Your instructions continue: "Now subtract the smaller of those two numbers from the larger one." In our example, 725 - 527 = 198. "Finally, reverse your new number, and add the two together"; 198 + 891 = 1,089.

"I'm seeing four digits in my mind. They're swirling around each other. There's a zero, and an eight, and…," you say, pretending to visualize ghostly numerals. After a moment, go on: "You have arrived at a new total that even you were unaware of. If you are thinking of the number one thousand eighty-nine, please stand up." Remarkably, due to the mathematical principle at work, everyone who followed your instructions closely—and arrived at a four-digit number—will be thinking of 1,089. (Those who did not will be thinking of a three-digit number, namely 198. This total is arrived at only when the first and last digits of the first three-digit number are one digit away from each other, as with 615.) Spectators will arrive at this total less than a third of the time, and when they do, all hope is not lost. Simply announce that those spectators not thinking of 1,089 were close, but in their case the same four digits—zero, one, eight, and nine—are arranged in a different order, 0198…otherwise known as 198.

TECHNICOLOR DIVINATION

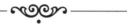

This mind-reading feat works as well for adults as it does for children.

EFFECT: "This is the first mind-reading miracle I learned," the performer tells his audience. "I began performing the feat in the first grade, to the amazement of my classmates—and my teacher." A spectator is invited to help, and selects one of six crayons. This is done while the magician's back is turned. The other five crayons are hidden in the volunteer's pocket. When the magician turns around to face the audience again, he gazes directly into the eyes of his volunteer. "I see the color of your selection as clearly now as I did when performing this feat as a young boy," he says. "You chose a light color. You chose blue." The magician is, of course, correct!

REQUIRED: Six different-colored crayons.

PREPARATION: None.

PERFORMANCE: Show six crayons, each one of a different color. "I knew I had a gift for the mystic arts at a very early age," you joke, as you display them.

Ask a volunteer to assist. As you turn your back, instruct her to select one of the colors, concentrate on it, and to hand it to you behind your back. "Next, place the other five crayons somewhere out of sight—in a pocket, perhaps. When I performed this in the schoolroom, my classmates found all sorts of interesting hiding spots for the remaining crayons."

With the selected crayon in your hand, turn back around to face your volunteer once again. While staring into her eyes and "divining" the color she is concentrating on, scrape the crayon over your thumbnail, leaving a small amount of the wax behind. Bring this hand (but not the crayon) out from behind your back, and place it on the spectator's shoulder. As your hand swings up in front of your body to grip her shoulder, quickly, casually, and coolly glimpse at the color on your nail. You are now free to describe the color she selected. After you reveal its identity, bring the crayon out from behind your back to prove the accuracy of your divination.

OVER AND OVER AND OVER

The method in play here is bold and simple, yet extremely effective.

EFFECT: Several spectators are asked to think of a four-digit number. Each spectator then calls out his selection, which is recorded on a slip of paper. The slips are folded and dropped into a bag. The slips are thoroughly mixed, and one is selected at random by a volunteer from the audience (*not* the magician). "Sir, is there a billet in your hand?" the performer asks. After receiving an affirmative answer, the magician asks him to open the slip and stare at the number written on it. "Repeat the number—all four digits—to yourself. Say it over and over and over in your mind. Keep saying 1995, 1995, 1995, 1995, 1995…" Amazingly, 1995 is the number the spectator is thinking of!

REQUIRED: A stack of index cards or other small slips of paper, a bag, and a pencil.

PREPARATION: None.

PERFORMANCE: Ask several members of your audience—perhaps ten—to each think of a four-digit number. "This can be a year of significance, the total in your bank account, the last four digits of your phone number—whatever four-digit number you decide on, make it of some significance to you," you say.

Ask each spectator to call out his number, and as he does, you write it down on a slip of paper, which is folded and dropped into the bag. At least, that's what appears to happen. Instead of writing down every number called out, you write the same number—the first number called out—on *every* slip of paper.

The working of the trick from this point forward should be obvious. Have the slips mixed and one selected from the bag (which you hold at its very edge), emphasizing the fairness of the procedure as your instructions are carried out. "I will not touch the bag or the slip of paper. Sir, please reach inside and remove one billet. Hold it close to your chest, open it and read the number printed on it to yourself, silently." Your back can be turned at this point, to heighten the impossibility of what is about to transpire.

"Sir, now that the number is foremost in your thoughts, I would like you to repeat it, over and over, to yourself, silently." Build up the impossibility of the proceedings and then say, "Keep repeating it to yourself, sir. Keep saying 1995, 1995, 1995, 1995, 1995…"

Have the number verified as you dispose of the bag, which is, in the parlance of magicians, "dirty" (in other words, its contents, if examined by a layman, would expose the working of the trick).

OVER AGAIN: The divination effect described above need not be performed exclusively with numbers or dates. For children, the names of pets or farm animals could be substituted. For adults, use the names of world leaders or celebrities, interjecting jokes and asides into your presentation. Mysterio once performed this feat for a Persian potentate, divining the name of one racehorse from a group of thirty-five.

HANDLED

The word *stooge,* has, to many magicians, come to have an unsavory connotation. A better term, perhaps, is *secret accomplice.* Mysterio, however, had no such qualms. His diary entry for March 19, 1919, includes the following description of a Second Sight act he'd seen at the Pantages Theatre in Portland, Oregon: "It was like no other mentalism act I'd ever seen. The only possible explanation is a stooge. And the end result—a tremendous effect on the audience—was well worth it."

EFFECT: Three coffee mugs are used, in addition to a spectator's watch. "When my back is turned," says the conjurer to an audience volunteer, "please place the watch under one of the three mugs. Then mix them up."

The spectator follows the magician's instructions. When the performer turns his gaze to the mugs on the table, he unerringly determines the location of the watch.

REQUIRED: Three coffee mugs and a personal object from a spectator, like a wristwatch.

PREPARATION: Before the show, a member of the audience must be brought into your confidence. A basic three-point code must be established, based on the position of the handle of one of the three mugs. **Figure 1** shows three mugs arranged on the table in a row. The left mug of the trio will act as the indicator. When the handle of the mug is tilted to the right, as in **Figure 2,** this tells you that the watch is concealed under the rightmost mug. When the handle is aligned (straight) as in **Figure 3,** the object is under the center mug. Any other orientation of the left mug's handle indicates that the watch is under it. Note that the position of the other two mugs should appear random in order to conceal the fact that the left mug is a "tell."

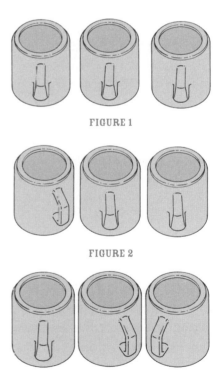

FIGURE 1

FIGURE 2

FIGURE 3

PERFORMANCE: "For this experiment in telepathy, I require a personal object from a member of our audience," you explain. Borrow a watch, a ring, or even a photograph from a spectator.

Explain the rules of the proceedings: "In a moment, I will turn my back to you—please excuse me in advance—and you, sir [pointing out your accomplice], will hide this object under one of the mugs on the table. Then, mix them up, further confusing the issue."

Your back is turned, and your secret accomplice follows your directions and codes the location of the object by positioning the handle of the mug.

"Though it ticks silently, the movement of your chronometer is loud and clear in my mind," you say. Lift the appropriate cup to disclose the wristwatch, and return it to its owner.

HANDLE-LESS: To repeat the effect, the method just described is adequate. But observant spectators may throw a kink into your plan, if their suspicions are aroused. As Mr. Mysterio once wrote, "If a spectator makes a request you cannot accommodate—if they ask to shuffle a pack when no shuffling will do—your reputation can suffer great harm. Prepare for every and any eventuality."

Alternative codes can be used to transmit the location of the watch to you. An easy way is to use three mugs that appear, to the untrained eye, to be identical but that to your eyes reveal a slight imperfection that can serve as a marker. Perhaps a small chip in the mug will tip you off, or an imperfection in its color. All your secret assistant needs to be sure of is that the watch is placed under the marked mug.

Still another method of determining the location of a hidden object is to commit to a sequence of positions—left, right, and center—under which the object will be hidden in the course of your performance. Though this sequence will appear random to your spectators, it will be anything but haphazard as far as you and your assistant are concerned.

DEVILISH DATE DETERMINATIONS

These impromptu mental feats are perfect for use in the office, since they involve an object nearly every businessperson has on hand—a calendar. Mysterio used these feats when visiting theatrical agents. Because the tricks were quick, baffling, and made an impression, they often opened doors for him at major talent agencies.

EFFECT: Any four dates on a calendar are selected and the numbers are totaled by the spectator who chose them. Instantly, the magician tells the spectator which four days he picked!

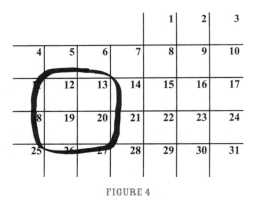

FIGURE 4

REQUIRED: A calendar.

PREPARATION: The memorization of a simple formula, described below.

PERFORMANCE: "I'd like you to select four dates in any month on this calendar," says the mind reader to a willing volunteer. "Just draw a box around any four adjacent days. The only requirement is that all four dates have to touch one another on the calendar. Add them up and tell me the total." For the sake of this explanation, assume the spectator selected the four dates as shown in **Figure 4.** The total of these dates (12 + 13 + 19 + 20) is 64. To determine the individual dates selected, follow this simple formula: Divide by four, then subtract four. This gives you the lowest digit in the group.

In this example, 64 ÷ 4 = 16, and 16 - 4 = 12. Twelve is the earliest date selected. To determine the other dates the spectator selected, add 1 (12 + 1 = 13); then you add 7 to your result (12 + 7 = 19); and for the final number chosen, you add 1 again (19 + 1 = 20).

THE FOLLOW-UP: The calendar is then handed to another spectator, who is asked to select a different month, and to choose three days in a vertical line. "Don't show me which numbers you've selected," the performer says. "Just give me the total of the digits." In this example, assume that the spectator has selected the numbers shown in **Figure 5**: 9 + 16 + 23 = 48.

This time, to determine the selected numbers, you divide the total by 3. This gives you the middle number selected. 48 ÷ 3 = 16. To determine the other two numbers, subtract 7 for the top number (16 - 7 = 9) and add 7 for the bottom number (16 + 7 = 23).

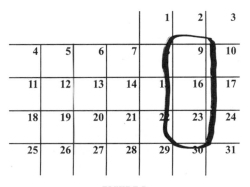

FIGURE 5

SIXTEEN DATES

This final feat of calendar wizardry is even easier to perform than the first two, as it requires no mental computation on the part of the performer. It was invented by Canadian wizard Mel Stover.

EFFECT: A spectator is invited to draw a square around any sixteen days on any month in a calendar. "You will now select four dates from those sixteen at random," the magician says. The spectator picks them, and totals their value. The magician reveals a prediction, made long before the feat began, that exactly matches the total of the spectator's randomly chosen dates!

REQUIRED: A calendar, a slip of paper, an envelope, and a pencil.

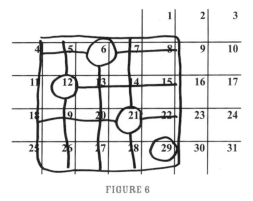

FIGURE 6

PREPARATION: None.

PERFORMANCE: A spectator is invited to select any month on a pocket calendar, and draw a square around sixteen dates in that month (it should be a four-by-four box—all of the dates must be contiguous) and show it around. (Make sure you get a look at it.) As soon as he does, you write a prediction of things to come. Due to the mathematical principle at work, the total of the four dates he is about to select will always be equal to double the sum of the numbers in either of the two diagonally opposite corners of the square. Either of the two diagonally opposite corners can be used.

Now for the selection process. "In the top row, circle one of the dates, and do not tell me what it is. Then, cross out the remaining dates in that row, and all of the dates in the column that lie beneath your selection." The spectator does so.

Continuing, the performer says, "Pick another date, this time from the second row—but not one of those that has already been eliminated. Then, cross out the remaining dates in *that* row, and the dates directly below it, too." A third date is chosen from the next row down in a similar fashion. Because of the elimination process, only one date will remain in the last row. **Figure 6** shows the circled and eliminated dates in each row and column.

Finally, instruct the spectator to add the values of these dates together. He does, and when your prediction is revealed, the spectator will be surprised that you knew the total of his "randomly selected" dates before even he did!

WITHOUT A DATE: The above effect can be performed even without the use of a calendar. Number sixteen slips of paper 1 through 16, and set them on the table in a four-by-four grid, as in **Figure 7**. Have a spectator select four of the numbered slips as outlined above in the calendar trick. If he follows the same procedure, the total of his selected numbers will *always* be 34. This can be predicted in advance in a number of ways—with 34 cents in the performer's pocket, $34 in his wallet, a simple written prediction in an envelope, or even with a message written on the back of the slips that the spectator selects, so that after the numbers have been chosen, the spectator himself can turn them over to reveal the magician's prediction.

1	2	3	4
5	6	7	8
9	10	11	12
13	14	15	16

FIGURE 7

LIKE A SORE THUMB

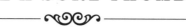

Mr. Mysterio was fond of the following phrase: "One of magic's most endearing qualities is its marriage to the element of surprise." In this strangely named trick, the climax is not evident until the very last moment, making for a surprising, strong effect.

EFFECT: A packet of cards is spread between the magician's hands. All of the cards have red backs. "It's difficult to spot the odd one, isn't it?" says the magician. "There might be a subtle mark on one of them, or there might be a slight imperfection in the printing of one card. Whatever the difference, I will tell you this: One of these cards is different from the others. I want you to use your intuition to pick it out." A spectator chooses one. "Excellent choice," the magician says. "How did you know?" Upon the delivery of this final line, the cards are turned over. All of the cards with the exception of the spectator's selection are fives of spades. His card is a five of hearts!

REQUIRED: Ten or more fives of spades from identical decks, one five of hearts from a matching deck, and a piece of double-stick tape.

FIGURE 8

PREPARATION: Stick a small square of double-stick tape to the center of the back of the five of hearts. Place it face down on top of the fives of spades (which are also face down).

PERFORMANCE: Spread the cards between your hands, face down. "Everyone is faced with a wide array of choices, on a daily basis," you say. "Today, you're going to make the *right* choice." At this point, you can mix them if you like, as long as the cards remain face down and the taped five of hearts stays on top. **Figure 8** shows this arrangement.

"These cards, from the back, look identical. One of them, however, is different. Touch the back of any card—the card you think is different from the rest."

Here, the spectator touches the back of any card in the packet. Whichever one he touches will be used. Before proceeding, you say, "Are you sure that's the one? In a moment, you'll wonder what would have happened if you'd chosen another card." If he changes his mind, fine. It doesn't matter.

Whatever card the spectator finally settles on, you remove from the spread. Drop this card on top of the packet—and onto the five of hearts with the double-stick tape on its back. Square up the cards, and lightly press on them, causing the selected card to adhere to the back of the five of hearts.

Say, "You selected this card," as you deal the top card—really two, stuck together—face down onto the table, "...not any of these." Here, you turn over the cards that remain in your hand, revealing them to be all fives of spades. When the last five of spades has been displayed, conclude the effect by turning over the double card and showing it to be the five of hearts. "I *knew* you were going to make the right choice!" Scoop up all of the cards and pocket them so that the double card cannot be examined.

INTERNATIONAL TASTE BUDS

The presentation of this effect leads your spectators away from the method used to accomplish the feat, a basic tenet of conjuring psychology.

EFFECT: The mentalist is blindfolded by his audience. "The often heard maxim is that when one of your senses is dulled or dead, other senses come to the fore. In this case, I have been blindfolded. I now offer a demonstration not of a heightened sense of smell or hearing, but of taste."

A packet of postage stamps is handed to the performer, who licks them one by one and sticks them to a blank sheet of paper. As he does so, he announces—correctly, of course, and in spite of his blindfold—the country from which each stamp originated!

REQUIRED: A bundle of international postage stamps (available in hobby or stamp shops), a sheet of paper, and a blindfold (which can be made from a bandanna).

PREPARATION: Familiarize yourself with the various stamps you will use, so you will know which country issued each stamp after only a casual glance.

PERFORMANCE: "It's often said that the blind have a heightened sense of hearing, the deaf an abnormally acute sense of smell, and the mute a strangely keen sense of vision. What I propose to demonstrate now is how, by simulating blindness, I can amplify my sense of taste to an extreme level."

FIGURE 9

The props are now introduced, and the stamps are shown to be different. The various nations that issued them are called out. The stamps are then handed to a spectator, who mixes them thoroughly.

Another spectator examines the blindfold, and then ties it around your head. Remarkably, even though the cloth is opaque (a spectator can even test this out for himself), by glancing down the bridge of your nose, as shown in **Figure 9,** you will be able to identify virtually any object held in your hands.

"Please hand me a stamp," you say. A spectator does so, and as you bring the stamp to your lips to lick it, peek at it and identify it. Lick the stamp, and then have it stuck to the blank page in front of you. Have a spectator do this, since you have been blindfolded and should maintain the illusion that you cannot see.

Once the stamp is stuck down, begin to describe the country that issued it. For example, if the stamp is of Chilean origin, say, "I sense—in fact, I taste—a distinctly South American flavor. A country that borders the sea, for miles and miles. Is the stamp from Chile?"

The rest of the revelations should be handled in a similar manner. If you have memorized the stamps, conclude the demonstration by announcing the value, country of origin, and even the image on the face of the two or three last stamps. Do this without handling them, commenting that your "heightened awareness" has allowed your "sixth sense" to come to the fore. "I can see nearby objects in my mind's eye. In your hands I see the following images...." After the spectators have confirmed your descriptions, remove the blindfold and take a bow.

UNDER THE INFLUENCE

Dozens of mental miracles utilizing the "multiple outs" principle have been devised over the years. Mr. Mysterio designed a beautifully simple effect that uses everyday objects that can be carried in the magician's pocket. It is presented here.

EFFECT: The performer removes three items from a small envelope: his business card, a quarter, and a piece of candy. "Everything seems to be on the up-and-up, doesn't it?" he says, as he lines up the objects on the table, in front of his audience. "But even though these objects are ordinary in every way, I've devised a way to divine which one of them you'll choose, before even *you* know which one you will select." A spectator is now asked to carefully consider the three objects and then select one. No matter which object the spectator chooses, the magician shows that he'd predicted the choice in advance.

REQUIRED: A manila "pay"-type envelope (sometimes called a coin envelope), a business card, a small slip of paper, a piece of wrapped candy (with an opaque wrapper), and a quarter.

PREPARATION: On the slip of paper, write, "It's money that interests you. That's why you selected the quarter." On the blank side of the business card, write the words, "Call me soon!" Unwrap the candy, and inside the wrapper (or on another tiny slip of paper, if necessary, write the words, "I knew you would pick me, so eat me!" Slip everything into the manila envelope.

PERFORMANCE: Remove the envelope from your pocket, and from it take the business card, candy, and quarter. Leave the slip of paper inside the envelope and set the envelope on the table.

Arrange the three objects in front of a spectator, in a row. Say, "To the untrained eye, it appears as if I've lined up three ordinary objects in front of you: a business card, a piece of candy, and a coin. And these objects *are* ordinary. There's nothing funny about them at all. What is unusual is that after considerable practice and testing I've devised a method to invisibly influence anyone who looks at these objects and chooses just one. Why don't we give it a try?"

A spectator is asked to carefully consider the objects on the table in front of her, and to carefully select one by pulling it toward herself. Once she has settled on an object, you continue: "How can I prove that I influenced your choice? Simple. I made a prediction, and here it is…"

Now you reveal a previously written prediction based on the spectator's ultimate selection.

If she chooses the quarter, dump the slip of paper out of the envelope and have her read what is written on it ("It's money that interests you. That's why you selected the quarter"). While she reads the message, pocket the remaining props.

If she chooses the candy, have her unwrap it as you pocket the other articles on the table. She reads the message inside the wrapper that says, "I knew you would pick me, so eat me!"

In the case of the business card, simply have it turned over. The message on the back ("Call me soon!") will be read. Tell her to keep the card as you pocket what remains on the table.

THREE DIRECT HITS

A showier version of the mental feat described below was developed by Mysterio for his stage presentations. The scaled-down version explained here is just as effective as Mysterio's original (which has been adopted by many famous present-day mentalists).

EFFECT: A spectator is asked to make three choices. "But before you begin making decisions, I will make the first of three predictions," the mentalist states. On a small slip of paper, the performer jots down a note.

The first choice the spectator makes is from a handful of poker chips in a variety of colors.

"Interesting," the magician says. "Let me make a second prediction." He jots another note.

Now the spectator is asked to roll a die until he arrives at a number he is satisfied with. The mentalist continues, "Perfect. One more to go." Here, a final note is jotted down and set aside with the others, in plain sight.

Finally, the spectator is asked to select a playing card. It is noted and remembered.

Despite increasingly impossible odds, the entertainer unfolds his predictions to reveal that he has scored three direct hits, predicting exactly which card, which number on the die, and which color the spectator selected!

REQUIRED: Three poker chips, three slips of paper, a standard six-sided die, a deck of cards, an opaque cup, and a pen.

PREPARATION: You must know the top card of the pack and must be capable of forcing it. Several methods of forcing are taught in chapter 2, on card magic. No other preparation is necessary.

PERFORMANCE: Begin by announcing your intent—to accurately predict three choices made by a spectator. Announce that your first prediction will be one of three different colored poker chips.

Pick up a slip of paper and the pen, and instead of writing the color of one of the poker chips on the slip, write down the name of the card on top of the pack. Fold the slip and set it in the cup on the table.

Now have one of the chips selected by a spectator. Have her announce the color of her selection. For the sake of this explanation, assume she selected the red chip.

"I will now make my second prediction, this time of a number that my volunteer will roll on this die," you say, as you write not a number, but *the color of the chip that was just selected.* Fold this slip and place it in the cup.

Now have the die rolled and a number selected (in this example, the number is five).

"There is only one more prediction I have to make," you say, "and this will be the most difficult of all. The first choice made was one in three. The second was one of six. Now I'll make the correct choice when my odds are one in fifty-two." On the final slip of paper, write, "You will roll the number 5." Fold the slip and place it with the other two.

Gesture toward the deck of cards and ask the spectator to cut off about half. Now perform one of the card forces from chapter 2. Your spectator will apparently "choose" a card at random, but will in fact end up with the card you previously memorized.

The conclusion of the trick comes with suitable buildup from your patter: "The choices you made were entirely yours, correct? And each successive choice was from an increasingly widened field, was it not? Despite those conditions, I predicted the following: that you would select the red chip…the number five…and the ten of spades."

As you remove the slips from the cup, take out the center slip first, with the prediction of the color on it. Then remove the slip with the prediction of the number on it. The slip that remains will, of course, have the name of the force card on it.

THE CENTER TEAR

EFFECT: A spectator is invited to decide upon a random piece of information. "I want you to lock this piece of information into your mind," the magician says. To facilitate this, on a small slip of paper, the spectator writes out his secret information. This can be anything; a word, a name, a number, or even a drawing. The billet is folded into quarters and handed to the mind reader, who tears it to shreds and sets the ragged pieces alight. As he stares into the flames, the magician announces the spectator's secret thoughts!

FIGURE 10

REQUIRED: Several small slips of paper approximately 3 inches (8 cm) square, a pen, a book of matches, and an ashtray or receptacle in which to burn the paper. You should be seated at a table to perform the Center Tear.

PREPARATION: Draw the outline of a circle in the exact center of each piece of paper, as in **Figure 10**. The circle should be approximately 1¼ inches (3 cm) in diameter. All the papers should look identical. Place the matches in your left trouser pocket.

PERFORMANCE: "I'd like you to concentrate on a specific thought," you say, as you hand a piece of paper to a volunteer from your audience. "To focus your mental energies,

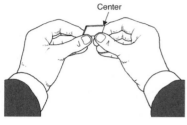

Center

FIGURE 11

FIGURE 12

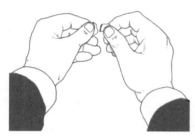

FIGURE 13

write that thought—it can be a word, the name of a loved one, or even your telephone number—in the center of this slip of paper."

After the spectator has written his word on the slip, have him fold the paper in half, and then in half again. Take the paper back from him.

"There's no one that knows what word you have in mind, is there? No one but you, that is? Correct? Good. Now I'm going to focus *my* mental energy on this paper, and on your thought."

Holding the paper at your fingertips, take note of the position of its center. This will be easy to spot, as shown in **Figure 11.** Hold the paper so that the center portion with the writing is in the upper right corner of the packet, facing you, and tear the slip in half as in **Figure 12.**

Place the left-hand pieces behind the right-hand pieces and tear the paper in half again, as in **Figure 13.** The center of the paper will be the topmost of the pieces. Drop all of the torn pieces, except for the center, into the ashtray. To do this, hold your right thumb on top of the center and let the other pieces fall. The bit of paper will cling to your thumb.

Reach into your pocket with your left hand and secure the matches. Holding the match book on top of the secret slip of paper in your right hand, light a match and set fire to the slips of paper in the ash tray. As you concentrate on the burning paper and are setting the matchbook on the table, both hands fall to your lap, below the level of the table. It is at this point that the slip is unfolded. With the right hand, which still holds the unfolded slip, pick up the matchbook and, in the action of replacing it in your right pocket, peek at the spectator's message. Now, in your most convincing tone, slowly divine the spectator's secret word.

STANDING ROOM ONLY: If you would prefer to use the Center Tear technique while standing, proceed as above, but in the action of lighting the torn pieces in the ashtray, purposely cause the match to go out. While the match is still burning, use your right thumb and fingers (with the hand held at your side) to slowly open the folded slip concealed in your right hand. Now, in the act of picking up the matchbook (ostensibly to light another match), it is an easy matter to glimpse the spectator's message on the billet. To conclude, light another match, burn the papers, pocket the matchbook (along with the secret slip), and read her mind.

ASHES ON THE ARM

Though recently revived by television magicians, this feat is as old as the hills. And there's a reason for its revival—the effect is a very good one. Mysterio frequently performed this feat in the 1920s, preparing for it "on the fly." One diary entry for December 15, 1911, mentions, "…and my clandestine preparations for the Ash Trick were nearly interrupted at a dinner party for King George V. Must remember to *always* lock the lavatory door while setting up tricks in the future."

EFFECT: As flames dance in an ashtray—the mentalist just having burned a billet on which a spectator wrote a secret word—the performer rolls back his sleeve. "I feel the answer to your question coursing through my veins," the magician says. So saying, he grabs a handful of the cooling ashes and rubs them vigorously on his bare forearm. Slowly and steadily, the faint trail of charred paper takes on a recognizable shape—the word or thought the spectator has concentrated on!

REQUIRED: A tube of lip balm, an ashtray, a slip of paper, a book of matches or cigarette lighter, and a pen or pencil.

PREPARATION: Before your performance, roll back your left sleeve and on your bare forearm, use the tube of lip balm to write out the name of a chosen card or number (you will force this word, number, or card later on) in large, bold letters. For this example, assume that you have written "3 H" on your forearm, indicating that your spectator has selected the three of hearts. Place this card in a position for forcing (as described in chapter 2).

PERFORMANCE: Begin by forcing the three of hearts on a spectator. After the card has been remembered and returned to the deck and the deck has been shuffled, say, "To further ingrain the name of the card into your memory, please write it down on this slip of paper."

Hand the spectator a small slip of paper and a pen, and have her follow your instructions. "Please fold the paper up, so I can't see the name of your card. Then, if you would be so kind, set the slip in the ashtray and light it."

As the ashes appear in the tray, roll back your left sleeve. Pick up a handful of ashes (once cool!) and rub them briskly on your left forearm. They ashes will adhere to the lip balm (which is invisible), eventually forming the "3 H" you drew on your arm earlier.

MORE THAN A CARD TRICK: Though described as the revelation of a selected card, Ashes on the Arm can be used to reveal many other bits of information. If you are able to obtain personal details about a spectator prior to your performance—say, a birthday or a phone number—having this apparently unknown information appear on your arm will make a tremendous impact. Other performers prefer to reveal numbers (which can be forced, or glimpsed by means of a Center Tear), names, or words via the ash trick, elevating a mere card trick to the near-miracle class.

INSTANT MAGIC SQUARE

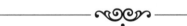

This mental feat is perfect for tableside entertainment, since the Magic Square can be sketched out on a scrap of paper. With a blackboard or large writing tablet, however, the same effect can be used for an audience of hundreds, with spectacular results.

EFFECT: A spectator is invited to call out a number between twenty-four and one hundred. "Thank you, sir, for your contribution to tonight's performance," the magician says. "And now, for a demonstration of magical mental ability, I present an example of a skill not seen since the days of Zerah Colburn, the child-prodigy lightning calculator of nineteenth-century America."

The magician sketches out a grid on a piece of paper and fills each square with a number. When the numbers in the squares are added—in as many as twenty-two different patterns—all patterns total the spectator's randomly selected number!

REQUIRED: A pen and paper.

PREPARATION: Memorize the information in **Figure 15,** opposite.

PERFORMANCE: "Ladies and gentlemen, I would now like to present, for your entertainment pleasure, a mental feat so startling, so impossible, that it has confounded the keenest minds in the most elite universities in the known world, as well as heads of state. To begin the demonstration, I will first sketch out a square."

Here, you draw a four-by-four grid on a piece of paper as illustrated in **Figure 14**.

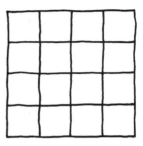

FIGURE 14

Continuing, you say, "Would you be so kind as to help me, sir?" Pointing to someone in the audience, he is asked to name any number between twenty-four and one hundred. As soon as he names the number, fill out the grid in the pattern you've memorized, which is outlined in **Figure 15**.

N	1	12	7
11	8	N-1	2
5	10	3	N+2
4	N+1	6	9

FIGURE 15

The letter N stands for the number named by your spectator, minus 20. If, for example, the spectator names thirty-six, N - 1 stands for 36 - 20 - 1 (15), N + 2 stands for 36 - 20 + 2 (18), and so on.

Fill out the grid rapidly, but not automatically. It should appear to the audience as if you are making rapid mental computations and filling in the squares of the board as a result of them, as opposed to simply regurgitating a series of numbers from memory. If the selected number is thirty-six, the finished square will look like the one pictured in **Figure 16**.

16	1	12	7
11	8	15	2
5	10	3	18
4	17	6	9

FIGURE 16

When the grid has been completely filled, say, "What does this mishmash of numbers mean, exactly? What do these digits denote?" You now begin the revelatory element of the trick, by adding all the rows (four) and columns (four) to show that they equal the freely chosen number.

Next, add the four corners. Then the four centermost squares. Then add both diagonals. Each sequence of four squares adds up to the spectator's selected number. In all, there are twenty-two different combinations of four squares that add up to the spectator's selected number.

Bert Allerton, who developed this Magic Square presentation, often involved his audience in the procedure, assigning different groupings of squares to various spectators, having them do the math and then revealing that all the totals are the same.

The key to the presentation of the trick is to make sure there is no dead time as you add the various totals. Keep it moving and reveal each successive total at an increasingly quickened pace, tracing the various formations on the grid as you complete the mathematics that involve them, as in **Figure 17.**

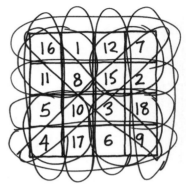

HIGHER MATH: To confound your audience even further (always a good thing), you can secretly determine the spectator's selected number *before* the performance starts. There are a number of ways to do this. One of them is the Center Tear, also described in this chapter. Before your performance, approach a spectator and ask him to concentrate on a number between twenty-four

FIGURE 17

and one hundred. "Write it on this slip of paper to help impress the number on your mind," you say. Rip up the slip of paper, performing the Center Tear as you do, learning what the secret number is. Before leaving the spectator, tell him, "At some point in my show, I may call on you and ask you to think of your number again. Can you do that for me?"

Now, in the course of your performance, call on the spectator whose number you already know and perform the feat as if reading his mind. Tell him to "just think of a number." Fill in the grid and then ask him for the number he was merely "thinking of." Proceed with the revelations as described above to conclude a multilayered piece of mathematical and theatrical deception.

COLOR CODED VIA KICKS

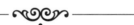

The principle involved in this effect is called the "instant stooge." Used sparingly, it can make miracles possible.

EFFECT: The magician approaches a spectator and invites him to amaze the audience. "You're going to display a talent to everyone here that even you did not know you had." So saying, the magician and his newfound friend play a guessing game. The performer places a card on the table face down, and asks the spectator to guess its color. Amazingly, time and time again, the spectator is proven correct. He is able to distinguish the red and black cards from each other, even though the cards are face down. Finally, he divines not only the color and suit of a face-down card, but its value as well!

REQUIRED: A deck of cards.

PREPARATION: Place the two of spades on top of the deck before you begin.

PERFORMANCE: After performing a series of tricks, scan your audience and look for an appreciative, attentive, and smart-looking audience member. Look for someone who is clearly interested in your performance. This is important.

Approach your prospective helper and while addressing him, say, "Would you like to help me with one final card effect?" If the response is positive and affirmative, continue by saying, "We're going to do something together that's quite remarkable. You're going to display to the audience your ability to sense the colors of different cards, without seeing their faces. You'll be able to tell the *red* cards from the *black* ones, without ever looking at them."

As you say the word "red," be sure you are standing close enough to the spectator to lightly tap the top of his foot with yours. This tap should be gentle, but not too gentle; you want him to know that you are not accidentally tapping his foot. Then, when you say the word "black," tap his foot again, this time twice. You can repeat the above line of patter (varied slightly), tapping his feet again (once for red and twice for black) to reemphasize the code you've established.

CONTINUE: "Are you ready to give it a try? Great. Let's start with one card." Look through the deck and set a black card on the table face down. Ask the spectator, "Is this card red or black?" As you say "black," step on his toes again, twice, indicating that the card is black.

Ninety-nine percent of the time, a willing and interested spectator will catch on quickly and play along with you. He'll announce, "It's black!" Turn the card over to reveal that he's correct. Indeed he is.

Continue along these lines. Place another card—a black one—face down on the table and code it to the spectator as before. Then place a red card face down on the table and have him "guess" its color too.

Next, say, "Let's make this a bit harder, using three cards." Place three cards on the table in an overlapping row, one red card between two blacks. Look at another spectator (not your instant stooge), and say, "Which card should our new Svengali identify?" Have him point to a card (the color of which you already know). Code its color to your assistant, and have him identify it (and then the other two on the table).

"Incredible, isn't it, folks?" You address the audience as you prepare for the final, knockout climax to the trick. The two of spades (or any other low spot card you know) is on top of the pack. Force it on a spectator (not your stooge) and tell him not to look at it. "Place it face down on the table in front of our talented friend." You know the value of the card, but no one else does.

Look at your assistant and again code the color of the card to him. "It's black? Excellent! But before we turn the card over, I want to take this test one step further. See if you can get the *suit* of the card, as well. There are two black suits, *spades* and *clubs*." Here, you press down on the spectator's foot when you say the word "spades." If the spectator is paying attention (and by this time, he should be, considering all he's been through), he will pick up on your signal and announce, "It's a spade!"

"Fantastic," you say. "There's only one more bit of information we don't know about the card: its value. Let's give it a try, shall we? See if you can determine the card's value, since you already know it's a spade." As you deliver this final line of chatter, press down twice, distinctly, on the spectator's foot. With any luck, he'll quickly announce that the card "is a two!"

Turn it over to reveal that he's correct, and have him take a bow to complete the miracle.

If you have the opportunity, approach your stooge after your performance and quickly explain to him that much of the fun of magic lies in its secrets, and that he should keep the secret of the trick he performed to himself. If this is explained to him in a friendly, courteous manner, chances are good that he will keep the secret for a long, long time.

LAYERS OF DECEPTION: Though not specifically discussed in this work, employing a marked deck with this trick can add an extra layer of deception to the trick. Instead of looking at the cards before sending their color to your accomplice, set them face down on the table, read their backs (via the marks on them), then send the color of each one to the spectator. Though he will be aware of the fact that you know the color of each card, he may not understand exactly *how* you know this information.

ONE WORD IN A MILLION

Though vastly more complicated methods exist for performing the effect described below (for his personalized version, Mysterio used a prop that cost over $500, a considerable sum in 1925), as simple as the modus operandi described here may be, it works.

EFFECT: The mind reader invites a spectator to assist him. The volunteer selects two books from a pile of several on the performer's table, decides on a page number at random, and then a word on his selected page. "At no time will I touch the book you are holding," says the mentalist. "Glance at your chosen page and the first word on it." The spectator does so, closes the book, and begins to concentrate on his word. One letter at a time, and not without a modicum of mental effort, the mind reader then spells out the word the spectator is thinking of!

REQUIRED: Two books, though a shelf full can be used. The books used in the demonstration should be of approximately the same length.

PREPARATION: None.

PERFORMANCE: Invite a spectator to assist you and have her select two books from the stack on your table. "I want to emphasize the fairness of the proceedings from this point forward," you say. "The choices you make here are your own. I am not influencing you in any way.

"Of these two books, which do you prefer? This one?" Hold up her selection and leaf through it, commenting on the contents, on the author, or any other feature of the tome that makes for an interesting talking point. At some point in your conversation, without being obvious about it, memorize two pieces of information about the book. On a page somewhere near its center, glimpse both the page number you have stopped at and the first word (or series of words) on that page. For the sake of this explanation, assume that you stop at page 155 and see that the first word on that page is *apple*. Continue flipping through the book casually for a moment after this glimpse, and then close the book. Hand it to the spectator.

FIGURE 18

"This is the book you chose, and the book we'll use. We will also, however, use the book you were not as enamored of." Pick up the second book. Now, addressing another spectator, begin riffling through the book in your hands, as in **Figure 18.** Tell him to call out "Stop!" as you riffle through the pages, so that together you can select one at random.

Now comes the only gutsy moment in the trick. When the spectator calls out "stop," you do stop. But instead of announcing the number of the page that he stopped you on, simply announce the number that you memorized in the book previously selected. If possible, time your riffling to stop at a point close to the page number in your mind.

After miscalling the page number, close the book in your hands and set it aside. The rest of the performance depends upon your buildup and presentation. Turn back to your first spectator. "Madam, please turn to page 155 in your book." She does so.

"There are hundreds of words on that page, correct? I want you to shift your gaze to the top line of the page, and begin reading the first line to yourself, silently. In fact, to make things even more focused and sharp, concentrate on the first full word on that page." She does so.

"Spell it out in your mind. Imagine writing out that word on a large black chalkboard in your mind. Have you done that?" When she confirms that she has, you can announce the word one letter at a time (for dramatic effect) or first describe the word and then announce it to build suspense. "You were thinking of the word *apple*, weren't you?" She confirms your divination, and you accept a hearty round of applause.

CELLULAR PSYCHIC

In Mysterio's time, the following effect would not have been possible without a costly, custom-made apparatus. Modern technology makes this miracle easy to do, and virtually foolproof. The effect is particularly well suited to casual performances at parties and other informal get-togethers.

EFFECT: Gathered among a group of spectators, the mind reader solicits donations from the crowd. "Please place a personal object here on the table, something from your pocket. A coin, a business card, a lipstick, a photograph from your wallet—whatever you would like to contribute to this experiment will be helpful, and it will be returned at the conclusion of the performance." Spectators pile ten, twenty, or thirty objects onto the table, and eventually an audience volunteer selects one of them entirely at random. The performer then hands an index card with a telephone number on it to one of the audience members. She dials the number and listens intently. Incredible though it may seem, a voice on the other end of the line announces loudly and clearly the name of the object selected only moments before!

REQUIRED: A cellular phone with a speakerphone function, a willing accomplice, and an index card with your accomplice's phone number written on it.

PREPARATION: Explain to your accomplice that at some point during your performance, you will call him from your cell phone, but will not talk to him—your phone will be on speaker, and your secret assistant should listen intently to what is happening on the other end of the line. He is to pay close attention to the objects you are discussing, and what you are saying. Place the index card in a convenient pocket before beginning.

PERFORMANCE: Before performing this effect, dial your accomplice on your cell phone, and activate the phone's speaker function. Place the phone in your breast pocket or another location that will obscure the phone's microphone as little as possible. Now your performance can begin.

Then, as previously described, invite several spectators to make donations to your cause. "Please loan me, for the purpose of a psychic demonstration, a personal object or two." After searching their pockets, most spectators will offer up the usual assortment of pocket change, keys, and chewing gum. Arrange these items on your working surface, and invite one member of the audience to lead the group in the selection of one of the objects. Stress the fairness of the proceedings, and as each object is eliminated, hand it back to its owner. When the final object has been selected, announce its name to the group, making sure (without being obvious) that your accomplice, who has been listening to your conversation all the while on the phone, can clearly hear the name of the item.

As soon as the name of the final selection is announced, your accomplice hangs up his phone.

Now hand the index card bearing your accomplice's phone number to a member of the audience with a cell phone. "Dial the number, please, and, in a loud, clear voice, tell everyone in the audience what you hear on the other end."

If your accomplice has a shred of theatricality in his body, the resulting conversation can be quite amusing. He should be instructed to mysteriously describe in general terms the selected object, dancing around its given name as long as possible. Only after mentioning its color, shape, texture, and so on should your accomplice name the object by its common name. This heightens the suspense, and builds tension up to the moment of the final revelation of the selected object.

KEEP IT RANDOM: Though many a magician will instantly see the possibilities of this method and transform the above-described trick into one involving a deck of playing cards, the temptation to do so should be resisted. When using a wide array of borrowed objects, an effect as strong as this one approaches genuine mind reading. Casting it in the light of a mere card trick is to steal the thunder of an otherwise powerful and convincing demonstration.

HEADLINE SENSATION

After Mysterio's death, a sensational publicity stunt was developed that has since been adopted by countless mentalists. In his notes, Mysterio describes a remarkable card effect that works along similar lines; in this book, his original notes have been adapted to make the trick into something even more incredible: that sensational publicity stunt. Imagine predicting the headline of a newspaper weeks or months in advance!

EFFECT: Several weeks in advance of his appearance, the mentalist mails an envelope to the owner of the venue at which he will perform. On stage on the day of his performance, the performer announces this fact, has the envelope brought forward and clipped to a clothesline hanging above the stage. "There my prediction will remain, in plain view, throughout the performance."

Eventually, a member of the audience comes forward with a copy of the local newspaper. The day's headline is read. The prediction is removed from the envelope and read out loud: It matches the paper's headline almost to the letter!

FIGURE 19

REQUIRED: In addition to two envelopes that nest one inside of the other (one of which will be addressed and stamped), you will need a duplicate of the smaller envelope, a clothesline, and a clip to which the smaller envelope can be attached above the stage (as shown in **Figure 19**), and a chair with large slats running horizontally across its back, as in **Figure 20.**

PREPARATION: In advance of your performance, place a blank piece of paper in the smaller envelope. Seal it and place it inside the larger one, and mail this package to whomever is responsible for the show you are to present in a few weeks' time. Call this person and explain that he is not to open the envelope until the day of the performance, as it contains a prediction of future events.

FIGURE 20

The day of your performance, buy a copy of the local newspaper and write out a sentence that is nearly identical to its lead headline (don't make it word for word; your prediction should be accurate, but not *too* accurate). Seal this into the duplicate of the smaller envelope and attach the envelope to the back of the chair. To do this, you can use a small, open pocket made from cardboard, a file folder, or even a bag, as in **Figure 21.** Make sure the arrangement is not visible to the audience.

FIGURE 21

PERFORMANCE: "Ladies and gentlemen, weeks prior to tonight's appearance, I mailed a prediction of events to come to Mr. Rubin, the sponsor of tonight's entertainment. Mr. Rubin, would you step forward, please, and bring the envelope I sent you?"

Rubin does so, and when he joins you on stage, you describe the circumstances further, explaining that the envelope he holds has not been opened, and that inside is another envelope, which contains your prediction of today's newspaper headline. You can even invite other audience members to examine the postmark, demonstrating that Rubin is not your accomplice. Next, have Rubin open the larger envelope and remove what he finds inside. Using the chair you've prepared, take the smaller envelope and clip it to the line that is hanging above your head. "We'll get back to that envelope in a while," you announce, as you invite Rubin to return to his seat and enjoy the performance. "I'll need your services again in a few minutes, sir."

After an adequate amount of time has passed and you have performed five or six other effects, invite Rubin back to the stage and hand him the day's newspaper. Have him confirm its date. "In a moment, sir, I would like you to read today's headline to

FIGURE 22

FIGURE 23

everyone gathered here. But first, let's take a look at what's in the envelope."

Now comes the only tricky moment in the entire performance. Using the chair with the envelope attached to its back as an impromptu ladder, retrieve the hanging "prediction" that has been in plain view throughout your performance. Remove the envelope from the clip with the hand that is *furthest* from your audience (and therefore, closest to the back of the chair, as shown in **Figure 22**). Address Mr. Rubin and ask: "Would you mind reading to everyone here the headline at the top of the front page?" As you ask this, step down from the chair, apparently steadying yourself by gripping its back with your hand. It is at this moment that you switch envelopes, dropping off the one just retrieved, and picking up the one containing your prediction. See **Figure 23**. This switch should take no more than two seconds to execute, and is completely covered by two natural actions: steadying yourself with the back of the chair and the fact that your spectator is now addressing the audience.

Now approach Rubin and hand him the envelope. "I want you, sir, to open the envelope and tell everyone here what you find inside." He does so, and removes the slip of paper on which your prediction is written. "Please read what is written on the slip," you tell him, as you hold up the newspaper. Of course your prediction and the day's headlines match almost exactly.

PREDICTION PRESENTATION POINTS: For maximum visibility, try writing your prediction in large, bold letters on a long strip of paper that is then folded up and placed in the envelope. This can then be unfolded and displayed prominently between the hands of your spectator while on stage. Even though he will read the prediction aloud at the conclusion of the trick, reinforcing the revelation with a visual element is always a good idea.

The misdirection you use to mask the switch of the envelopes cannot be too strong. Think of other elements you can use to erase this moment from the memory of your audience. If you work with an assistant, perhaps this is the moment he comes on to the stage to retrieve a prop or object from your table, or to assist you or your spectator in some way.

Headline predictions can be used to generate headlines of other sorts: ones that will build your reputation as a mind reader and magician. Invite members of the press to your performance, or, at the very least, let them know you will make a headline prediction well in advance of the date of publication. You may also wish to use the editor of the paper as the audience member you bring on stage. Though Mysterio's notes make no mention of a newspaper-headline prediction, in one entry titled "Getting Publicity," the great prestidigitator did pen the following lines:

"Always involve the newsmen—even those from this newfound 'radio' business—in your performances when you can. If I have learned one lesson from that brash American, Houdini, it is that there is no such thing as too much publicity. Keep your name before the public constantly, and the public will constantly appear before you, buying tickets and patronizing your performances. Ink and newsprint are as vital to the career of the magician as cards, handkerchiefs, and steamer trunks full of tricks." ◌

CHAPTER VIII

PARLOR MAGIC

CONJURING ON STAGE

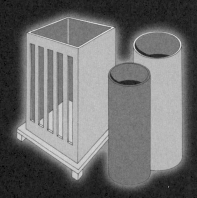

A S YOUR CAREER IN MAGIC PROGRESSES, your opportunities to perform will increase. Many amateur, up-and-coming magicians cut their teeth in social situations, conjuring informally at parties, while at dinner, or whenever the opportunity strikes. The tricks best suited to these situations are described in chapter 3, "Close-up Magic"—pocket tricks and impromptu miracles that amaze, yet are best suited for audiences of fewer than fifteen people, and often fewer than five.

In contrast, the enterprising magical entertainer will seek out (and be sought out by, if he's worth his salt) venues with larger audiences. For these situations, the tricks in this chapter are more suitable, as are effects described in the next chapter, on handkerchief tricks.

In Mysterio's day, *parlor tricks* was a common term, as was the phrase *drawing-room conjuring*. Today, few homes are outfitted with drawing rooms or parlors. Still, the conjuring conceits offered in the pages that follow are perfectly suited for these mid-sized shows. Some of the tricks in this chapter are also simply "bigger" than the effects in other chapters.

There will always be a call for entertainers who can stand before a group and keep it enthralled. The tricks outlined here will give you a good working knowledge of material that is well suited for these sorts of situations.

SLEEVED

— ❧ —

EFFECT: "There's a common misconception about the way magic works," the magician says. "Very few tricks require the magician to sneak things in and out of his sleeves. In fact, here…let me take off my jacket, so you don't think I would stoop so low as to use *my* sleeves." As the magician removes his jacket, he is nearly as startled as the audience when, from inside the folds, he produces a full glass of orange juice!

REQUIRED: A straight-sided glass full of juice (or a bottle of beer, if it seems appropriate for the crowd). You must wear pants with a back pocket, and a jacket or sport coat.

PREPARATION: Place the glass, which is three quarters full of the beverage of your choice, in the rear right pocket of your pants. It should protrude from the top of the pocket, as in **Figure 1.** Put on your jacket. You're ready to perform.

PERFORMANCE: This is an excellent trick with which to open an impromptu performance. After introducing yourself, tell the assemblage that your sleeves play no part in your sophisticated brand of conjuring. "Sleeves are so passé," you joke. "In fact, let me remove my jacket for this first trick."

FIGURE 1

Begin taking off your jacket. As you do, the "dirty work" takes place. While your left arm exits its sleeve, your right hand boldly reaches into your back pocket and grabs the glass. After the left arm is free of its sleeve, pull your right arm and hand—which is holding the glass—out of your right sleeve. **Figure 2** shows this. Before the glass of juice is produced, look at the audience and pause momentarily. Say something pseudo-dramatic like, "Of course, magicians occasionally bend the truth in the service of good drama—and if I'm a hundred percent honest, this trick *does* use my sleeves. Watch!" Triumphantly (but not smugly!) produce the glass. Toast the audience, take a sip, then take a well-deserved bow.

FIGURE 2

MAGIC PITCHER

This versatile prop can be made with a minimum of expense, but will repay you many times over; the effects it makes possible are many.

EFFECT: The magician pours a quantity of milk from a clear pitcher into a paper cone. "No one drinks evaporated milk anymore, do they?" the magician asks. "That's because evaporated milk isn't made anymore!" The performer wads up the cone into a compact ball of paper. The milk has vanished without a trace.

REQUIRED: A Magic Pitcher. Most professional magicians call this a Milk Pitcher, as milk is the liquid most often used in conjunction with this device. For the record, any liquid can be used.

To construct the prop, first secure a clear plastic pitcher with a ridged, fluted, or patterned design on its exterior. The pitcher should be clear, but the pattern around it should be sufficiently "busy" to make seeing directly through its sides difficult.

Two other items are required to construct the pitcher: glue that firmly bonds plastic pieces together, and a clear plastic vessel—another pitcher, a carafe, or a large cup—that fits inside the first pitcher. This smaller vessel should be approximately $^3/_4$ inch (2 cm) shorter than the larger pitcher and, when placed inside it, should be at least $^1/_4$ inch ($^7/_{10}$ cm) smaller in diameter. Center the smaller vessel inside the pitcher, and glue the two pieces together. When finished, you will have created a double-walled Magic Pitcher. **Figure 3** shows a top view of the pitcher.

For the basic vanish of a quantity of milk, you will require a sheet of newspaper in addition to the filled pitcher.

FIGURE 3

PREPARATION: Fill the space between the inner and outer walls of the pitcher with milk.

PERFORMANCE: Roll the sheet of newspaper into a cone. As you do so, you can patter about evaporated milk as outlined above, or pretend to spot funny or interesting headlines in the paper as you roll it up. Read them off as a way to kill time and extend what might otherwise be a quick trick.

Once the cone has been rolled, hold it in your left hand and begin, with your right hand, "pouring" milk into it. If you carefully tilt the pitcher into the cone, the liquid will run into the inner chamber of the Magic Pitcher as opposed to pouring out of it. Keep pouring until at least half of the pitcher's contents have been "emptied" into the cone.

To convince the audience that there is actually milk going into the cone, at some point during the proceedings, allow a small stream of liquid to actually flow into the paper. It will drip out of the bottom of the newspaper cone. As it does this, attempt to catch it in the pitcher.

Because of the pitcher's double-walled construction, after the pouring, it will appear from the outside as if half of the milk has actually been poured into the cone. Set the pitcher aside, utter your most convincing magic words, and crumple the cone into a ball. The milk has vanished.

SQUARE CIRCLE

This versatile production device was invented by British magician Louis Histed, though other performers like the Chautauqua entertainer Karl Germain experimented with similar ideas in the first quarter of the twentieth century. From this magical device, nearly any small object—even a live animal—can be produced.

EFFECT: The performer shows his audience a brightly decorated cabinet. "It was built from the boards of an old steamer trunk that once traveled the world with that famous magician of yesteryear, that headliner in vaudeville, Mr. Mysterio," the performer announces as he shows the open-fronted cabinet empty. Inside the cabinet rests a large, open-ended tube. This, too, is shown to be empty. The cabinet and tube are nested together, and from their center the performer produces a massive quantity of articles—silk handkerchiefs, streamers, party favors, and even a live rabbit.

REQUIRED: A Square Circle is composed of four parts. The outer cabinet (the square) is approximately 10 inches (25 cm) square, and 15 inches (38 cm) high. It is open at the top and bottom, and its front panel is cut into a pattern, like the bars shown in **Figure 4.** The interior of the cabinet is lined with black velveteen on all sides. The tube (a.k.a. the circle) that sits inside the cabinet can be made of cardboard or metal, should be open on both ends, and decorated to match the cabinet. The load chamber, which contains the items to be produced later, is of a diameter slightly smaller than the tube. It is also made of cardboard or metal, and is covered on the outside by black velveteen, to match the interior of the square cabinet. The last piece of the prop is the base upon which everything sits. This is slightly larger than the square cabinet, and sits on four short legs. These pieces are illustrated in **Figure 4.**

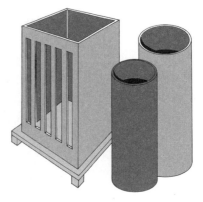

FIGURE 4

PREPARATION: The load chamber is placed on the base, filled with the items you wish to produce, then covered by the tube. The cabinet is nested over the tube.

PERFORMANCE: The prop is introduced and displayed to the audience, and the cabinet is lifted off the base and shown to be empty. It is then replaced on the base and the tube is lifted out of it and also shown to be empty. Because the load chamber and the interior of the cabinet are both covered in the same deep plush velveteen material, the load chamber and all it conceals are rendered invisible when viewed through the front panel of the cabinet. So, while the tube is displayed and the lines are delivered about the cabinet and its origins (and hence its strange, magical qualities), anyone looking through the front panel of the cabinet will see nothing—nothing but a black void and apparent nothingness, that is.

The tube is nested inside the cabinet again, and now the production commences. To keep this portion of the performance lively and interesting, develop a running line of chatter to accompany what can be, in the hands of an unthinking conjurer, a mere display of items crammed into a box. If producing handkerchiefs, comment on their fashionable colors ("a perfect match for your eyes," you could say to a fetching female audience member). If staging this effect at a birthday party or celebration, use the prop to conjure up party favors or a gift for the guest of honor.

Whatever items are produced from the prop, make the final production a spectacular one; live animals are not out of the question, though they can be hard to work with. A round fishbowl full of water can be produced as a finale. If the production is the last item in your program, the final object produced from it could be a banner announcing the end of your performance. One that says "Good Night" or "Thank You" will always bring you a rousing round of applause and end your performance on an upbeat, positive note.

TABLE LIFTING

"The spiritualist movement, has, thankfully, faded somewhat in these recent years," Mysterio wrote in his diary on December 26, 1931. "Perhaps Houdini's campaigning had some positive effect on the charlatans after all." Spiritualists claimed not only that the dead could talk to them and through them, but that ghosts could manifest themselves in physical ways. One method of mimicking a popular, startling manifestation—the animation of a table—is explained here.

EFFECT: While seated around a table, the magician and his spectators place their hands on the bare tabletop. As if lifted by spirit hands, the table seems to rise off the floor!

REQUIRED: A lightweight card table, two sturdy wooden or metal rulers, and a secret assistant, an audience member who's been prepped beforehand.

PREPARATION: You and your assistant hide the rulers under the bands of your watches. When it comes time for your performance, sit at opposite ends of the table. Your sleeves should hide the rulers from sight.

PERFORMANCE: In the course of performing several tricks, turn the conversation to spiritualism. "Though the movement is perhaps less prominent today than it was in the first quarter of the twentieth century," you say, "spiritualist camps still exist, and there are many believers who walk among us. Perhaps there is one among the audience tonight. Let's attempt a demonstration."

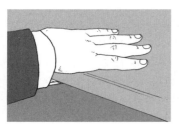

FIGURE 5

Have all those seated around the table place their hands lightly on its top. It is at this point, in the act of instructing the assembled group, that you and your secret assistant wedge the concealed rulers between your hands and the underside of the tabletop, as in **Figure 5.**

Have the lights dimmed, as if conducting a séance. Call out to the spirits, "Appear for us! Make yourselves known!" When the appropriate dramatic mood has been set, the table can be rocked back and forth by the "ghosts" you have conjured up. To cap off the demonstration of spiritualist phenomena, have the "spirits" lift the table a few inches off the ground.

SPIRITS AFOOT: As the table tilts back and forth, it is a simple matter for you or your assistant to wedge the tip of your shoe under one of its legs, as in **Figure 6.** This will allow even greater force to be exerted on the table and makes wild rocking back and forth and tipping of the table even more dramatic.

FIGURE 6

TORN AND RESTORED NEWSPAPER STRIP

The plot of this trick is easy to follow, and for that reason it is a classic. Study it carefully and present it well, and it will be come a highlight of your program.

EFFECT: A strip of newspaper is torn into several pieces and then restored. A small bundle of newspaper falls from the restored paper; the audience, of course, suspects that this bundle contains the torn pieces. This bundle is opened to reveal a whole, unblemished piece of paper!

REQUIRED: Three column-wide strips of newspaper, approximately 10 to 12 inches (25 to 30 cm) long, and a glue stick. Though not necessary, you may wish to cut out columns made up only of text, so that they will look the same when substituted for each other. Large pictures or advertisements can ruin the illusion.

PREPARATION: One of the strips of paper is folded into a compact bundle and glued to the back of another strip, as in **Figure 7.** The third strip of paper is folded into a compact bundle and held at the base of your right second and third fingers in the finger-palm position (described on page 128). Your fingers should curl around the paper naturally.

PERFORMANCE: Display the strip of paper (the one with the secret bundle glued on the back) in the right hand, and then tear it in half. Square up the torn pieces and tear these in half as well. Square up again and tear the pieces one more time. You can continue tearing the pieces up,

FIGURE 7

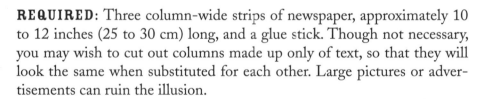

but don't shred them into confetti-sized pieces. Stop when they're about the size of the secret package.

Place all the torn pieces in front of the secret packet that's glued to the back of the strip in your right hand. Fold over the torn edges, tightening these separate pieces into a compact bundle. In the process of adjusting this bundle of torn pieces, turn over the entire packet. This will bring the glued packet of paper into view. Note that the edges of the torn pieces should be compact enough to hide completely behind the duplicate strip of paper when it is unfolded, so be sure that you've scrunched up the torn pieces tightly before proceeding.

Begin unfolding the glued piece of paper. As the strip unfolds, "accidentally" drop the concealed bundle of paper from your right hand. Remember, it has been there all along, while you were tearing up the strip of paper.

Act embarrassed, as if you have exposed the working of the trick, as you display the restored strip of paper.

When the audience finally requests to see the paper that dropped to the floor, put the restored strip in your pocket. Pick up the paper off the floor and unfold it to show that it, too, is a single, solid strip of paper.

IDEAS: You may want to write a message on the strip of paper you are going to drop on the floor. Something like "I don't know how it works either!" might be worthwhile.

If you don't want to hold the packet of paper in your hand throughout the trick, try dropping it from your sleeve, your belt, or elsewhere.

MIRAGE IN YOUR POCKET

In contrast to many of the effects in this chapter, Mirage in Your Pocket only works if performed one-on-one. An entirely different effect would be achieved if the trick were worked in front of a larger audience.

EFFECT: The magician places a plate in a spectator's hands. "Let's go on a trip," he says. "This dish will help in visualizing the imaginary journey you're about to take through the desert." As the performer patters about the heat of the sun, endless dunes of sand, and unquenchable thirst, he touches the spectator lightly on her temples. Then, in an effort to make the imaginary journey more realistic, he helps the spectator close her eyes, gently resting his fingertips on her eyelids. "Imagine that your trek through the desert is nearing its end, and you've run out of water," the performer says. "Think about your empty canteen, and your desire for a drink of water." No sooner does the magician utter these words than the spectator hears a distinct "clunk!" on the plate. When she opens her eyes, a glass of water has appeared on the plate in front of her!

REQUIRED: A plate (not a saucer; you want something with a bit of heft to it) and a straight-sided glass full of water. Your pants must have a back pocket and you should be wearing a jacket.

PREPARATION: Fill the glass three quarters full with water and place it in the back right pocket of your pants. The top of the glass should stick out of your pocket; your jacket will conceal it from prying eyes. Surprisingly, even with the glass in your pocket, you have a relatively free range of motion, which means that the trick can be set up well in advance of your performance.

FIGURE 8

PERFORMANCE: With the glass in place, set the pseudo-theatrical stage: Talk about an imaginary journey through the desert, and the mind's ability to create images so vivid that they appear to be real.

Set the dish in her hands, which you instruct her to hold out in front of her body, as in **Figure 8.**

Continue your discussion about the power of the imagination, delivering the above lines about the desert heat. As you do so, tell the spectator that you are going to tap her temples with your fingers three times, and that after the third tap, you will place the tips of your index fingers on her eyelids.

Suiting your actions to your words, tap her temples gently with the tips of your index fingers three times. On the count of three, if she has followed directions, the spectator will close her eyes. This is where the deception takes place.

Instead of placing the tips of the index fingers from each hand on her eyelids, you

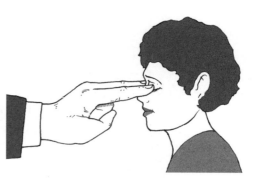

FIGURE 9

place the tips of two fingers on your left hand gently on her eyelids. See **Figure 9.** There's no need to rush this, since her eyes will be closed and you will have conditioned her to expect the fingers from each hand to be in play. Many will recognize this as an old schoolyard dodge.

Note: It's important to remember that if your spectator wears contact lenses, you should not perform this effect on her. Pressure on her eyelids may cause problems with the lenses. Always ask!

If everything has gone according to plan, your right hand will now be free, though your volunteer will believe that both of your hands are touching her eyelids. This allows you to, while continuing your semi-serious/semi-goofy story about the desert and the mind's eye, reach into your back pocket, remove the glass, and gently set it on the plate in her hands.

To complete the mystery, bring your free hand in front of her right eye and instruct her to open her eyes as you remove "both hands." Of course, when she opens her eyes, she will see both of your hands pointed toward her, and the glass on the dish. Offer her a drink. She'll need it. After all, she's been on an exhausting journey.

EGG IN NEWSPAPER

"Though many of the feats I will perform tonight will be of a supernatural nature, I can assure you that they are all accomplished by entirely *natural* means." So began Mr. Mysterio's opening address, the words he used at the beginning of each public performance he gave. In the case of this trick, a common household object—something entirely ordinary—is the basis for what spectators perceive to be a spectacular and complicated trick.

EFFECT: The magician breaks an egg ("An ordinary piece of hen fruit," he calls it) into a clear glass. Then, he leafs through a section of his daily newspaper, folds it in half, and pours the egg into its folds. Amazingly, the sticky, messy yolk and white of the egg vanish from the folds of the paper. Each page is shown. The egg really is gone!

REQUIRED: A section of newspaper (tabloid size works well), a glass, a large zipper-style plastic bag, wide clear adhesive tape, and an egg.

PREPARATION: Using the tape, affix the plastic bag to an interior page of the newspaper, as in **Figure 10.** Tape or glue a duplicate page over the bag to conceal its presence when the newspaper is flipped through.

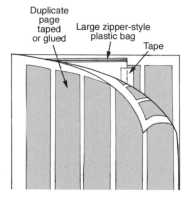

FIGURE 10

PERFORMANCE: "And now, a feat with a small, ovoid object." Here, you introduce the egg. Crack it and dump it into the glass, disposing of the shell.

Display the newspaper and leaf through it, one page at a time. "It's not apparent on first glance," you say, "but the paper seen here is a new blend of hyper-absorbent ink and overly porous fibers. Allow me to demonstrate its vacuumlike qualities." When finished, fold the paper in half. Make sure the plastic bag concealed in its folds is easily accessible and open when you begin the trick.

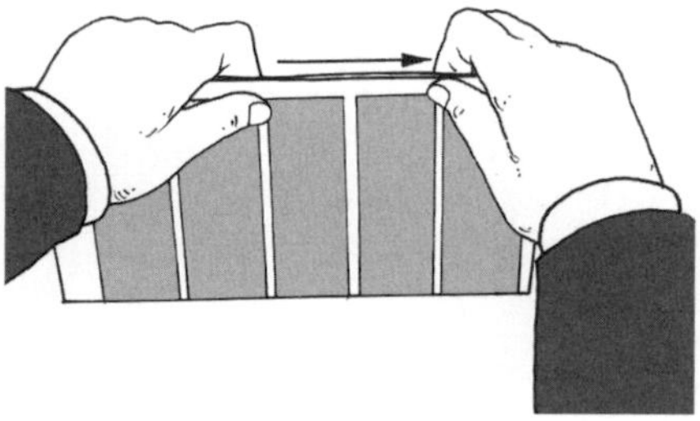

Use the index finger of the hand that holds the paper to wedge open the plastic bag. Then, pour the egg into the paper (in actuality, of course, it is poured into the plastic bag).

Remove your index finger from the bag and as you pass your free hand over the paper, use your fingertips to seal the bag shut by pressing on it through the paper, as in **Figure 11.** You can now show that the egg has vanished by rotating the paper slowly in a circle, opening out the pages, and leafing through them one at a time.

FIGURE 11

OTHER INGREDIENTS: The gimmicked newspaper used in this effect can be used to vanish other incongruous substances, including liquids. Because the concealed bag is of the resealable variety, a well-constructed routine will allow you to reproduce the vanished liquid from the folds of the paper by pouring it back into the pitcher or glass from whence it came.

HYDROSTATIC MIRACLE

This effect combines a scientific secret with a visual element that is hard to beat. Though well suited for parlor and stage performances, the effect can also be worked up close.

EFFECT: The magician fills a clear glass tumbler with water and places a small piece of paper over the glass's mouth. "Some of you in the audience today may be familiar with the scientific principle I am about to demonstrate." Here, the magician upends the glass and, amazingly, the water does not spill! It remains suspended in the glass, defying the law of gravity. At a shake of the magician's hand, reality returns, and the water falls out of the glass and into the pitcher from whence it came.

FIGURE 12

REQUIRED: A clear glass tumbler, a sheet of paper to cover its mouth, a circular piece of clear plastic (construction of which is described below) that just covers the mouth of the glass, glue that dries clear, and a pitcher of water.

PREPARATION: To create a plastic disk of the appropriate size, trace a circle around the rim of the tumbler. Cut out a clear disk of the same size as this traced circle. Cut out a second disk slightly smaller than the one just created, and glue the two pieces of clear plastic together, creating a double-thick circle that will sit snugly inside the mouth of the tumbler, as in **Figure 12.**

Fill the pitcher with water and drop the clear plastic disk inside. The tumbler and paper are on your table.

PERFORMANCE: From the pitcher, fill the tumbler approximately three quarters full with water. "In a moment, I will demonstrate how to defy scientific principles. I will show you an unexplainable feat in complete opposition to all physical laws."

Dip the paper into the pitcher, "to moisten it," you say. As you do, pick up the clear disk (which is inside the pitcher) and hold it behind the paper. Place the paper and the disk over the mouth of the glass, making sure the disk is seated securely in the mouth of the glass.

Turn the glass upside down while holding the paper (and disk, though its presence is unknown to the spectators) gently against the mouth of the glass, as in **Figure 13.**

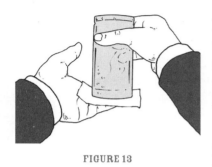

FIGURE 13

Remove your hand from the paper. Because it is wet, the paper will stick to the plastic disk and the mouth of the glass. Say, "There is an old scientific principle at work here." Deliver the next line with as much ire or humor as you like: "*A miracle* holds the paper in place."

Slowly pull the paper away from the mouth of the glass and crumple it into a ball with your free hand as you say, "This, on the other hand, has nothing to do with science." The water is apparently suspended inside the glass! Flick the edge of the glass or give it a brisk shake (over the pitcher, of course) as you deliver the final line of the routine: "And this is the conclusion of the experiment!" The disk and water fall into the pitcher, creating the perfect applause cue.

ONE DROP MORE: The final moment of the trick, in which the water falls out of the glass, can be done without shaking or touching the glass with your free hand, but requires additional preparation. A small hole must be drilled in the glass near the base. This must be done with special equipment, and should not be attempted by anyone but a skilled craftsman. The performance of the effect is exactly the same as described above; however, the magician's thumb must be held over the hole in the base of the glass throughout. When the thumb is removed from the hole, the disk and water will fall into the pitcher of their own volition.

RABBIT REQUIRED

Though few contemporary magicians work with live animals, the snow-white rabbit continues to be associated with magicians. Below is a method to simply and quickly produce one from an apparently empty box.

EFFECT: The magician shows a plain wooden box to the audience inside and out, front and back. "I realize that it's not a black top hat," he confesses to the audience, "but it's the best I can do." The lid is placed on top of the box, and when lifted again, a soft white rabbit is produced from the interior of the box!

REQUIRED: A rabbit or other animal, and a sturdy, rectangular wooden box about the size of a shoe box, with a simple removable lid. The lid is *not* hinged to the box. Make sure the box is large enough to accommodate the animal. You'll also need to construct or buy a black fabric bag with snap fastenings (not Velcro) that will comfortably hold the animal. Lastly, you'll need a spool of heavy monofilament fishing line.

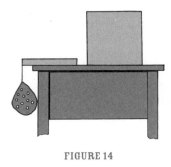

FIGURE 14

PREPARATION: Place the rabbit in the secret bag, hang the bag from the back of the lid, and set the lid on top of the box, with the secret bag hanging outside the box, but behind it, so that the box itself conceals the bag from the view of the audience. If the lid of the box is heavy enough, or if you can weight it down, you can hang the secret bag off the back edge of your table, with the load bag hanging over the table's edge, as shown in **Figure 14** (which shows the bag hanging behind the box as well as off the table edge). In Mysterio's day, it was common to have a servante (a secret shelf) attached to the rear of a performer's table. This shelf could easily accommodate props that the audience was not intended to see, including secret bags, like the one used in this effect.

Attach the fabric bag to the lid by a short length of monofilament. This is shown in **Figure 15.** The bag hangs from the back of the lid as shown in the illustration, but can also hang from the other side of the lid if put in position by the magician. This is the basic secret of the effect—the lid conceals the animal as the magician shows the box "empty." The bag should be outfitted with snap fasteners that make opening and closing it both easy and silent (which is why Velcro should not be used to close the bag).

FIGURE 15

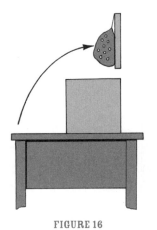

FIGURE 16

PERFORMANCE: Begin by tilting the box toward the audience and showing it empty. It is completely free of preparation and can be shown from all sides if you like. Replace the box on the table and pick up the lid by tilting it up and away from the table as shown in **Figure 16.** Tilting the lid up in this way keeps the rabbit bag hidden from the audience.

From the perspective of the audience, the lid is clearly empty. Set the lid down directly in front of the box, allowing

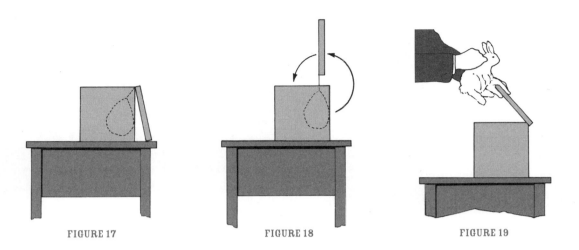

the bag to enter the box as you do so, as shown in **Figure 17.** Now turn the lid over. "I want you to see all sides of every piece involved in this trick," you say to the audience. Because the bag is already in the box, this flip-over of the lid will not reveal the working of the effect, as shown in **Figure 18.**

You can now set the lid onto the box, utter a mystic incantation or deliver more patter about the magician's best friend, the rabbit, and then lift the lid partway, open the bag, and produce the rabbit, as shown in **Figure 19.**

CHANGE BAG

Mysterio's notes on the prop used in this trick: "Its uses are endless! One should be in the prop trunk of every working magician."

EFFECT: Limitless effects are made possible with this clever device. The magician can cause a quantity of silk handkerchiefs, placed in the bag, to vanish (which is proven by turning the bag inside out). Likewise, the bag allows the performer to know ahead of time which of ten different colored poker chips a spectator will select—before even the spectator knows. The bag can also be used to switch an unprepared deck of cards for a prepared deck (perhaps one that has been set up or stacked).

REQUIRED: A Change Bag (construction of which is described below) and twenty plastic balls, eleven of which match exactly, and nine of which are different colors.

PREPARATION: Depending on your requirements, the size of your Change Bag may vary. The construction is essentially the same in all cases. You must sew together a basic bag with two pockets, only one of which is apparent to the audience. **Figure 20** shows this bag in its simplest form. Two pieces of fabric make up the bag, one for the outside and one for the inner flap or wall that separates the bag into two compartments.

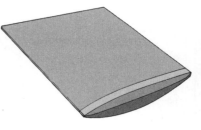

FIGURE 20

FIGURE 21

FIGURE 22

PERFORMANCE: Operating the Change Bag can be done by feel alone. If, for example, you are vanishing a quantity of handkerchiefs, it is a simple matter to place them in one of the two pockets, and then hold this pocket closed as you turn the bag inside out, as shown in **Figure 21.**

If you're using the Change Bag to force one of a number of slips of paper on a spectator, simply drop the unprepared billets into one compartment and then, with your index fingers, close off this compartment so that when a spectator reaches inside, the only slips he can select from are the prepared batch you placed in the bag before the performance, as shown in **Figure 22.** This same technique can be used to determine the color of an object selected from the bag (apparently at random), the value of a playing card, and so on. The bag can be used to switch two similar items in the same way.

COMPLICATED CAMOUFLAGE: Disguising a Change Bag as an ordinary object may take considerable time and thought, but the extra effort will be worth it when you create a prop that is virtually above suspicion. Adding drawstrings to the top of the bag, as in **Figure 23,** is a common embellishment. Some performers add handles to the top of the bag so that it looks like a handbag, as shown in **Figure 24.** Whatever design you

FIGURE 23   FIGURE 24

choose, the advice offered by Mysterio to those interested in constructing a Change Bag is both commonsensical and salient: "Line the interior of the bag with, at the very least, a dark fabric. Even though spectators will likely not peer into the bag, do whatever you can to camouflage its interior. A busy, pattered cambric will also suffice for this purpose."

MENTAL CELEBRITY PHOTOGRAPHY

At one time, this effect, performed with cards, was sold by virtually every magic shop in the world. "I often recommend this trick to students," Mysterio wrote, "as an effect that can help them bridge the gap between sleight-of-hand and tricks requiring apparatus."

EFFECT: An empty picture frame is shown and placed on the magician's table. It is covered with a cloth as the performer introduces several index cards, on which have been written the names of different celebrities. "Everyone has a favorite," the performer says. "Mine is Marilyn Monroe. A bit old-fashioned, I know." The performer mixes the cards and then has one selected by a member of the audience. When the cloth is removed from the picture frame, inside of it is a photograph of the celebrity selected at random by the audience member!

REQUIRED: A standard picture frame. For maximum visibility, it should accommodate an 8-by-10-inch (20-by-25 cm) image. Also required are a photo of a celebrity that will fit into the frame (the photo may be trimmed from a magazine), a piece of black silk fabric that will cover the photograph, and a larger, opaque cloth that entirely covers the frame when assembled.

PREPARATION: Glue the celebrity photograph to the backing of the picture frame. Over this, lay the black silk. Then, reassemble the frame so that the top edge of the silk hangs outside the frame proper, as shown in **Figure 25**. The goal is to make the frame look empty while concealing the picture inside. When assembled, the frame should be loose enough to allow the silk to be pulled from its inside without any effort.

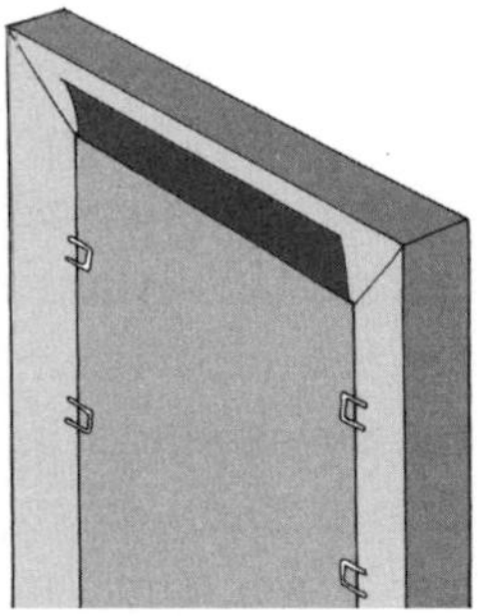

FIGURE 25

On file cards or other similar-sized cards (the backs of playing cards will work in a pinch), write the names of twenty or thirty celebrities, including the name of the celebrity in the photograph. Place the card with this known name on top of the stack. You will force it on a spectator during the performance.

Set the prepared frame on your table with the opaque cloth nearby. The cards with the celebrity names are also nearby.

PERFORMANCE: "Everyone has a favorite celebrity," the performer says. "Picking a favorite can be tough, though. Who's in the tabloids? Who's out of them? What movies have you seen recently? Who would you like to be?"

Introduce the picture frame and show it to be empty. Place it back on your table and cover it with the cloth. Pick up the stack of index cards and name some of the celebrities they represent. If you've chosen wisely, a number of funny, topical comments can be made about the individuals you're discussing. Be sure to maintain the position of the celebrity name to be forced (on top of the stack). Use the cross cut force (described on page 46) or a Change Bag to force the chosen celebrity name.

Now for the build-up. "You've selected a celebrity, one of the many great golden gods of Hollywood. Excellent. Please indulge me for a moment. Imagine this person's face. Imagine every nuance of their chiseled features: their hair, their smile, their eyes, their smile. Imagine how those elements, when combined, add up to that 'it' factor that separates the mundane from the famous, the little people from the shining stars. Please name the celebrity you've selected in a loud, clear voice so that everyone gathered here knows his or her name."

The spectator does so.

Dramatically remove the cloth from the picture frame and, as you do, pull out the fabric that, until now, has been concealing the portrait of the celebrity just forced on the audience volunteer. "Isn't *that* what he looks like?" Dispose of the cloth (and the silk inside it) as you show the frame around and confirm that the picture that has appeared inside it does, indeed, match the name of the celebrity selected "at random" by your audience volunteer.

VANISHING WAND

This trick can stand alone, or serve as a magical interlude between other effects. The principle at work—what magicians call the "shell"—has a wide variety of applications in the world of magic.

EFFECT: The magician wraps his wand in a sheet of newspaper. The newspaper tube is then crushed into a ball—and the wand is gone!

REQUIRED: A magic wand, black and white paint, a sheet of stiff paper or poster board, and a half-sheet of newspaper.

PREPARATION: Cut a piece of stiff paper or poster board to the length of the wand you will use, roll it around the wand, and glue it into a tube. Then paint it to exactly resemble the wand—black with white tips, as shown in **Figure 26.** Some performers prefer to use the cardboard center of a clothes hanger as a paper wand. Place the real wand in your jacket pocket and the paper (shell) wand on your table near the sheet of newspaper.

FIGURE 26

PERFORMANCE: Pick up the "wand" (actually a paper shell) from your table and use it in a number of tricks. When the time comes to perform this effect, begin your patter by saying, "Few laymen realize that the magician's wand is his most prized possession. Without it, he is powerless. Luckily, I have trained my wand—it's an educated object, I'll have you know—so that it will always be at my side. Observe."

Roll up the wand shell in a sheet of newspaper, and twist together the ends so that "nothing can get in or out," you say. Now tear through the center of the paper and the wand shell once. Then ball up the paper into a tight bundle and toss it to the floor.

"It's gone," you say, "but not far." Reach into your pocket, produce the solid wand, and proceed with your performance.

SOLID DECEPTION: To further prove the paper wand is solid, some performers outfit the paper wand with wooden tips. These can be easily made out of short pieces of dowel, obtainable at any hardware store. With these solid tips in place, the wand can be rapped against the tabletop, proving it to be solid. Even when rolled into the newspaper, these wooden tips do not get in the way of vanishing the wand.

VANISHING BOWL OF WATER

This effect uses a classic magical principle to accomplish a stunning vanish in the middle of an otherwise bare stage.

FIGURE 27

FIGURE 28

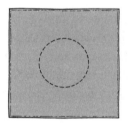

FIGURE 29

FIGURE 30

EFFECT: An assistant delivers a large bowl to the magician, who stands at center stage. The magician places the empty bowl on a tray, and fills it with water. The bowl is then covered with a cloth and the assistant exits the stage, leaving the magician in its center, holding the covered bowl in his hands. The performer throws the bowl high into the air, where it—and its contents—vanish completely!

REQUIRED: A well-rehearsed assistant, a specially prepared bowl, a tray, two large opaque cloths, several large pieces of cardboard, glue, and other basics of handicrafts. A table should be on the stage during your performance.

PREPARATION: The bowl, cloth, and tray should all be prepared in advance of your performance. **Figure 27** shows how a shelf (which can be held in place with waterproof glue) is built into the bowl. Furthermore, the bottom of the bowl is outfitted with a flat hook, which must engage with a lip that has been permanently fixed to the tray. The hook on the bottom of the bowl should easily engage with the tray, as shown in **Figure 28.** However, the marriage of the two pieces should not be loose—the tray needs to support the weight of the bowl and the water inside. Be sure that the hook is sturdily attached, and that the same is true of the slot in the tray.

   To prepare the cloth, trace the outline of the rim of the bowl onto two or three pieces of stiff cardboard. Cut out these circles, glue them together, and then glue (or sew) them into the center of the two pieces of cloth, as in **Figure 29.** Hem the edges of the cloths together. The end result is a single piece of fabric with a large circle in its center. When held from the edge of the disk, it appears that a large bowl is being covered by the cloth, as in **Figure 30.**

PERFORMANCE: The magician is met at center stage by his assistant. She carries the tray with her, on top of which is the pitcher of water, the bowl and the cloth. The magician removes the bowl from the tray, displays it, then sets it on the tray, being sure to engage the hook underneath the bowl with the slot on the tray. He next picks up the pitcher of water, and fills the bowl with it. Make a showy presentation of this—pour the water at a considerable distance from the bowl, making the quantity of water you're filling it with look like much more than is actually being poured. Set the pitcher on a side table, then remove the cloth from the tray, covering the bowl with it. Be sure to center the cardboard disk hidden inside the cloth over the mouth of the bowl.

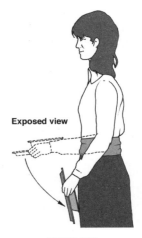

Exposed view

FIGURE 31

Grip the disk through the fabric as you pretend to remove the bowl from the tray. This is the key moment in your performance: As the bowl is apparently lifted from the tray (really, you are only lifting the cloth with the cardboard inside), your assistant tilts the tray backward, toward her body. This is shown in **Figure 31.** Because the bowl is attached to the tray, and because of the shelf inside it, the bowl will stick to the tray and the water will not spill.

Your assistant casually exits the stage as you approach the footlights, focusing all attention on the bowl that is apparently between your hands. Pretend to struggle with it, and then, when the dramatic tension has built up sufficiently (and when your assistant is finally out of sight), toss the cloth in the air. The bowl is gone!

FIGURE 32

THE CONVINCER: If you are able to palm a damp sponge in your hand (or steal one off of the tray as you pick up the cloth and your assistant walks off with the bowl and tray), you can heighten the illusion of the bowl actually being under the cloth before it vanishes by squeezing the sponge at an opportune moment and causing a stream of water to splash on the stage, as in **Figure 32.**

Because of this apparent "accident" (apparently you've spilled something on the stage just before the bowl vanishes), the audience is further convinced of the presence of the bowl under the cloth, even though it's not really there. ౷

CHAPTER IX

HANDKERCHIEF MAGIC

SILKEN SORCERY

"EVERY MAN CARRIES ONE, MAKING THE ORDINARY POCKET HANDKERCHIEF THE PERFECT ARTICLE WITH WHICH TO MAKE MAGIC."

I N MYSTERIO'S NOTEBOOK, this sentence headed the section on tricks with handkerchiefs. Said notebook was written in the 1920s, at a time when the above statement was true. Sadly, it is not nearly as common, in modern times, for gentlemen (or ladies) to carry pocket handkerchiefs.

But this fact is of little importance to the enterprising entertainer. Pieces of fabric, often referred to by magicians as "silks" (since silk is the preferred medium in which these tricks are worked) can still be stretched, changed, vanished, and transposed in the context of the modern miracle show.

Outlined in the chapter that follows are tricks performed with or upon handkerchiefs, and tricks performed *by* handkerchiefs. Very often, performers will use a cleverly constructed pocket square to cause an item to vanish from a spectator's hands, or to make other objects appear.

Mysterio concluded his observations on handkerchief tricks with the following thoughts: "Conjuring tricks with handkerchiefs offer many advantages to the modern performer. In most cases, they travel well, require little space, and many of them produce an effect large enough to be seen on the world's grandest stages."

THE DISSOLVING KNOT

This effect is the first you should learn with handkerchiefs. It is a magical "standard"; that is, it is known to nearly every aspiring wizard—and all magicians of experience as well.

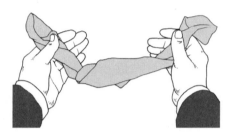

FIGURE 1

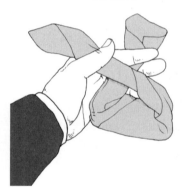

FIGURE 2

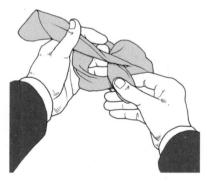

FIGURE 3

EFFECT: The magician ties a knot in the center of a handkerchief. At his command, the knot dissolves!

REQUIRED: A handkerchief. Silk works well, though a hankie of any material can be used.

PREPARATION: None.

PERFORMANCE: Hold the handkerchief by its diagonally opposite corners and roll it up, rope-fashion, by twirling it in a circle, as shown in **Figure 1.**

"When is a knot not a knot?" you ask the spectators.

As you pose this question, you apparently tie a knot in the center of the handkerchief. Cross the corners of the silk, creating a loop, as shown in **Figure 2.** Note that your left thumb clips one end of the handkerchief to the base of your index finger while the other end is held between the index finger and middle finger.

Your right hand now reaches through the center of the loop and grasps the end of the silk clipped between your index and middle finger, as shown in **Figure 3.** This end is pulled down and through the loop. At the same time, the left middle finger pulls down near the center of the fabric, creating a bight (a closed loop) in it, as shown in **Figure 4.** As the end of the handkerchief is pulled through the opening, the bight is tightened, creating a slip knot, as in **Figure 5.**

The handkerchief can now be dangled from one hand, and the knot appears to be entirely ordinary.

FIGURE 4

YOUR FINAL LINE OF PATTER: "A knot is not a knot when it's not!" Tug gently on the ends of the handkerchief, and the knot will visibly dissolve!

MIXED MEDIA: A dissolving knot can be tied in items other than handkerchiefs. Try using it with ropes, ribbons, or even articles of clothing. Once you have mastered the basic technique, its applications will become obvious in a wide variety of situations.

FIGURE 5

PLUCKED OFF

This excellent variation on the Dissolving Knot is always well received by audiences, since its outcome is so unexpected. It is perfectly suited for a stage performer working in pantomime.

EFFECT: The magician ties a knot in the center of a handkerchief. Running his hand over it, he plucks the knot off the silk entirely—in other words, a loop of fabric actually slides off the handkerchief and into the magician's hand, where it is displayed to the audience.

REQUIRED: Two matching silk handkerchiefs 18 inches (45 cm) square, preferably of a solid color.

PREPARATION: Cut a length from one of the handkerchiefs and sew it into a loop approximately two inches (5 cm) in diameter. When sewn together, the loop should appear as much like a knot in the center of a handkerchief as possible, as shown in **Figure 6.** Be sure to hem any loose edges of this fabric so that it will withstand repeated

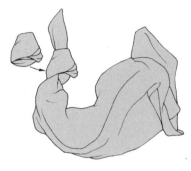

FIGURE 6

use. This false knot and the matching handkerchief are placed in a convenient pocket before the performance, the knot looped over one end of the silk.

PERFORMANCE: Display the handkerchief to the audience, concealing the knot from view in your left hand, as shown in **Figure 7.** Tie a Dissolving Knot in the center of the silk as described on page 276. Keep the false knot concealed in your left fingers as you tie the knot and display it to the audience. No palming is required, as the false knot is well camouflaged by the handkerchief.

Next, reach across your body and grasp the corner of the handkerchief concealing the false knot with your right hand. Slide the knot down the length of the silk toward the dissolving knot. Use your right hand to tug on and loosen the dissolving knot, which vanishes. The audience is unaware of this fact, however, due to the fact that the false knot is exposed at the same moment the other knot vanishes.

With the right fingers, slide the false knot partway down the length of the silk. The audience will be surprised to see it move freely along the length of the fabric. Finally, pluck the knot from the silk entirely, toss it in the air, and

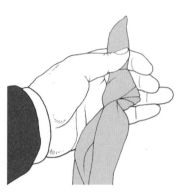

FIGURE 7

catch it to emphasize the impossibility of what has just transpired, then pocket the knot and the silk to conclude the effect.

FIGURE 8

Repeating the effect (once or twice, at most) is easy. Steal the knot (as if palming it) out of the pocket after depositing it there the first time and then repeat the steps outlined above. Alternatively, instead of placing the knot in your pocket, simply *pretend* to place it there, but keep it palmed instead. Then repeat the effect.

THE HOLY VERSION: For an added comedic touch, some performers prefer a visual, gag-type ending to this trick. A hole approximately 2 inches (5 cm) in diameter is cut in the center of the handkerchief before the performance. If the silk is held from one end, the audience will not notice the hole. The effect can then be performed as described above, and after the knot has been plucked from the handkerchief and deposited in your pocket, the silk can be shown to be missing a piece—apparently the knot just removed, as shown in **Figure 8**—which is entirely logical if a piece of the fabric actually had been magically removed from it. Of course, if the effect is performed twice in rapid succession, two holes in the handkerchief are entirely appropriate (and may be funnier than one hole).

WITHOUT LETTING GO

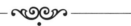

As much a challenge as a magic trick, this is a good item to keep in your arsenal of impromptu tricks. It can be performed at the dinner table or in casual situations.

EFFECT: The performer ties a knot in the center of a handkerchief without letting go of the ends.

REQUIRED: A handkerchief.

PREPARATION: None.

PERFORMANCE: Mysterio's notebook was particularly lacking in details on how to perform this stunt. Instead of a detailed description and presentation, he sketched out a rough drawing explaining the method behind the effect. **Figure 9** is a fleshed-out, professional interpretation of his original drawing, and it explains the position your arms must be in to tie the knot. Note how the arms are crossed, one hand running under the elbow of the opposite arm. With the handkerchief stretched out on the table before you, if each hand grabs a diagonally opposite corner as the hands are straightened, the knot is formed.

FIGURE 9

HAUNTED KNOT

EFFECT: As if possessed by a spirit, a knot tied in the corner of a borrowed handkerchief flip-flops back and forth. It responds to the magician's commands and requests as if alive! Then, just as amazingly, its magical charge fades away, and the handkerchief is shown to be entirely ordinary.

REQUIRED: A handkerchief, preferably made of cotton. Silk handkerchiefs will work for this effect, but the sturdier the fabric used, the better. Thick cloth table napkins work well too.

FIGURE 10

PREPARATION: None.

PERFORMANCE: Tie a knot in the corner of a sturdy handkerchief. As the knot is tied, insert the tip of your left thumb into the fold of fabric created near the knot, as shown in **Figure 10.**

Moving your thumb will cause the knot to animate. Tilt your thumb forward, and the handkerchief bows. Pull your thumb backward and the knot returns to its upright position. With carefully studied movements, the knot (or the "spook I've captured," as you refer to it) can be caused to shake his head back and forth (answering questions "yes" or "no" depending on the direction of the shake), bob up and down to the beat of his favorite tune, and much more.

PRODUCING A HANDKERCHIEF—METHOD 1

EFFECT: Without speaking a word, the magician shows both hands empty, front and back. He rolls back his sleeves, reaches into the air and produces a bright silk handkerchief from the ether.

REQUIRED: A length of fine black silk thread and a silk handkerchief. The thread should be approximately 10 inches (25 cm) shorter than your arm's length.

PREPARATION: Tie one end of the thread to a button-hole in your jacket. The other end is pinned to a corner of the handkerchief, which is folded into a compact bundle and tucked under the lapel of your jacket. **Figure 11** shows this setup.

FIGURE 11

PERFORMANCE: No words need be spoken to perform this effect. Show your hands front and back, and then roll up the sleeves of your jacket. As you do, slip your thumb into the loop of thread hanging down from your lapel.

To cause the handkerchief to appear, pull your hand and the thread forward and away from your body in a quick, direct action. **Figure 12** shows this. When your fingers reach the end of the thread, the handkerchief will be at the tips of your fingers. Because the thread used to perform the trick is shorter than your arm, when the silk appears your arm will not be in an unnatural, overextended position.

FIGURE 12

Note: This production makes an excellent opening to a flashy silent stage act. If you are willing to prepare for the trick over and over again, you can break the thread after the hankie has appeared so that the cloth can be used in another trick.

PRODUCING A HANDKERCHIEF—METHOD 2
(FROM A CANDLE)

This is a classic method of producing a handkerchief, and should be performed quickly, with no patter.

EFFECT: The magician lights a candle. From its flame, he plucks a silk handkerchief!

REQUIRED: A candle, a candlestick, a silk handkerchief 18 inches (45 cm) square, and a box of kitchen matches.

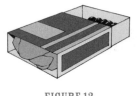

PREPARATION: Open the drawer of the matchbox halfway. Roll the handkerchief into a compact bundle (leaving one corner protruding and easily accessible) and tuck it into the empty end of the drawer, as in **Figure 13.**

PERFORMANCE: Display the candle in the candlestick. Pick up the box of matches with your right hand. With your left fingers, remove a match from the box. Then use your left hand to close the box. This forces the handkerchief into your waiting right hand, as shown in **Figure 14.** Strike the match on the side of the box and light the candle. Set down the box at the same moment the candle is being lit. Blow out the match and dispose of it. Finally, to produce the handkerchief, clip the free end between your right thumb and first finger as you apparently reach for the flame of the newly lit candle. Allow the handkerchief to cascade from your fingers and into view, as if it had been plucked from the flame. Be careful, of course, to keep the fabric from catching fire as you do so.

FIGURE 14

HANDKERCHIEF THROUGH THE ARM

The following effect is simple in execution, but powerful, particularly for the volunteer assisting the performer, who will both see and feel the magic happen. Brooklyn magician Al Baker devised the method.

EFFECT: The prestidigitator encircles a willing spectator's forearm with a handkerchief, and knots the ends of the handkerchief twice. There seems to be no possible way to free it without untying it. The magician, making a mockery of the laws of physics and nature, quickly and visibly pulls the handkerchief—which is still tied—through the spectator's arm.

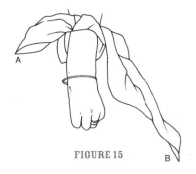

FIGURE 15

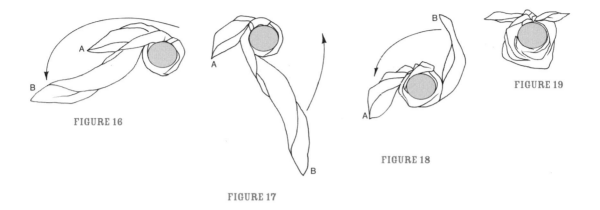

FIGURE 16

FIGURE 17

FIGURE 18

FIGURE 19

REQUIRED: A silk or cotton handkerchief that is 18 inches (45 cm) square or larger (larger is better). You should master the Dissolving Knot, taught on page 276, before learning this effect.

PREPARATION: None.

PERFORMANCE: After a willing spectator has been selected from your audience and joins you on stage, ask her to face you and extend her arm. After she does so, tie a Dissolving Knot around her forearm. **Figure 15** shows the spectator's arm *after* the tricky knot has been tied around it. Be sure that the Dissolving Knot is snug against the spectator's arm, so that it does not prematurely untie.

The ends of the handkerchief (A and B in the illustrations) must now be tied together one more time, but in a very specific way. End B (on the right side of the spectator's arm in **Figure 15**), is pulled to the left, *over* the spectator's arm again, as in **Figure 16**. In a continuing action, end B is looped down, under and completely around the spectator's arm, encircling it entirely, as shown in **Figures 17 and 18.**

Throughout this process, end A has not moved. To complete the mechanics of the trick, tie the ends of the handkerchief together in a simple, strong knot, as shown in **Figure 19.**

"It would appear impossible for this simple square of silk to free itself from your appendage, wouldn't you agree?" Based on the knotted condition of the hankie, that statement should seem accurate to anyone but a magician. "And yet, a momentary rearrangement of the molecules that make up the handkerchief is all that it takes," you say as you tug on the knot in the hankie. As you do so, the Dissolving Knot does what

it was meant to—it dissolves—and the handkerchief, still tied together at the ends, apparently and miraculously penetrates the spectator's wrist, as shown in **Figure 20.**

SOFT GLASS

FIGURE 20

U. F. Grant was a distant relative of the famous U.S. president and general Ulysses S. Grant and one of the "idea men" (illusion designers) behind Mysterio's full evening show. Grant invented this variation of a classic handkerchief effect. The method he devised eliminates the need for a specially prepared handkerchief, making the trick virtually impromptu.

EFFECT: A red handkerchief is placed in a glass tumbler. A white handkerchief is draped over the mouth of the glass and held in place with a sturdy rubber band. "Even though the red hankie is locked inside the solid glass, it can be easily extracted without removing the rubber band," the magician says. "All I need to do is soften the glass." Reaching under the white handkerchief, the magician extracts the red hank! The rubber band is removed and everything can now be examined.

REQUIRED: A straight-sided drinking glass, a rubber band, and two handkerchiefs (one white, the other red). The white handkerchief should be large enough to cover the glass completely, and should be opaque.

PREPARATION: None.

PERFORMANCE: Hand out the glass and have it inspected. As your audience examines it, explain, "Everyone knows how glass is made. Sand is heated up, melted, and blown into shape. Well, if you know what you're doing, you can soften a piece of glass even when it's cold. Watch this."

Place the red hankie in the tumbler and push it down toward the bottom. Grip the base of the glass between your thumb and index finger, as in **Figure 21.** As you cover the

FIGURE 21

tumbler with the white handkerchief, the secret move takes place: The glass is allowed to turn upside down, pivoting between your thumb and index finger, as in **Figure 22.**

FIGURE 22

Drape the white handkerchief over the bottom of the glass (apparently the top) and snap the rubber band around it. "The red handkerchief is like a prisoner," you say. "But by softening the glass, I can free it from captivity." Reach under the white hankie and *slowly* remove the red handkerchief from the glass.

To end your performance, pretend to "heal" the "soft" bottom of the glass, remove the rubber band and white handkerchief from around the tumbler's base, and as you set everything aside, under cover of the white handkerchief, turn the glass back over so it is mouth up.

DEKOLTA'S VANISHING HANDKERCHIEF

This mechanical method for vanishing a handkerchief was devised by Buatier deKolta, one of history's most creative conjurers. In addition to tricks with handkerchiefs, deKolta devised a famous illusion in which a die approximately 3 inches (8 cm) square visibly grew to over fifty times its original size. Mysterio's stage show frequently included another deKolta invention, the Vanishing Lady.

EFFECT: The magician tucks a silk handkerchief into his closed right fist. With no sleight-of-hand or awkward moves, the handkerchief vanishes.

REQUIRED: A deKolta Pull (construction of which is described below), and a handkerchief. A jacket must be worn when performing this effect.

PREPARATION: A deKolta Pull is a container small enough to fit into the magician's hand. A pull can be made from either a hollow ball or plastic egg with a hole cut in its side, or a small canister, like those sold at pharmacies to hold pills. At the end of the container opposite the hole, a length of elastic is permanently attached (a large knot inside the canister will keep the elastic firmly in place). At the free end of the elastic, a safety pin is tightly tied. See **Figure 23** for illustrations of both styles of pulls.

Run the elastic through the belt loops of your pants, and attach the safety pin to the rearmost belt loop, as in **Figure 24.** When properly positioned, the container should be concealed by your jacket, as it hangs near your right hip. See **Figure 25.**

The handkerchief should be in your left pants pocket.

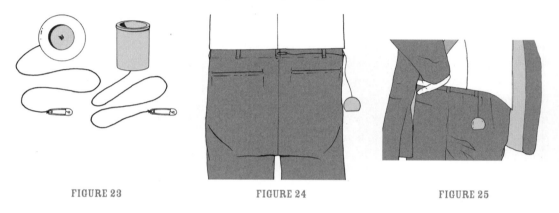

FIGURE 23   FIGURE 24   FIGURE 25

PERFORMANCE: Reach into both of your trouser pockets at the same time, as if searching for something. As you remove the silk from your left pants pocket, grasp the pull in the palm of your right hand. The elastic will be concealed behind your arm, and your right fingers curl naturally around the pull.

Direct all attention to the handkerchief and say, "The silk fibers that make up this hankie are surprisingly reactive to friction." Close your right fingers around the pull as your right arm is raised just above your waist, with your arm extended in front of your body. You should feel tension from the elastic when your arm is extended.

Turn the right side of your body toward the audience and tuck the silk into your fist (and the pull). When the entire handkerchief is inside the pull, relax the grip of your right hand slightly. The elastic will go to work, and the pull will secretly fly out of your hand, under your coat.

Don't stop here! Now that the work has been done, capitalize on the opportunity at hand. Focus all attention on your right hand, which apparently contains the handkerchief. Pause for a few beats. Roll up your sleeves, if you like. Then rub your right fingers together, "to create friction between my skin and the silk fibers." Finally, open your hand to show that the handkerchief is gone.

Mr. Mysterio was fond of saying, "Delay the magic moment to heighten the effect." His mantra was taken from S. W. Erdnase's classic, *The Expert at the Card Table*, which states: "The resourceful professional, failing to improve the method, changes the moment." Even though the dirty work is done before the handkerchief is shown to be gone, the magical moment is delayed to increase the level of impossibility and further separate the method from the effect.

MORE THAN A HANKIE: The deKolta Pull was first used to vanish handkerchiefs. Attaching a different sort of container to the end of a length of elastic allows you to vanish other objects in similar fashion. Using a small squeeze-style coin purse (as illustrated in **Figure 26**) in place of the bottle or ball described above allows you to vanish handfuls of coins, dice, folded playing cards, or nearly any small object that will fit inside.

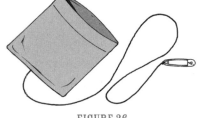

FIGURE 26

HANDKERCHIEF TO GOLF BALL

The simple gimmick you will construct to perform this routine may seem obvious to savvy magicians, but to an unknowing layman this trick will prove startling.

EFFECT: The magician removes a white silk handkerchief from his pocket. Tucking the hankie into his fist, he squeezes it tightly. When his hand is opened, the handkerchief has been transformed into a golf ball.

REQUIRED: A hollow "practice" golf ball (these are made of a light yet durable plastic and are available at sporting goods stores), a regular golf ball, and a small white silk handkerchief (silk compresses into a smaller space than cotton). The practice ball and regular golf ball should look alike.

PREPARATION: Cut a hole $1^1/_2$ inches (3 cm) in diameter in one side of the hollow practice ball. Place it in your right trouser pocket, along with the real ball. The handkerchief is placed in your left trouser pocket.

FIGURE 27

PERFORMANCE: "I'm not much of a golfer," you say. Reach into your trouser pockets with both hands, as if searching for something. Grasp the hollow ball with your right hand and the handkerchief with your left hand. Withdraw your left hand from your pocket first. Attention will be focused on the handkerchief. No one will suspect that your right hand conceals the hollow ball in its naturally curled fingers. **Figure 27** shows the ball concealed in classic palm.

"In fact, I'm such a bad golfer," you say, "I've nearly given up the game." Here, you wave the white hankie as if it were a signal of surrender on the battlefield.

Make a fist with your right hand, around the hollow ball. Slowly, tuck the hankie into the ball, starting with the center. "Note that I said *nearly*. I haven't given it up entirely." As you deliver the line "…haven't given it up entirely," pause dramatically and then open your right hand. The silk has turned into a golf ball! Examine the ball (keeping the hole concealed from the audience as you do so), and then place it in your right trouser pocket.

To "prove" the ball to be real, as an apparent afterthought, remove the *real* ball from your pocket. Toss it to an audience member.

ESCAPE!

EFFECT: The magician's wrists are tied together. Then a length of rope is threaded through the magician's arms and tied in a loop. There is no way for the magician to free himself of the rope loop. Or is there? After turning his back for only a moment, the magician is free of the rope!

REQUIRED: A length of rope and a pocket handkerchief.

PREPARATION: None.

PERFORMANCE: Have a spectator tie your hands together with the handkerchief. Then, let her tie another piece of rope through the circle created by your arms. Have her tie several knots in this rope loop, to make sure you cannot easily free yourself from it.

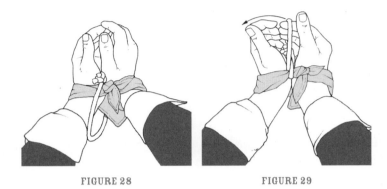

FIGURE 28   FIGURE 29

To escape, turn your back on the audience. Thread a small piece of the rope through the handkerchief that is securing your wrists, as in **Figures 28 and 29.** Loop this over your hand. You are free of the rope, which you hold on to as you turn around to show your audience that you have escaped, à la Houdini! For a variation on this effect, you can tie a spectator's wrists together, looping the rope that ties them together through your tied wrists. Follow the procedure described above to separate yourself from the spectator.

THE GO-GO VANISHER

This versatile device can be used in conjunction with other tricks—or perhaps to vanish an object that will appear elsewhere later—or as a stand-alone feature. It was devised by Stewart James as an alternative to another standard vanishing cloth trick, the Devil's Handkerchief.

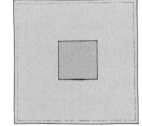

FIGURE 30

EFFECT: An egg is placed on the magician's outstretched hands. "As quickly as they come, so do they go," he says. A fancy handkerchief is whisked over the magician's bare hand. The egg is gone!

REQUIRED: A Go-Go Vanisher. This is a specially made cloth, constructed by sewing two handkerchiefs together at the hems. In the center of one of the handkerchiefs, cut a hole approximately 4 inches (10 cm) across, as illustrated in **Figure 30.** The size of the hole can vary based on the size of the objects to be vanished. Patterned handkerchiefs will help to hide the hole, though a Go-Go Vanisher can be constructed from virtually any sort of fabric.

PREPARATION: None.

PERFORMANCE: Lay an object like an egg on the table, or in the palm of your hand. Place the Go-Go Vanisher on top of it, making sure that the secret hole is positioned directly over the object, and grasp one corner of the cloth. With a rapid cross-wise snap, pull the vanisher over the object, which will be carried inside and should end up near the corner of the vanisher diagonally opposite that which you are holding.

The Go-Go can vanish objects in other ways, too.

For example, if the cloth is set down with its opening nearest to the table, you can toss an unbreakable object—for example, a ball—underneath it by lifting up one corner, as in **Figure 31**. In actuality, you toss it the ball into the opening of the Go-Go Vanisher. Later, when the cloth is lifted, the object is gone.

FIGURE 31

FIGURE 32

OTHER VANISHING CLOTHS: To vanish a small object like a ring, watch, or coin, sew a small pocket into the corner of a handkerchief, as in **Figure 32.** The opening of the pocket is outfitted with two small strips of Velcro, so that a small item like a coin can be placed inside or changed with another item at the performer's discretion.

When ready to vanish an object similar to that which is inside the secret pocket, simply fold the prepared corner of the handkerchief underneath and into the center of the hankie proper, as in **Figure 33,** and give the hidden object to a spectator to hold through the layers of fabric, while "going south" with the real item. Later, to cause the item apparently still covered by the handkerchief to vanish, grasp a free corner of the hankie, shake it out, then show it on both sides to prove that the object is gone.

FIGURE 33

FIGURE 34

THE DEVIL'S HANDKERCHIEF: The forebear to the Go-Go Vanisher is the Devil's Handkerchief, the traditional vanishing cloth preferred by magicians, Mr. Mysterio included, for centuries. Devil's Handkerchiefs are made with a double thickness of fabric, like the Go-Go. Instead of having a hole cut in the center of one side of the hankie, though, the pocket in a Devil's Handkerchief is at its hem, as in **Figure 34.** The Devil's Handkerchief should be made from a patterned material, like gingham.

To use the Devil's Handkerchief, the cloth is first formed into an impromptu bag by gathering its corners together in one hand, as in **Figure 35.** The object that will disappear is then dropped into the secret pocket of the handkerchief, as shown in **Figure 36.** When opened out, the object is concealed between the layers of the cloth, which can then be shown on both sides.

"The performer must be careful, of course, to allow the proper corners of the cloth to drop," Mysterio wrote on January 21, 1908. "My pet canary Percival made an unexpected appearance in last night's performance when, in a moment of mental weakness, I transposed the ends of the Devil's Hank. Instead of vanishing, he flew out of the secret pocket and into the flies of the theater. It was quite an embarrassing moment. Fortunately, no members of the press were present at the performance."

FIGURE 35

FIGURE 36

SILKEN LUNCH

The device described below is very useful, and inexpensive to construct to boot.

EFFECT: A silk handkerchief (or group of silks) is stuffed into a paper lunch bag, which is blown up like a balloon. "Cover your ears if you must," the magician says. "This won't be quiet!" When the performer pops the bag with a loud bang, it is ripped to shreds. The handkerchiefs have vanished!

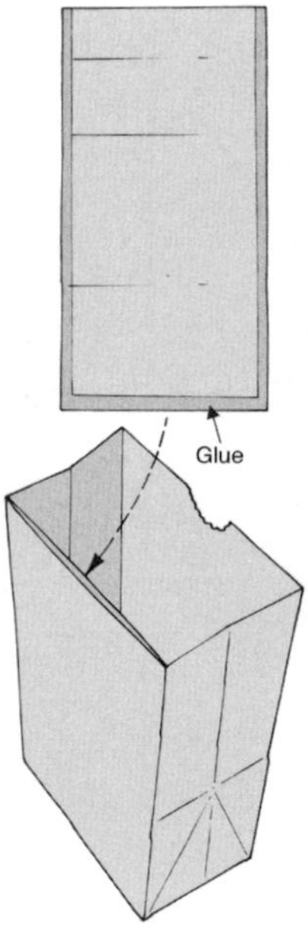

REQUIRED: Two paper lunch bags, rubber cement or glue, and a quantity of silks.

PREPARATION: Cut away one side of a bag and apply glue around its edges, as shown in **Figure 37.** Slide this extra piece into the other bag while the glue is still wet, creating a hidden pocket in the bag. After the glue has dried, the bag can be folded flat. From the outside, it appears to be nothing more than a standard brown paper lunch bag.

Glue

FIGURE 37

PERFORMANCE: Unfold the bag and, as you open it out, insert your right thumb into the secret compartment. This gives you easy access. Set the bag down on your work table and pick up the silk (or silks) you plan to vanish. Stuff the handkerchiefs into the secret compartment, inflate the bag, and then twist its neck so that the air will not escape. Warn your audience about the loud noise to come. Pop the bag and tear away its front, as shown in **Figure 38.** The silks are gone!

ALTERNATIVE LUNCHES: Instead of vanishing hand-kerchiefs, the prepared bags can be used to transform the silks into other small, lightweight objects, or cause them to change color. Begin your performance with, for example, a red handkerchief hidden inside the bag. Place a white handkerchief into the secret compartment, then inflate and burst the bag as usual. The white silk has been magically dyed red.

FIGURE 38

With a modicum of creative thinking, other effects can be devised. A red handkerchief can be transformed into an apple. Silks tied together can magically untie themselves when placed in the bag.

KLING KLANG

Credited to Mysterio's compeer from England, Colonel Stodare, Kling Klang is an odd name for a straightforward yet mystifying trick that never fails to please.

EFFECT: An egg is placed in a long-stemmed goblet and covered with a handkerchief. "The goblet is covered both to make it proof against sleight-of-hand," the performer states, "and to keep the light out. Like a butterfly's chrysalis, the egg can only work its magic in total darkness." A red handkerchief is rolled into a compact bundle between the magician's palms, where it turns into a white egg! The goblet is uncovered to reveal the red silk where the egg reposed only a moment before.

REQUIRED: A stemmed goblet large enough to hold an egg, two identical silk handkerchiefs 18 inches (45 cm) square, a white cotton handkerchief, a length of white cotton thread, and two realistic plastic eggs (one with a hole in its side).

FIGURE 39

PREPARATION: Attach the egg with no hole in it to the center of the white cotton handkerchief, using a 6-inch (15-cm) length of thread, as shown in **Figure 39.** Set this parcel, egg side up, on your table. Carefully fold one of the silk handkerchiefs and place it under the white hankie (the one with the egg attached) so that it's not visible to the audience. Tuck one corner of the other silk hankie into the hole of the other egg, as shown in **Figure 40.**

FIGURE 40

PERFORMANCE: Pick up the glass in your left hand and the egg-handkerchief combination in your right hand. "This small, ovoid object works best in total darkness. Though snow white itself, it is in the darkest, inkiest void that it will make a magical transposition. Allow me to demonstrate."

Place the egg and the silk hidden under it in the goblet as the cotton handkerchief is turned over to cover all. Gently shake the goblet so that the egg taps its side, proving that the hen fruit is inside and that no trickery has taken place…yet.

Retrieve the second egg and silk from the table, keeping the egg palmed in your right hand. It is easy to keep the egg concealed there since the hand holds and displays the silk handkerchief at the same time. Use both hands to effect a marvelous minor miracle. Gradually work the visible silk handkerchief into the hollow egg. The silk apparently grows smaller and smaller, finally disappearing. Concentrate on your right hand, eventually opening it and registering surprise at the transformation from silk to egg.

"And now, we lift the veil," you say as you remove the covering from the goblet which has been on your table and in full view throughout the presentation. The imitation egg is removed from the goblet as the cloth is raised, revealing what is apparently the same handkerchief that vanished from your hands only a moment before.

THE INVISIBLE HEN

Joseph Karson popularized this trick to modern magicians as the Chinese Egg Bag. But this endless production of eggs from a silk handkerchief is at least a hundred years old, likely predating even Mr. Mysterio's professional debut in 1906.

EFFECT: A handkerchief is shown front and back and is then formed into a makeshift bag. "This is embarrassing," the conjurer says, "but in the case of this trick, the magic words happen to be 'cluck, cluck.'" When the bag is upended, out drops a solid, white egg! The magician produces twelve eggs from the cloth in rapid succession, dropping each one into a hat on his table. The hat is then tossed into the audience, which expects to be showered with eggs. Instead, the hat is empty—all the eggs have vanished!

REQUIRED: Two heavy handkerchiefs or bandanas, a hat (which may be borrowed), a length of thread, and a plastic egg.

FIGURE 41

PREPARATION: Sew the handkerchiefs together on all four edges and attach one end of the thread—which should be approximately half as long as the handkerchiefs—to the egg. Attach the free end of the thread to the center of one hem of the handkerchief, as in **Figure 41.**

PERFORMANCE: Borrow a hat from an audience member (a baseball cap will do if no one is wearing a beaver top hat, as was so often the case in Mysterio's day). Set the hat, mouth up, on your table. "Ladies and gentlemen, allow me to introduce Clara, the invisible hen." So saying, you show the handkerchief as in **Figure 42.** The egg is concealed from the view of the audience.

FIGURE 42

Form the handkerchief into a bag by gathering up the corners, as shown in **Figure 43.** First fold the hankie together at the top, holding those corners with one hand. Then pick up the lower corners with your free hand. Deliver the line above about the magic words ("cluck, cluck"), then tip the makeshift bag to one side, allowing the egg to roll out of it and into the hat.

You must now reload the handkerchief (stealing the egg out of the hat) so that the same object can be produced repeatedly, creating the illusion of five, ten, or even a dozen eggs being produced when in fact only one is in play. Let go of the lower corners of the hankie, and allow the handkerchief to momentarily cover the hat. Then lift the hankie by the corners on either side of the thread. This lifts the egg back out of the hat and prepares you to reproduce the egg again.

Produce as many eggs as you see fit via the method described, and conclude the effect by pocketing the handkerchief (and attached egg). Pick up the hat and toss it toward a spectator

FIGURE 43

nearby. If your theatrical charade has been successful, she will be shocked to discover that the hat is empty.

A CONVINCING TOUCH: To add a further illusory layer to the Invisible Hen routine, begin with a real, raw egg in the hat. After producing two or three eggs as already described, reach into the hat and remove the genuine article. It can be cracked into a glass or handed out as a "souvenir" to prove the existence of your imaginary chicken.

FLASH COLOR-CHANGING SILK

Sometimes the boldest, simplest methods are the best.

EFFECT: The magician passes a red handkerchief through his fist, turning the handkerchief green!

REQUIRED: Two handkerchiefs 18 inches (45 cm) square. One is red with a white border, the other is green with a white border.

FIGURE 44

PREPARATION: Sew the handkerchiefs together around all four edges. The end result is a white-bordered handkerchief that is red on one side and green on the other, as in **Figure 44.**

PERFORMANCE: Best performed in pantomime, the trick virtually works itself. The red side of the hankie is displayed between the hands. Forming your left hand into a fist, the handkerchief is passed through it, by pulling it down and through the fist with the right fingers, as shown in **Figure 45.** As the hankie emerges from the bottom of the fist (if you insist on using patter, you could call your clenched fist an "organic tunnel of mystery"), the green side is exposed, creating a visible color-changing effect. The green side is then displayed to the audience to conclude the trick.

OTHER TUNNELS OF MYSTERY: Instead of performing the effect in silence and using your fist, pass the hankie through a small paper tube, or a hole cut in a piece of poster board, to cause its color to change. Patter themes can be built around an ungimmicked prop of this nature and, at the same time, take some of the "heat" off the special handkerchief.

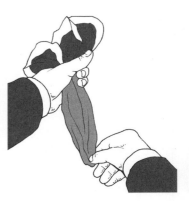

FIGURE 45

THREE HANDS-OFF KNOTS

Though big and showy, this trick requires little by way of props and can be prepared on the fly.

EFFECT: Three silk handkerchiefs are displayed, along with a length of ribbon. The ribbon is threaded through the sides of a paper bag. The silks are vanished. When the ribbon is removed from the bag, the missing handkerchiefs are discovered tied to it!

REQUIRED: Two red, two white, and two blue silks, all 18 inches (45 cm) square, two identical 36-inch (90 cm) lengths of ribbon, a rubber band, a paper bag with slits cut in its side, and another bag, prepared as described in Silken Lunch (page 292).

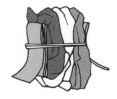

FIGURE 46

PREPARATION: Tie one handkerchief of each color onto one length of ribbon, and push them all close to the center of the ribbon. Accordion-pleat the silks together into a small bundle. Then, pleat the ends of the ribbon on top of the handkerchiefs and encircle the entire package loosely with the rubber band, as in **Figure 46**. Be sure that both ends of the ribbon are easily accessible.

Place the prepared bundle in the unprepared paper bag, the loose silks on top of it, and the loose ribbon on top of all.

PERFORMANCE: Invite three spectators to join you on stage. "Give my helpers a round of applause for their efforts," you say, to both put the volunteers at ease and kill time as they join you on the platform.

Remove the loose ribbon from the bag, and hand it to one volunteer for examination. Take the loose silks from the bag next, along with the prepared bundle, which is concealed inside the silks. The empty bag can now be examined by your volunteers, if you like.

Retrieve the ribbon and the bag, and drop the ribbon back into the bag. Then drop in the silks—apparently to free your hands, but really to deposit the prepared bundle in the bag. As you do this, pick the prepared bag up off your table and show it empty. Take the loose silks out of the unprepared bag again (this time leaving the prepared bundle behind) and place them in the secret compartment of the prepared bag. Blow up the bag, twist its neck, and hand it to a volunteer for safe keeping. "Hold it tight. Don't let anything in or out of that bag," you instruct him.

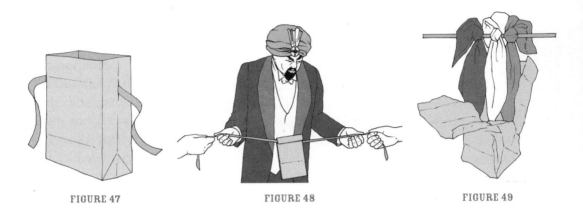

FIGURE 47   FIGURE 48   FIGURE 49

Reach into the unprepared bag and pull the ends of the prepared ribbon free from the rubber band. Thread them through the slits in either side of the bag, as in **Figure 47.** Fold over the top of the bag, then hand the ends of the ribbon to the unoccupied spectators, one on your right, the other on your left, as in **Figure 48.**

Vanish the silks from the blown-up bag by popping it and tearing it open. To complete the transposition effect, tear the bag away from the ribbon, as in **Figure 49,** to disclose the missing silks tied onto it. The loose ribbon in the bag can be taken away with the torn-off section.

CUT AND RESTORED SILK

EFFECT: Two silks are placed in a paper cylinder (perhaps made of a rolled-up magazine cover, in a pinch). The magician snips through the center of the tube, apparently slicing the handkerchiefs in half. In fact, the halves of the tube are separated, showing the silks in two pieces. With a magic pass and incantation, the silks are both made whole again.

REQUIRED: Two identical silk handkerchiefs, a piece of stiff letter-sized paper, a pair of scissors, and two rubber bands.

PREPARATION: Roll the paper into a tube, and place both handkerchiefs in the tube and both rubber bands around it, as shown in **Figure 50.**

PERFORMANCE: Remove the handkerchiefs from the tube and display them to the audience. As you replace them in the tube, say, "I am about to perform a bit of visual deception. You can see the ends of the handkerchiefs protruding from each end of the tube, can you not?"

Remove both silks from the tube a second time, this time secretly sliding one of the rubber bands over them, and toward their center.

As you hand the tube to a spectator for examination and ask him to unroll it and check it out, switch two ends of the handkerchiefs so they are now in the configuration shown in **Figure 51.** Your hand covers the rubber band at the center and, to the spectators, everything appears copacetic. Retrieve the paper and rubber band from the spectator and roll the paper into a tube around the handkerchiefs, concealing their real condition in the process. Encircle the tube with the rubber band.

Grip the ends of the tube and pull on the silks slightly, then hand the scissors to a spectator and invite him to cut through the

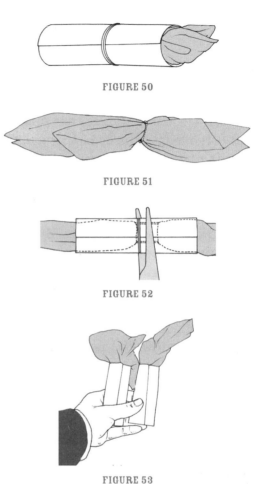

FIGURE 50

FIGURE 51

FIGURE 52

FIGURE 53

center of the tube. Be sure to pull on both handkerchiefs as he does this, so that he cuts through the rubber band (as shown in the X-ray view in **Figure 52**) and not the cloth.

"These poor, innocent, beautiful silk handkerchiefs have clearly been cut in two," you say as you separate your hands, one half of the tube in each. "Thankfully, they are as easy to restore as they are to cut. Observe." Place both halves of the tube in your left hand, as shown in **Figure 53.** Grip one end of each handkerchief and with a deft pull, remove them both from the tubes simultaneously. As they unfurl, it will appear as if both silks have been restored in midair.

CORDS OF PHANTASIA

This is one of the most overlooked tricks in all of magic. Though popular in Mysterio's day (and made into a feature by his contemporary, Dante), it is rarely seen by modern audiences.

EFFECT: Two lengths of rope are tied around a folded paper fan. The magician then ties four bright silk handkerchiefs to the ropes, and secures them in place with another knot from the ropes. Two spectators assist the magician, holding the free ends of the ropes. "On the count of three, you will witness a miraculous penetration of solid through solid," the performer says. True to his word, at the conclusion of the count, the fan and silks (still knotted) are pulled free from the ropes, which remain in the spectators' hands!

FIGURE 54

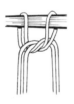

FIGURE 55

REQUIRED: Four silk handkerchiefs 18 inches (45 cm) square, a folding paper fan (or a magic wand or other skinny object of approximately the same size), and two pieces of soft cotton rope 6 feet (1¾ m) long.

PREPARATION: None.

PERFORMANCE: Invite two spectators to assist you. "You will act as the eyes and ears of the audience," you say. Hang the ropes over the fan, as shown in **Figure 54,** and tie them into a single knot, as shown in **Figure 55.** "So far, all I've done is secured this fan with these two lengths of rope, correct?" The spectators nod their heads in assent, since that is all you have done.

Hand the ropes to the spectators so that each one receives two ends of the same piece. Next, tie the handkerchiefs in single knots around the ropes, as shown in **Figure 56.** Use single knots, and don't tie them too tightly. "So far, everything looks fair, correct?" As you say this and the spectators confirm that you have tied

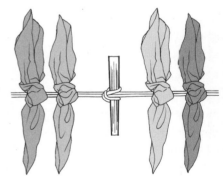

FIGURE 56

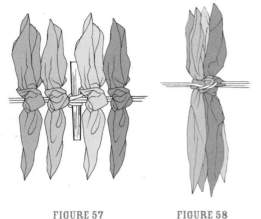

FIGURE 57   FIGURE 58

the handkerchiefs to the rope, slide them down the ropes, toward the fan, as in **Figure 57.**

Ask each spectator to hand you one end of rope. Tie these into a single knot around the silks and fan, as shown in **Figure 58,** and then hand the ends of these ropes back to the spectators. By tying the last knot, you have switched two ends of the ropes in full view of the audience.

"Up to this point, everything has been aboveboard, has it not?" you say. "I secured the fan to these ropes with a knot, the silks to the ropes with knots, and tied another knot around the entire arrangement. Everything is held in place securely, and is free of trickery, correct?" Your assisting spectators should have no trouble agreeing with these statements.

"Now for the tricky part," you say. "On the count of three, please pull on your ropes firmly." Begin counting to three, and as you do, work the fan loose from the center of the ropes. As you do so, grip the ends of the handkerchiefs with your other hand. On the count of three, as the spectators pull on the ropes, you pull the fan free of them. Amazingly, the handkerchiefs will be pulled free of them as well, with their knots intact, and each spectator will be left holding one end of each rope in his hands, as shown in **Figure 59.**

FIGURE 59

PULL-APART SILKS

This trick can be presented with a spectator's assistance, or by the performer "in one." "Each performer should make a trick his own; try not to mimic exactly that which you have seen or read," Mysterio wrote. "Even the simplest trick can become a showpiece if properly presented."

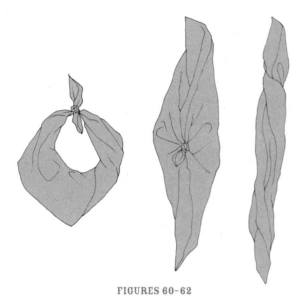

EFFECT: Two handkerchiefs of contrasting colors are tied together, one looped through the other. The linked silks are dropped into a borrowed hat or bag. The magician reaches in and removes, with one hand, the red handkerchief only. It is still tied in a loop. He then removes the green handkerchief, leaving no clue as to how the two cloths melted through each other.

REQUIRED: Two silk handkerchiefs of contrasting colors and a hat or bag (which may be borrowed).

FIGURES 60-62

PREPARATION: Tie the green handkerchief into a loop as shown in **Figure 60.** Place the knot at the silk's center, and roll the silk in a ropelike fashion, concealing the knot, as shown in **Figures 61 and 62.**

PERFORMANCE: "Magicians are often accused of using mirrors or smoke to misdirect their audiences and accomplish their feats. For the following experiment, I will use neither, but will admit to the device I do use to accomplish it: darkness."

Show both handkerchiefs and tie the red one into a loop, as shown in **Figure 63.** Loop the green silk through it, and tie it—apparently—into a loop as well. In fact, you tie a square knot, as described in the

FIGURE 63

Genuine Dissolving Knot (page 204), in the visible ends of the green handkerchief.

"What could be fairer? I've tied both of these handkerchiefs into loops, and both loops are tied together. Now for the motivating magic, which happens under the cover of darkness."

Drop the silks into the borrowed hat. Do this very openly, to "prove" that your actions are anything but sneaky. After the appropriate pause, reach into the hat and upset the false knot in the green handkerchief, causing it to open. This can be accomplished with one hand and with relative ease.

"The powers of darkness work quickly," you say. With one hand (which is shown empty, though this fact is not stated in an obvious way), remove the green handkerchief from the hat. Because you tied and hid another knot in it before the performance began, the handkerchief is still tied in a loop. Now the red silk can likewise be removed from the hat and both can be handed out for examination.

MYSTERIO'S THOUGHTS: After learning the secret to the above mystery, Mr. Mysterio jotted a quick note about it for future consideration: "Work this effect up into an audience participation extravaganza. Much can be made out of the trick if the silks are handed to a spectator apparently tied together, only to be discovered untied. With the right patter, and worked into a longer routine, this would certainly be sensational."

Instead of placing the handkerchiefs in a bag, an adept performer (as Mysterio himself was) can manipulate the false knot in front of the audience and, in the action of handing the silks to a spectator, cause them to visibly melt apart.

SELF-UNKNOTTING HANKIE

This is one of the most visual, charming, and mysterious tricks that can be performed with a handkerchief.

EFFECT: The magician ties a silk handkerchief into a knot. "And now, for a visible, incredible haunting," he says. "I will now throw a spirit into this piece of fabric. Once the apparition has inhabited the handkerchief, he will make himself known to all of us. Watch!" The magician makes a magical pass at the knotted silk. Visibly, slowly, and eerily, the knot unties itself!

REQUIRED: A silk handkerchief approximately 18 inches (45 cm) square, a piece of black bonded nylon (or heavy-duty cotton) thread 40 inches (1 m) long, and a small black bead.

PREPARATION: Sew one end of the thread to a corner of the handkerchief and at the opposite, free end of the thread tie the bead, as shown in **Figure 64.**

FIGURE 64

FIGURE 65

PERFORMANCE: Shake out the handkerchief, showing it to be apparently free from trickery. The thread should hang down toward the floor when you have finished displaying the silk in this manner.

Roll the silk into a ropelike shape by twirling the opposite corners (one of which is attached to the thread), then tie it into a loose knot with the thread running through its center, as shown in **Figure 65.** Allow the bead to fall to the floor, and in the act of pattering about the spirit that you will cause to inhabit the handkerchief, step on the bead.

"Hauntings rarely happen in the light," you explain, "and it's even rarer to capture a ghost in the company of so many attentive and skeptical individuals. Watch as the spirit goes to work."

Begin pulling the handkerchief upward, away from the bead on the floor. Amazingly, due to the arrangement of the thread through the knot, the silk will visibly untie itself, one end snaking up through the knot and out the other side! As soon as the knot is untied, remove your foot from the bead on the floor and allow the handkerchief to go limp. "The spirit has made his presence known and is now free from his earthly constraint. Please thank him for his appearance with a hearty round of applause." So concludes the performance.

OTHER HOOKUPS: Using a shorter thread, the bead can be held in your free hand and subtly pulled on to make the handkerchief untie. If you begin your performance with the handkerchief tucked into the breast pocket of your jacket, the thread could also be attached inside said pocket, making the effect entirely self-contained. Then, at the conclusion of the trick, the handkerchief goes back into your pocket where it began.

TWENTIETH-CENTURY SILKS

This effect was conceived by the New York magician and confidant of Mr. Mysterio Frank Ducrot. In addition to helping Mysterio develop several clever lines of patter, Ducrot, who operated Martinka's Magic Shop, supplied his friend with innumerable gimmicks and props over the years.

EFFECT: The magician ties two handkerchiefs together and places them in a clear drinking glass. Another handkerchief, this one of a contrasting color, vanishes from between the performer's hands. When the previously tied hankies are unfurled, between them—tied in place by two secure knots—is the missing silk!

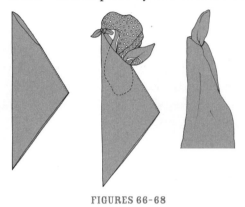

FIGURES 66-68

REQUIRED: Four silk handkerchiefs approximately 18 inches (45 cm) square. Two of them should be of a matching solid color. The other pair should be of a contrasting color or pattern, but with a border that matches the solid-colored silks.

PREPARATION: Fold one of the solid-colored silks in half and then sew a discreet pocket into the folded hankie, as shown in **Figures 66 and 67.** Before your performance, tie the corner of one of the patterned silks to the corner of the silken pocket. Tuck the remainder of the patterned silk into the secret pocket, leaving its other corner (which matches the solid silks in color) protruding from the end of the pocket, as shown in **Figures 67 and 68.**

PERFORMANCE: Display the two solid-colored silks and apparently tie them together. What actually happens is that the unprepared solid-colored silk is tied to the exposed corner of the patterned silk that is hidden in the silken pocket, as shown in **Figure 69.**

Drape the tied silks over your neck, with the knot behind your head. Now display the duplicate patterned silk and explain what is about to transpire: "You will witness—no, actually you will *not* witness—the fastest magical translocation the world has ever known. It happens at a speed so blinding, no scientist has been able to accurately determine the actual speed at which the effect occurs. Observe."

Here, you roll the duplicate patterned handkerchief into a ball and vanish it from between your hands. This can be accomplished by various means: Use a deKolta Pull (page 285), or vanish it via sleight-of-hand, as follows.

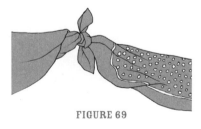

FIGURE 69

Roll the handkerchief into a ball, starting at one corner and working it in a circular motion between the palms of both hands. Your goal is to make a compact and tight ball that can be easily palmed. It helps to knot one corner of the silk in advance of this action.

Once the ball has been made, hold it in the palm of your right hand and perform a false transfer with it, apparently placing it in the left hand, which closes around it. In actuality, the balled-up handkerchief is retained in the right hand, which uses its thumb to hold back on it as it is apparently placed in the left hand. Reach into your right pocket "for a dose of magical dust," you say, and deposit the handkerchief there. Remove the "dust" and sprinkle it over your left hand, which is then opened to show that the silk is gone.

"And now for the lightning-fast part," you say. "The vanish was slow and deliberate—I do it that way because it looks better." Grasp the handkerchiefs around your neck, one in each hand, and quickly pull them into view, unfurling the concealed patterned silk from the pocket as you do so. The vanished silk makes its surprising, rapid, and magical return!

SHOWER OF SWEETS

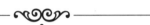

"This is a capital trick for children, but as everyone loves sweets and chocolates, it plays well for the older set, as well." So wrote Mr. Mysterio about the following conjuring classic, a production of candy from a borrowed handkerchief.

EFFECT: The performer borrows a handkerchief and lays it over an ordinary tray or plate. Picking up the fabric at its center, he sets the plate on a table. "If only what I were about to do involved money," the performer says with a wry grin on his face. "Even so, I suppose that a plateful of candy isn't a bad thing to conjure up." The performer shakes the handkerchief and from it falls a large quantity of wrapped candies and chocolates! A second shake and even more confections are produced. The magically produced sweets are handed around to the audience for sampling.

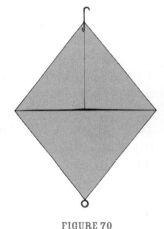

FIGURE 70

REQUIRED: In addition to a handkerchief and a plate, you will need a small bag, as shown in **Figure 70.** It is triangle-shaped, and has a small ring sewn to one corner and an S-shaped double hook arrangement on the opposite corner. The lower of the two hooks accommodates the ring, and the upper hook is used to hold the bag in its concealed position." Also required: a quantity of chocolates or candies to fill the bag.

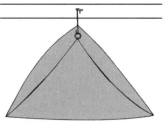

FIGURE 71

PREPARATION: Fill the bag with chocolates and close it by looping the ring over the smaller hook. Hang the bag from the back of your table by the larger hook, as shown in **Figure 71.** Set the plate on the table directly in front of the hanging bag.

PERFORMANCE: Borrow a handkerchief from a member of your audience. If one is not available, be sure you have one available that will adequately cover the secret bag.

"I'm frequently asked if I can conjure money from the ether," you say as you display the handkerchief front and back. It is clearly free of any concealed devices or trickery. Lay the handkerchief on the table, just overlapping the edge, so that the hook that the secret bag is hanging from is near the center of the handkerchief. Pick up the plate and show it to the audience as you continue your patter. "In addition to the unprepared handkerchief just displayed, we will use this sturdy platter. Unfortunately, it will *not* be used to display a massive quantity of magically acquired gold bullion."

Handing the plate to a spectator, instruct her to hold it firmly, with two hands. "For though I am not about to produce blocks of precious metal or even coins of slightly lesser value, I do propose to produce something marvelous." As she steadies her grip on the plate, tell her to knock her knuckles against it, to make sure it is solid. "Listen, everyone, to the quality of the plate!" As you give these final instructions, lift the handkerchief from the table, and at the same time, the concealed bag. The bag remains concealed in the folds of the handkerchief. Your audience should be paying attention to your volunteer, who is rapping on the plate, while you do this.

Hold the handkerchief over the plate. ("Be careful that the secret bag is not seen at this point," Mysterio wrote. "If you are on a raised stage, take especial pains to ensure that spectators seated below do not have an opportunity to look up into the folds of the handkerchief.") Then, with an imperceptible movement of your fingers, lift the ring over the small hook on the bag, opening it and allowing the sweets concealed inside to cascade down onto the plate. They can now be passed out to the spectators for sampling.

DOUBLE YOUR CHOCOLATE: To produce a second quantity of sweets, simply sew two similar bags back to back, and release the loads of chocolates one at a time. The first production will come as a surprise (though not much of one, since you have built up the production and anticipation of it with your patter). As the audience reacts to the appearance of the first quantity of candy, open the second bag. The element of surprise will be in full effect in this case, making the appearance doubly astounding. ⌒

CHAPTER X

ILLUSIONS
STAGE-FILLING CONJURING

· ∽ᴑᴓᴑ∽ ·

MR. MYSTERIO began writing an introduction to this chapter on illusions—stage-filling magic tricks involving human beings—in 1935. From his pen came the following words:

"I have been distressed, recently, to read several volumes on stage magic in which the authors have seen fit to lay bare the secrets of certain stage illusions for no reason that I can divine, other than the mean-spirited joy of exposure and a desire to profit thereby. The tricks and techniques they discuss cannot possibly be replicated, let alone performed, by the amateur, involving as they do costly and complicated properties. My book will contain *only* illusions that can be performed with but a modest investment in properties that can be constructed with relative ease."

The goal of this chapter, then, is not to reveal the methods behind classic illusions like P. T. Selbit's Sawing through a Woman or the classic Maskelyne/Kellar Levitation (which involves a complicated and costly arrangement of wires, steel, winches, and counterweights, not to mention a specially prepared stage). Those secrets will be saved for another volume, for, realistically, the construction of the necessary apparatus for most major stage illusions is beyond the abilities of the beginning magician. In fact, most major stage illusions are custom-built, having been designed to the measurements of specific performers and assistants.

Such should be the case with the effects outlined in this chapter, as well. Though general measurements are provided in each description, each trick should be built with an eye for the person or persons who will use it. Just as the patter for each trick is adapted to a particular personality, so should the magician's props be adapted to his height, weight, and personality.

PRODUCTION PANELS

─────── ❦ ───────

This most basic of production illusions is quite effective, and can be constructed relatively quickly and inexpensively.

FIGURE 1

EFFECT: Two large panels, on rolling wheels, are passed in front of each other on the stage. When the panels are separated, the magician's assistant appears from between them.

REQUIRED: Two large panels, approximately 7 feet (2¹⁄₈ m) high and 4 feet (1¹⁄₄ m) wide, as shown in **Figure 1**. The panels are mounted on sturdy wooden bases, which have been outfitted with casters or wheels (also shown in the illustration). The bases are approximately 3 feet (90 cm) wide. Three assistants are required to perform the illusion (two of them are visible; one will appear from behind the panels), unless you plan to perform some of the actions outlined below yourself.

PREPARATION: Rehearsal with your assistants is necessary to perfect the timing and choreography of the production. Before your performance, the person you will produce is concealed behind one of the two panels. Mark the center of the stage with a piece of tape so that the person you are going to produce knows where it is as he walks across the stage. The panels can be decorated with a company logo or any other design you like; whatever is suitable for the current show.

PERFORMANCE: The panels begin at either side of the stage, an assistant next to each one.

The music begins and your assistants push their respective panels across the stage. One panel will pass in front of the other, as shown in **Figure 2**. The concealed assistant simply walks along behind the upstage panel (that is, the panel closer to the rear of the stage) as it is pushed, also shown in **Figure 2**.

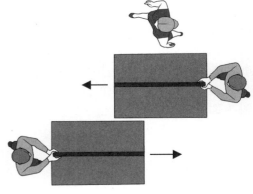

FIGURE 2

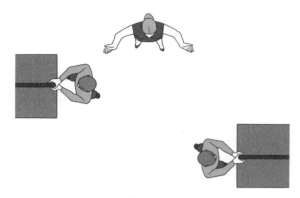

FIGURE 3

As the assistants reach the center of the stage, the concealed person stops on her mark and stands at the ready, facing the audience. The panels continue moving in opposite directions toward the wings of the stage, and as they do, the concealed assistant makes her appearance, as shown in **Figure 3.**

NO WHEELS REQUIRED: With care, this effect can be built even more inexpensively. The panels need not be mounted to casters. Instead, sturdy handles can be affixed to the panels on either side. In this way, the panels can be carried about the stage by your assistants instead of being wheeled.

BROOM ILLUSION

This visual escape illusion can be constructed at a moment's notice, on a minimal budget, yet makes for a large, showy effect.

EFFECT: The magician invites a member of the audience to the stage to assist him. The volunteer is tied to a sturdy broomstick with a solid piece of rope. The rope is looped around the spectator's body five or six times in as many directions, encircling her from shoulders to ankles, and then the rope is tied into a sturdy—and real—knot. Despite the utter fairness of the proceedings, at the magician's command, the rope apparently melts through the spectator's body, setting her free of the broom!

REQUIRED: A broomstick, a piece of rope that's at least 15 feet (4½ m) long, and a 2-inch (5 cm) wooden peg that matches the broomstick in color.

PREPARATION: Drill a hole in the center of the broomstick and place the peg in the hole prior to performance. The peg should fit into the hole snugly, but not too tightly. No overt amount of force should be necessary to remove the peg from the hole.

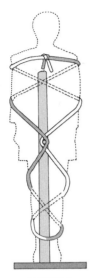

FIGURE 4

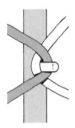

FIGURE 5

PERFORMANCE: "For this next illusion, I require the assistance of a willing spectator." Invite someone from the audience to assist you with the illusion, or use an assistant of your own if you prefer.

Once the volunteer has joined you on stage, invite her to examine the rope and ask her to stand with her back against the broomstick (which can be mounted in a stand, if you like, or held in place by an assistant).

Wrap the rope around the volunteer's body starting at her ankles, and starting with the center of the rope, as shown in **Figure 4.** Continue winding the rope around the volunteer's body as shown in the illustration. The key to the success of the illusion is the way in which the rope is wound over the spectator. In the illustration, you will note that one half of the rope is shaded, and that this portion of the rope is always wound *over* the other half of the rope. Additionally, the illustration shows exactly how many times the rope should be wrapped.

When you reach the peg, cross the ropes over each other as shown in **Figure 5,** which is an enlarged illustration of the rope and broom. Notice that there are the same number of crossovers of the rope above and below the peg. This is essential to the working of the illusion. When the rope reaches the top rear of the broom, tie the ends together.

Turn the volunteer so that her side faces the audience and, as you do so, discreetly pull out the peg but hold the rope in place. "She is tied from top to bottom, head to toe," you say as you swing her to her side, apparently to display her condition from every angle. "What is about to occur is, seemingly, impossible. Watch."

With your free hand, pull on the knot in the rope and at the same moment, let go with your other hand, which now holds the broom steady. The rope will apparently penetrate the volunteer's body entirely, freeing her from the broom. When it does, toss both the broom and rope to the ground, take the volunteer's hand, and join her in taking a bow. As the audience applauds, send her back to her seat.

VARIATIONS ON A THEME: For the conjurer interested in dressing up this illusion further, in place of a broom, any one of a number of props can be produced—a barber's pole, a tilting lance, whatever makes sense for the performance. As long as the wrapping is followed as shown in the illustrations, the volunteer can be bound to any object, and almost any type of binding can be used. For example, strips of wide, white cloth can be substituted for the rope, creating a mummylike effect when wrapped around the volunteer.

DARING PRODUCTION

Mysterio's notebook entry under this illusion read: "Though many magicians call this illusion the Mummy Case, I have titled it differently, for I feel the method is rather bold." Sometimes a bold and simple method can have big and surprising effects in a magic show.

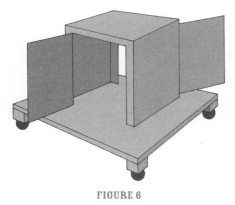

FIGURE 6

EFFECT: The magician shows a large box to be empty; he opens the front and back doors, and the audience can clearly see through it. The doors are closed and the box is shown on all sides. When the doors are again opened, the magician's assistant appears inside the box!

REQUIRED: The box, and an assistant. The box can be made of cardboard or plywood, depending on your budget and requirements. Regardless of the method of construction, the box should have four sides as well as a front and back door that open in *opposite* directions, as shown in **Figure 6.** If possible, the box should be on a platform with wheels, so that it can be easily moved about the stage, though this is not necessary for the success of the trick.

PREPARATION: Before your performance, your assistant is inside the box.

PERFORMANCE: Display the box at center stage and open the *back* door first. After you do this, your assistant steps out of the box and hides behind the back door, as shown in **Figure 7.**

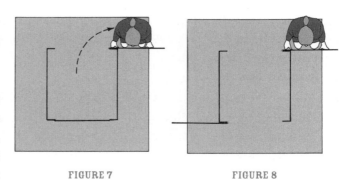

FIGURE 7   FIGURE 8

Then open the front door of the box. The audience can see through it, as in **Figure 8.** The back door conceals your assistant. Walk behind the box as if to say (without saying as much) that the audience can see through it and that it is empty.

Close the front door of the box. After you do this, your assistant should step back inside. Then close the back door. If the box has wheels or is on a mobile platform, turn it 180 degrees so that the audience can see its exterior from all sides.

Finally, after the appropriate dramatic and magical gesture, open the front door of the box to reveal your assistant!

COMMENT: Mysterio alluded to an alternative name for this illusion, the Mummy Case. For years, Floyd Thayer's Los Angeles–based illusion-building firm (among others) built a prop that worked on the method described here. In the Thayer illusion, an imitation mummy was removed from the case and displayed, then returned to the case; after the doors had been closed and reopened, the mummy was revealed as having transformed into a living, breathing Egyptian princess. This was accomplished by hanging the imitation mummy on the back door (on a hook) and then having the concealed assistant remove it and take its place when the doors were opened for the second time. In other words, many effects are made possible once the basic prop has been built. Other transformations, productions, and even vanishes are made possible by the same simple prop.

SILKEN SWITCH

This transposition illusion was developed in the spirit of the great illusionist Dante, who featured a similar effect, entitled the Black and White Illusion, in his highly successful touring show, *Sim Sala Bim.*

EFFECT: The magician and a male assistant display a large cloth to the audience. The assistant holds one end of the cloth and the magician the other, then the assistant rolls himself into the cloth. When the performer unrolls the cloth a moment later, the assistant inside it is found to be a *female.* A moment after that, the male assistant reappears in the center aisle of the theater!

REQUIRED: A large sheet of heavy, opaque cloth at least 6 by 8 feet (1³/₄ by 2¹/₂ m) and two well-trained assistants. You must be working on a stage with a rear curtain. Easy access from the backstage area to the theater is also necessary.

PREPARATION: Position one of your assistants just behind the center opening of the curtain, as in **Figure 9.**

PERFORMANCE: Display the cloth with your male assistant by holding it parallel to the rear curtain, as shown in **Figure 10.** You stand on one end and the assistant on the other, approximately 6 feet (1³/₄ m) in front of the rear curtain, where the female assistant is waiting. Make sure that the bottom of the cloth brushes the stage floor—you don't want the audience to catch a glimpse of your assistants' feet as they maneuver.

When the cloth is in position, the female assistant walks out behind it to the center of the cloth. At this moment, the male assistant steps behind the cloth (still gripping its upper corner with his hand, as shown in **Figure 11**) and begins rolling himself into it—at least, this is what the audience believes. The cloth must remain taut as he moves into this position.

The moment the male assistant is out of sight of the audience, he lifts one arm to allow the female assistant to step between

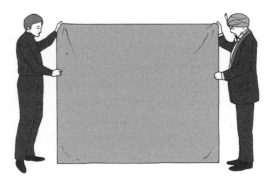

FIGURE 10

him and the edge of the cloth that he is holding, as in **Figure 12.** The female assistant now takes over his grip on the cloth, and the male assistant walks off stage through the back curtain, as in **Figure 13.**

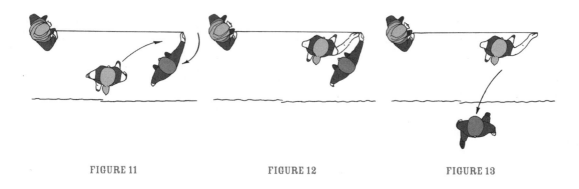

FIGURE 11   FIGURE 12   FIGURE 13

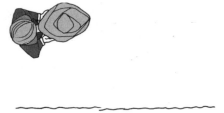

Now the female assistant, with help from you, is wrapped in the cloth as if she were a mummy, as shown in **Figure 14.** At your command, when the cloth is unwrapped, the transformation is revealed. While the wrapping has been going on, the male assistant runs to the back of the theater and lies in readiness for the climax of the trick.

FIGURE 14

A moment after the transformation is revealed on stage, the male assistant reveals himself in the midst of the audience and runs down the center aisle of the theater to join you and your female assistant on stage, making for the perfect applause cue.

SACK ESCAPE

Mysterio often wrote notes to himself, apparently meant for future reference. The following jotting seems appropriate for the escape illusions described below. "The Houdini legend is strong and compelling to audiences. Use it as a presentational hook in upcoming performances."

EFFECT: The performer is tied into a large cloth sack. Spectators do the tying, precluding the possibility of any tricky knots. Within seconds, the performer opens the cinched mouth of the bag and steps out.

REQUIRED: A large canvas sack with grommets around its opening, as shown in **Figure 15.** The sack should be large and sturdy enough to hold you or your assistant. A piece of rope 10 feet (3 m) long, a trustworthy onstage assistant, and a large sheet are also required.

FIGURE 15

PREPARATION: None.

PERFORMANCE: Invite one or two spectators to the stage and allow them to examine the props. "You will find the bag, rope, and sheet to be completely free of trickery, because they are. The escape I am about to attempt will be accomplished entirely by natural means. I resort to no secret aids, no cunningly concealed tools, and no divine intervention," you say. "My wits and agility are all that are required."

Feed the ends of the rope through the grommets at the top of the bag, being sure that the center of the rope is visible on the *inside* of the mouth of the bag. This is the basic secret of the trick.

Step inside the bag. Before ducking down inside it, explain what is about to transpire: "I will be tied into this bag by these good people. My challenge is to escape in record time." As you duck down into the bag, two things happen: One, your onstage assistant gives the audience volunteers reassuring instructions as to what they are to do; and, two, you take up a considerable amount of slack in the rope by pulling down on its center from inside the bag, as shown in **Figure 16**. Hold tightly to approximately 3 feet (90 cm) of rope by wrapping it around your hand. As you do, the audience volunteers will cinch up the mouth of the bag and tie it off with a number of strong knots, as you and your assistant have instructed them.

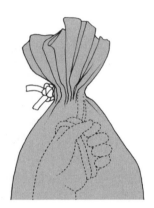

FIGURE 16

After the bag has been sealed, your onstage assistant instructs the audience volunteers to stand back. She holds up the sheet in front of you (or covers you with it) and you make your sudden escape from the sack by releasing your grip on the rope from inside, loosening the opening of the bag, and stepping out of it.

MYSTERIO'S COMMENT: "While this escape is simple in its working, its presentation will not be entertaining unless it is built up properly with lots of bally and talk. Stress the difficulty of the feat appropriately and you will have a marvelous pack small/play big effect to add to your show. Additionally, the clever performer will find a way to add small touches to the trick, like a change of costume made between the time when he is placed in the sack and the time when he makes his escape. It would also be effective to appear after the escape smoking a cigar, as my compeer Les Levante did in his Steel Trunk Mystery."

THE TIP-OVER BOX

This quick production of a person can, like the Daring Production (page 313), be made with inexpensive or more costly materials, depending on the performer's needs. The trick is quick and surprising.

EFFECT: The magician displays a large box on the stage and tilts it toward the audience, which can see that it is empty. The box is then set back down on the stage and the magician claps his hands, at which point one or two assistants spring from the box, materializing out of thin air!

REQUIRED: A large box (like an oversized chest for shipping) that sits on a solid platform, and at least two assistants. The box can be made of cardboard, or can be a wooden packing case made by a carpenter. If at all possible, the platform should be on wheels.

PREPARATION: The bottom panel of the chest is removed and attached to the platform in a perpendicular position, as shown in **Figure 17**. In this way, the chest

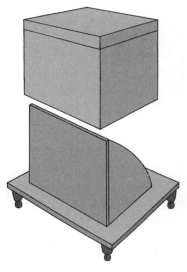

FIGURE 17

can be tilted back and forth, but its "bottom" will not move. Your assistant (or assistants, if you have two and both will fit into the box) crouches down behind the panel inside the chest, which sits upright on the platform.

PERFORMANCE: Wheel the chest to center stage with the help of an assistant, who stands on the other side from you. With his aid, tilt the front of the chest forward as in **Figure 18,** lift the lid, and show the interior empty. Because the interior panel of the chest does not move, it perfectly conceals the assistant(s) inside and appears to be nothing more than the bottom of the box, as far

FIGURE 18

FIGURE 19

as the spectators are concerned. **Figure 19** shows the box after it has been tilted 90 degrees toward the spectators. You stand on one side of it and your assistant stands on the other, which helps to hide the second assistant crouched down behind it as the box is shown empty.

To produce the assistant, simply tilt the box backward, setting it back down onto the platform, and close the lid. Give the box a complete revolution if you feel it necessary to show all sides of it, and once you have, await the appropriate dramatic crescendo in the music or for the necessary magical moment. Open the lid of the box, and out pops your surprising human production, as in **Figure 20.**

FIGURE 20

TIPPED AGAIN: The Tip-over Box can be combined with the Sack Escape (page 316) to create a startling illusion. Cut a hole in the top of the box as shown in **Figure 21.** Make sure the hole is large enough to accommodate the tied top of the sack used in the Sack Escape. Your assistant is tied into the sack, which is inside the Tip-over Box. She escapes from the sack as previously described, and then the sack is pulled through the top of the box. The box can then be

FIGURE 21

tipped over and shown empty—not only has your assistant escaped, she has vanished from the box as well.

If you work with twins ("If ever you are so fortunate as to find a set of twins willing to work in your illusion show, be sure to pay them well," Mysterio wrote in his diary), once the sack has been pulled through the top of the trunk and the trunk itself has been shown empty, the twin of the assistant who has just escaped and vanished from the box can run down the aisle of the theater for a spectacular "reappearance" in the center of the audience.

DOUBLE BOX ILLUSION

"In 1915, when the Cunard Line lost a number of my prop cases, I was forced to improvise a show with materials on hand at the theater," Mysterio wrote. "An inexpensive version of the Double Box Illusion was the first I constructed, and it occupied a prominent spot on my program. It proved a decided hit."

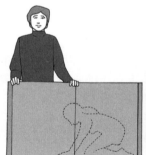

EFFECT: The magician approaches the center of the stage, where an assistant is waiting next to two collapsed boxes. The boxes have no lids or bottoms. They are unfolded by the performer and his helper, and one box is nested inside the other. At the conjurer's command, a *third* assistant appears from inside the nested boxes!

REQUIRED: Two assistants and two large boxes as pictured in **Figure 22.** The smaller of the pair, which we'll call box A, measures approximately 28 by 28 by 36 inches (71 by 71 by 90 cm) and has a hole cut in its rear, as shown. The edges of both boxes are hinged together with tape (if made of sturdy cardboard or foam core) or metal

FIGURE 22

hinges (if constructed from lightweight plywood). The boxes should be decorated in contrasting colors or patterns.

PREPARATION: Before your performance, fold both boxes flat, as in **Figure 23,** and place them on the stage, where an assistant holds them upright. The assistant who will be produced hides behind box B, as shown in the illustration.

PERFORMANCE: The key to the illusion is, first of all, casually handling the props, and, second, a certain speed or

FIGURE 23

cadence to the way they are used on stage. Enter and approach the assistant, who hands you box A. In its folded condition, the box can be briefly displayed to the audience. Do not unfold it during the display, as this would reveal the hole. Instead, simply make a sweeping gesture with it (almost waving it in the air) while it is still folded. The audience will intuitively understand that nothing is concealed in the box.

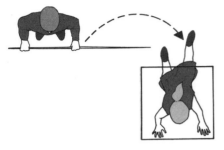

FIGURE 24

Set up box A by unfolding it (taking care to keep the hole out of the audience's line of sight) and placing it on the stage very near box B, which is still folded. As you unfold and arrange box A (as if getting its position "just right"), the concealed assistant crawls from behind box B and into box A through the hole, as in **Figure 24.**

Once she is inside, your onstage assistant helps you to display box B—unfolded and open—and demonstrate that it is empty. The two of you lift it toward the audience and look through it, and then place it on the stage, directly over box A. The nested boxes can now be turned around to show all sides. Finally, the secret assistant stands up and makes her appearance; you lift her out of the boxes and she takes her applause. The illusion is complete.

THE EXCHANGE ILLUSION

The element of surprise in this illusion is strong, and the fact that it is not a quick vanish or production makes it ideal for a closing effect.

EFFECT: The magician dons a long, hooded robe. His assistant is then tied into a sturdy cloth bag. The bag is concealed from the view of the audience behind a three-fold screen at the center of the stage. The supposed magician then claps his hands and, when his costume is removed, he is revealed to be the assistant! The actual magician is discovered tied inside the bag, behind the screen!

REQUIRED: A capable assistant who is approximately your height and build, a cloth sack with grommets in its top (as described in the Sack Escape, page 316), a three-fold screen approximately 6 feet (1 $^3/_4$ m) high, and two matching costumes with long hoods that mask the faces of the wearers.

PREPARATION: Mastery of the Sack Escape is required. Hang one of the costumes on the back of the screen prior to the performance.

FIGURE 25

PERFORMANCE: Most of this illusion should be performed to suitable musical accompaniment. Still, it should be introduced by you from the stage. "Ladies and gentlemen, what I am about to present is an escape illusion, a seemingly impossible feat." Introduce your assistant and, as you do, don the costume as shown in **Figure 25** (which shows the screen, sack, magician, and assistant on stage). Be sure to keep your face turned slightly from the audience once you are wearing the costume. This will make it easier to conceal your—and your assistant's—identity.

Now tie your assistant into the bag as described in the Sack Escape. Place the sack behind the three-fold screen. After the screen is in place, your assistant immediately frees himself from the bag and puts on the duplicate costume. He then stands behind the screen, waiting to switch places with you. While your assistant is doing this, be sure to keep attention focused on yourself with a steady line of patter.

When you judge that the time is right, walk over and step behind the screen as if you're readjusting it. It is at this point that the assistant takes your place, continuing on your path around and behind the screen, and then walks off stage, or to its side. **Figure 26** shows the path of the performer, the assistant behind the screen, and the path that the assistant takes once he has switched places with the magician. Where the assistant goes (on stage or off) depends on how quickly you, the performer, can take off the costume, hang it on the back of the screen, get into the bag, and tighten the rope that closes it.

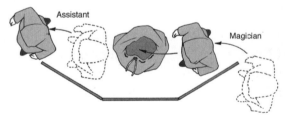

FIGURE 26

At the climactic moment, the assistant walks back toward the screen and, staying well in front of it, moves the screen to one side, exposing the sack to the audience. He unties it. Out from inside comes the performer, and when the robe is removed from the other person on stage, he is revealed to be the assistant!

SUBSTITUTION TRUNK ILLUSION

This is one of the most popular, baffling, and entertaining stage illusions of all time, and was a favorite of the late, great Harry Houdini. "It was his reputation-making, most sensational and best trick," Mysterio wrote.

EFFECT: The magician's assistant is placed in a large cloth bag, which is tied shut.

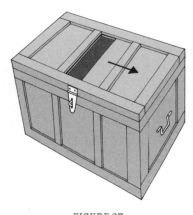

The bag is placed in a sturdy wooden trunk, which is locked by a member of the audience. Then the performer, invoking the spirit of Harry Houdini, stands on top of the trunk and proposes to show the audience the fastest escape the world has ever seen. The magician raises a curtain above his head, and when it is lowered, in his place stands the assistant. The trunk is unlocked, and the bag inside it is untied. Inside is discovered the magician!

FIGURE 27

REQUIRED: In addition to a well-trained assistant, you'll need a large packing crate with a secret, sliding lid as shown in **Figure 27**; a large sack with grommets at its mouth, as described in the Sack Escape illusion (page 316); a piece of rope 10 feet (3 m) long; an opaque curtain approximately 12 feet (3½ m) high and 5 feet (1½ m) wide, with lightweight aluminum rods sewn into both ends, as shown in **Figure 28**; and a padlock with which the trunk can be secured.

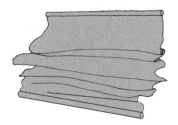

PREPARATION: Repeated rehearsal with your assistant is the key to successfully performing this effect.

FIGURE 28

PERFORMANCE: Place your assistant in the cloth sack and have her "secured" in it by two spectators from the audience, who tie its mouth tightly with as many knots as they desire. Your assistant will be able to escape from this sack easily, using the technique described in the Sack Escape illusion.

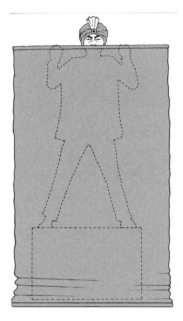

FIGURE 29

FIGURE 30

Once tied in the sack, your assistant ducks down into the packing crate and the lid is locked down on top of it. You stand on top of the crate in a wide stance, as shown in **Figure 29,** holding the curtain in front of you. Because a lightweight aluminum bar has been sewn into the foot of the curtain, it hangs down easily and hides the front of the crate effectively.

As you step up on top of the box, your assistant, now free of the sack, slides open the secret panel on the top of the box and stands up, then crawls out of it and stands behind you, on the back edge of the lid of the crate, crouched down, as shown in **Figure 30.** Lower the curtain enough so that the audience can see your head and say, "This happens very quickly, on the count of three. Don't blink or you'll miss it!" Raise the curtain again and count to three, out loud. On "three," release your hold on the curtain, which is caught by your assistant, who stands up so that the audience can see her head, and that she has taken your place. As you let go of the curtain, drop down into the box and quickly close the secret door.

All that remains is for your assistant to lower the curtain and reveal herself completely, after which she jumps down from the top of the box and unlocks it. While she does this, you shimmy into the bag and pull on the rope inside it to take up the slack and re-close it.

When the box is finally unlocked, the bag is untied and you are seen to have changed places with your assistant in the blink of an eye!

ARABIAN TENT ILLUSION

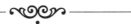

For the one-person production, this easy-to-build illusion is difficult to surpass. It was devised by U. F. Grant, who invented more than a thousand magic tricks and owned several magic manufacturers, one of which is still in business today.

EFFECT: The performer builds a small tentlike structure on stage, showing each piece of it on both sides as he does. Clearly the props are free of trickery. The magician reaches inside the tent and produces an endless quantity of silk scarves and even a glass bowl full of fish. Then, at the magician's command, the roof of the tent bursts off and out of its center is produced the magician's assistant.

REQUIRED: Large sheets of cardboard, foam core board, or lightweight plywood are required to construct the device for this illusion. Cut the material as shown in **Figure 31,** and hinge the roof together along its long edge and the two wall sections, as illustrated. If building the illusion from wood, three or four small, heavy-duty hinges will do nicely. If constructing it from cardboard or foam core, heavy adhesive tape can be used as a hinge. Be sure to leave approximately ½ inch (1¼ cm) between each panel if hinging together pieces of foam core or cardboard, to allow the sections to swing back and forth freely.

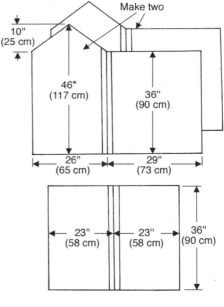

Decorate the sides and roof (inside and out) of the tent appropriately. Other things you'll need (besides two assistants) include silk streamers, a goldfish bowl, and whatever other articles—even live animals—you intend to produce from the tent. A bag to hold these articles is also required.

FIGURE 31

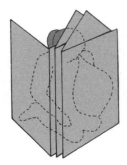

FIGURE 32

PREPARATION: Fill the bag with the various articles that will be produced. The assistant who will burst out of the tent should hold on to the bag or, if it is outfitted with straps, sling it over her shoulder. Stack the pieces of the tent on the stage, with one assistant holding them up and the other concealed behind one of the walls, as shown in **Figure 32.**

PERFORMANCE: Much like the Production Panels illusion (page 310), the Arabian Tent requires precision timing to be deceptive. Have the visible assistant hand you one of the wall pieces, which you stand up as shown in **Figure 33.** Next, put the other wall section of the prop in place, opening it out as you do to show that it conceals nothing. It is at this moment that the secret assistant crawls from behind the roof of the tent inside the tent proper, as shown in **Figure 34.**

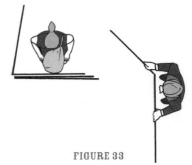

FIGURE 33

Conclude the construction portion of the illusion by picking up the roof and placing it on top of the tent proper. Now, from inside the tent (through a strategically cut hole, or perhaps by lifting the roof), the various articles carried by the secret assistant may be produced. The climax of the trick comes when the roof of the tent bursts off and the assistant makes her appearance.

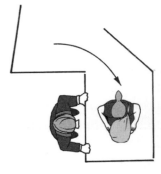

FIGURE 34

MAGICAL MOTIFS: As is the case with many illusions described in this chapter, the Arabian Tent can be decorated to suit the circumstances in which you are performing. If, for example, you are performing at a Christmas party, the tent can be decorated to represent a house, and from it can be produced various presents and Santa Claus. At Halloween, the tent can be painted to represent a haunted house, from which a ghost makes its appearance (your assistant, suitably dressed in costume).

In the event that you are hired to perform for a corporation and would like to introduce a new product or produce the CEO, the Arabian tent can be customized with the firm's logos, and only a modicum of training will be required to teach the company CEO how to act as the secret assistant in the illusion.

STUPENDOUS SUSPENSION

This is the most complicated illusion described in this chapter, and also one of the most impressive. The suspension of a human being in mid-air is a timeless classic of magic.

EFFECT: A spectator—virtually anyone from the audience—is invited to the stage to assist the magician. She lies on a wide wooden board that is supported by two ordinary sawhorses. "Who among us has never dreamed of flying?" the magician asks. "Tonight, now, I will make that dream come true for my willing volunteer." The spectator is told to close her eyes. The magician then removes the sawhorses that support the board she is lying on. With no visible means of support, the spectator remains suspended in mid-air!

REQUIRED: A secret support—made of sturdy metal bars or pipes—is required, in addition to a board that's long enough for a person to lie down on. The board is permanently attached to the support by two metal flanges, which are bolted securely through the support. If the support is made from metal piping, many of the joints can be threaded, making the illusion easy to break down and transport. However, the joints that support the bulk of the suspended spectator's weight must be welded securely, to provide solid support.

The base of the support is disguised by a rug. The board is apparently supported by a pair of sawhorses (or chairs, or other similar objects). The other requirement is a cloth that, when draped over the board, hangs down in front of it and conceals the center bar of the metal support. All of the properties are clearly shown, with suggested measurements, in **Figure 35.**

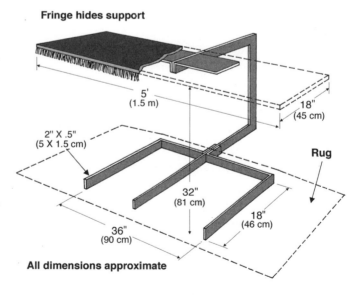

FIGURE 35

PREPARATION: With the apparatus in place on stage, drape the cloth over the board so that it hides the center bar of the support.

PERFORMANCE: Select a member of the audience to assist you and invite her to sit on the board at its center. To be safe, try to choose a spectator who weighs less than 125 pounds (57 kg).

Help her up onto the board (a step stool may be required), then help her lie down on it. Stand behind the spectator and the board, your left leg directly in front of the center bar of the metal support, as in **Figure 36.**

Wrap the spectator in the cloth that covers the board. ("For your safety," you say sarcastically.) Now, being careful not to move so far that you reveal the hidden support, remove the sawhorses that support the board. Pause after removing the first sawhorse, to allow the illusion to register in the minds of the audience. The sight of a human being balanced precariously on a board that is resting—at one extreme end—on a single sawhorse is a sight that requires more than five seconds to grasp completely.

Remove the second sawhorse dramatically, showing the spectator and the board floating in the air! See **Figure 37.** Replace the sawhorses, unwrap the spectator (masking the center bar of the support with the cloth again), and congratulate her on her maiden voyage. Send her back to her seat as you ask the audience to give her a hearty round of applause.

FIGURE 36

FIGURE 37

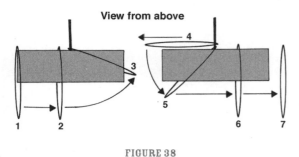

View from above

FIGURE 38

PASSING A HOOP: Traditionally, magicians have passed solid hoops over floating ladies to "prove" that there is no connection between the floater and the magician or any stage props. Using a solid hoop (or one made of rope tied into a circle), **Figure 38** shows how *two* passes must be made with the hoop to avoid the center support and pass over the lady smoothly and effectively.

WALKING AWAY: If the suspension illusion is performed close to a backdrop, the magician need not stand in front of the center support and conceal it with his leg. As **Figure 39** shows, the center bar can be concealed behind the curtain with only a modicum of preparation before the performance.

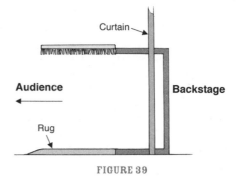

FIGURE 39

Another method for performing the illusion also involves hiding the support behind the curtain. If a sturdy support is attached to the board as shown in **Figure 40,** an assistant behind the scenes will need to counterbalance the spectator's weight. The support for this method of performing the suspension is less costly to build, but the illusion must be performed on a stage with curtains. ❧

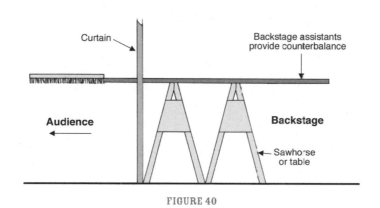

FIGURE 40

AFTERWORD

·~∞~·

SECRETS ARE ONLY THE BEGINNING...

"LEARNING HOW, in principle, to saw a woman in half without harming her is but the first small step on the road to becoming a magician," Mr. Mysterio wrote. "Reading a book of secrets without actually *performing* any of the tricks in it is meaningless. The man who reads a book and calls himself a magician is no more a magician than the man who attends a performance of *Hamlet* and calls himself an actor.

"There is certainly much to be said for the knowledge found in books. It is important to understand something fully before it can be put into practice. Let us say, then, that learning how to conjure begins on the page, but must then be translated to the stage (no matter how large or small that stage be)."

In many ways, these sentiments echo the advice Mysterio offers in the introduction to this book. And although they were written many years ago, the words should still resonate loudly with modern-day miracle-makers. Owning this book does not make you a magician. Putting the tricks in it to use is what pushes you across that line and changes your status from layman to miracle-man.

But even then, after you have taken the plunge and begun to perform tricks and stunts from this text, your work is not done. Considerable care must be taken to "sell" the idea of magic to your audiences, even when you are not performing.

A great talent in his day, Nate Leipzig was a success on the vaudeville circuits and at exclusive private gatherings. His impeccable sleight-of-hand magic was not flashy or Houdini-like in any way. It was upper-class conjuring, and it made Leipzig a legend in his own time. In social situations, those best suited to the performance of intimate close-up magic, Leipzig followed a dictum that served him well. It will serve you well, too, should you choose to follow it. When asked to perform for a group—in an informal setting, that is—Leipzig always politely refused. He would perform only if pressed hard by his audience; that is, he made certain that his potential spectators truly did desire to see him work—he was never quick to pull a pack of cards from his pocket and demonstrate five or ten tricks at the drop of a hat. (And in his day, all men wore hats.)

As W. Somerset Maugham wrote in *Mr. Know-It-All*:

"'Do you like card tricks?'

'No, I hate card tricks,' I answered.

'Well, I'll just show you this one.'

He showed me three."

In plain English: Know when to stop. Understand that there is a limitation to how much magic an audience is willing to digest in a single sitting (or, for that matter, how much ballet, violin, or poetry an audience can stomach in a single sitting). Select your audiences wisely, pay attention to their mood, and select your material wisely too. A few well-chosen, well-performed effects that leave 'em wanting more can do wonders for your career as a conjurer.

Whatever material appeals to you, make sure that it has been, as Mysterio recommends, rehearsed repeatedly, until you can perform it without a moment of hesitation. Tricks in your repertoire should come as easily as breathing or walking. Presenting them to a group should be a thing of joy, not a tense interlude in which you are unsure of what line or move comes next.

Unfortunately, practice does take time. What's more, mistakes are inevitable. The best way to learn how to perform a trick and make it sensational is to do it, repeatedly, for a live audience. Unless your family is very large, or you have an endless number of sympathetic and supportive acquaintances, this means that at some point you will have to conjure for strangers who may or may not like what you show them. But through repeated showings, *especially* for critical audiences, your sense for what is good entertainment and what makes for good, mystifying conjuring will develop.

ROUTINES

Just as important as creating a flow and rhythm to each trick is creating a program (a "set list," to use a modern term) that holds together. There should be no fumbling in the performance of an individual trick, and, similarly, there should be no hesitation when you're called upon to present ten or fifteen minutes of magic at a cocktail party or in front of a paying audience.

Once your repertoire is established and you have a number of effects on which you can rely, spend time grouping them together logically. Strive for variety in your program. Mix together tricks with different themes, and keep your audience interested by involving spectators and borrowing objects from them on a regular basis. Conversely, there is a time and place for a single, well-chosen trick. Understanding the difference is important.

PARTING ADVICE TO STUDENTS

Mysterio's notebook included a section headed "Parting Advice to Students." It is reproduced here in its entirety.

"Before sending budding bafflers on their way, I always do my utmost to impress upon them that each performance, successful or otherwise, contains a lesson. Each failure shows the performer what *not* to do, while each success shows the performer *how it can be done*. And there are still more valuable lessons to be learned.

"Was each line delivered at the right moment, for maximum impact? How well was your misdirection covered, in sleights involving that interesting art? Were you able to control the attention of the audience in *exactly* the way you desired?

"For an attentive performer, the questions never cease and the journey never ends. There are always ways to make even the oldest trick new, ways to improve the presentation or performance of virtually every effect you know. Even the simplest of feats can be refined to the point that it becomes a masterpiece."

OTHER RESOURCES

·~◦~·

MAGIC SHOPS

Since the middle of the nineteenth century, magicians have sought out professionals who could supply them with the tools of the trade. For Mr. Mysterio, primary suppliers included Martinka's in New York (the company is still in business, though now in New Jersey), Thayer's in Los Angeles (now Owen Magic Supreme), and Davenports in London (still run by the Davenport family). The following businesses come highly recommended as purveyors of fine prestidigitatorial products:

Abbott's Magic Company
124 St. Joseph St.
Colon, MI 49040
www.abbottmagic.com

Browser's Den of Magic
875 Eglinton Ave. W., Unit 10
Toronto, Ontario
M6C 3Z9
Canada
www.browsersden.com

Davenports Magic
7 Charing Cross Underground
Arcade
The Strand
London WC2N 4HZ
United Kingdom
www.davenportsmagic.co.uk

Eddie's Trick Shop
70 S. Park Square
Marietta, GA 30060
www.eddiestrickshop.com

H&R Magic Books
3839 Liles Lane
Humble, TX 77396-4088
www.magicbookshop.com

Hank Lee's Magic Factory
P.O. Box 789
Medford, MA 02155
www.magicfact.com

Hocus Pocus Magic
1492 N. Clark #104
Fresno, CA 93703 USA
www.hocus-pocus.com

Magic, Inc.
5082 N. Lincoln Ave.
Chicago, IL 60625
www.magicinc.net

Martinka & Co., Inc.
103 Godwin Ave.
Midland Park, NJ 07432
www.martinka.com

Owen Magic Supreme
734 N. McKeever Ave.
Azusa, CA 91702-2394
www.owenmagic.com

Stevens Magic Emporium
2520 E. Douglas Ave.
Wichita, KS 67214-4514
www.stevensmagic.com

Tannen's Magic, Inc.
45 W. 34th St., Suite 608
New York, NY 10001
www.tannens.com

Twin Cities Magic
250 E. Seventh St.
St. Paul, MN 55101
www.twincitiesmagic.com

MAGAZINES

Genii Magazine
4200 Wisconsin Ave. NW, Suite
106-384
Washington, D.C. 20016
www.geniimagazine.com

MAGIC Magazine
6220 Stevenson Way
Las Vegas, NV 89120
www.magicmagazine.com

FRATERNAL ORGANIZATIONS

**The International Brother-
hood of Magicians**
11155C S. Towne Square
St. Louis, MO 63123
www.magician.org

*Founded in 1922, the Interna-
tional Brotherhood of Magicians
(IBM) is the largest magic club in
the world. Its monthly journal,*
The Linking Ring, *is sent free to
members worldwide, and like the
SAM (below), the IBM hosts an
annual convention. Mr. Mysterio
was invited to join the IBM by its
second president (also secretary of
the treasury under Franklin D.
Roosevelt), William W. Durbin.*

**The Society of American
Magicians**
National Administrator
P.O. Box 2900
Pahrump, NV 89041
www.magicsam.com

*Founded in 1902, the Society of
American Magicians (SAM) is the
oldest magician's club in the world.
Its assemblies meet in most major
metropolitan centers in the United
States (and many international
locations as well). The society hosts
an annual convention and
publishes an excellent monthly
magazine,* M-U-M, *which is sent
free to all members. Mysterio was
inducted into the SAM (as
member 1045½) in the back
room of Martinka's Magic Shop
in New York City, where the
organization was founded.*

The Magic Circle
Centre for the Magic Arts
12 Stephenson Way
Euston
London NW1 2HD
United Kingdom
www.themagiccircle.co.uk

*Considered by many to be the most
prestigious magical organization
in the world, the Magic Circle
operates from its own luxurious
headquarters in the heart of
London. Membership in the
Magic Circle is by examination
only; in other words, you must
audition for a panel of experts
before becoming a member. The*
Magic Circular *is the organization's monthly magazine.*

SUGGESTED READING

The serious student of the art will only begin his exploration of the magical arts with this book. It has been said that more books have been written about magic than any other performing art. Though hard to substantiate such a claim, it is not hard to believe it. The list that follows is composed of books that describe all aspects of the art, from the basics of card conjuring to the essentials of stage illusions as well as the stories of great illusionists of the past. There are lessons to be learned from every work on the list, be it a subtle nuance of presentation, the hard-won experiences that can only be gleaned by working in a trouping magic show, or the step-by-step instructions of an awe-inspiring routine for the Linking Rings. Some of the books listed below are out of print, and others are available only from specialty dealers in conjuring supplies. All are worth seeking out and studying.

Bamberg, David. *Illusion Show.* David Meyer Magic Books, Glenwood, Illinois, 1991.
The finest autobiography of a stage magician ever written.

Bamberg, Theo, and Robert Parrish. *Oktio on Magic.* Squash, Chicago, 2008.
A volume replete with staggering stage tricks, hand shadows, and reminiscences of one of the twentieth century's most artistic and accomplished magicians.

Ben, David. *Dai Vernon: A Biography Vol. 1 (1894-1941).* Squash, Chicago, 2005.
Critically acclaimed, this is the first of a two-part biography of the greatest sleight-of-hand magician of the 20th century.

Blaine, David. *Mysterious Stranger: A Book of Magic.* Villard, New York, 2002.
A book that tells Blaine's story and teaches several blockbuster tricks.

Christopher, Milbourne. *The Illustrated History of Magic.* Thomas Y. Crowell Company, New York, 1973.
An enlightening and entertaining account of magic's rich history.

Christopher, Milbourne. *Panorama of Magic.* Dover Publications, New York, 1962.
Thoroughly illustrated with fantastic vintage artwork from the collection of the author.

Downs, T. Nelson. *The Art of Magic.* Downs-Edwards Company, Buffalo, New York, 1909.
One of the ten cornerstones of any magic library, this title teaches essential sleight-of-hand tricks.

Erdnase, S. W. *Artifice, Subterfuge, and Ruse at the Card Table.* S. W. Erdnase, Chicago, 1902.
The card magician's bible and a bestseller since 1902. No serious magician should be without a copy.

Firman, Pete. *Tricks to Freak out Your Friends.* Chicago Review Press, Chicago, 2007.
Fun effects from a funny British magician.

Ganson, Lewis. *The Dai Vernon Book of Magic.* Harry Stanley, London, n.d.
One of the ten best books on sleight-of-hand magic ever written.

Ganson, Lewis. *Dai Vernon's Tribute to Nate Leipzig*. Harry Stanley, London, n.d.
Leipzig's tricks made him famous. Find out why.

Hilliard, John Northern. *Greater Magic*. Carl Waring Jones, Minneapolis, Minnesota, 1938.
A book that every magician should own, with hundreds of pages and over a thousand illustrations. Contributions from modern magical masters make this book outstanding.

Hoffmann, Professor. *Modern Magic: A Practical Treatise on the Art of Conjuring*. Routledge, London, 1876.
The first popular book to reveal professional magic secrets, and still relevant today.

Hofzinser, Johann Nepomuk. *The Magic of Johann Nepomuk Hofzinser*, compiled by Ottokar Fischer, translated by Richard Hatch. Modern Litho, Omaha, Nebraska, 1985.
This important work teaches the great Viennese conjurer's methods. Now out of print.

Holden, Max. *Programmes of Famous Magicians*. Max Holden, New York, 1937.
Learn how great conjurers structured their shows.

Hugard, Jean (ed.). *Encyclopedia of Card Tricks*. Max Holden, New York, 1937.
A handy reference work full of tested and workable card tricks.

Hugard, Jean, and Frederick Braue. *Expert Card Technique*. Carl Waring Jones, Minneapolis, Minnesota, 1940.
Along with Erdnase's book, a bible for the advanced card magician. Track down the third edition, if you can.

Hugard, Jean, and Frederick Braue. *The Royal Road to Card Magic*. Dover Publications, New York, 1999.
An excellent and near-complete introduction to card tricks and sleights.

James, Stewart (ed.). *The Encyclopedia of Rope Tricks*. Squash, Chicago, 2005.
The biggest and best book of tricks with rope in the English language.

James, Stewart. *The Essential Stewart James*. Magicana, Toronto, Canada, 2007.
An introduction to the work of this enigmatic Canadian that details fifty impossibilities only he could have invented.

Jarrett, Guy E., and Jim Steinmeyer. *The Complete Jarrett*. Hahne, Burbank, California, 2001.
Describes the work, life, and illusions (with annotations) of this singular genius.

Jay, Ricky. *Learned Pigs and Fireproof Women*. Villard Books, New York, 1986.
Fantastically written and illustrated, this book illuminates the lives of some of the most unusual entertainers in history, including Max Malini.

Kreskin. *How to Be a Fake Kreskin*. St. Martin's Press, New York, 1996.
A good introduction to mind magic and similar effects.

Neil, C. Lang. *The Modern Conjurer and Drawing-Room Entertainer*. C. Arthur Pearson, London, 1903.
An excellent book for those interested in parlor magic. Out of print.

Parrish, Robert. *Words about Wizards*. David Meyer Magic Books, Glenwood, Illinois, 1995.
Brief biographical sketches of some of the world's finest magicians from a man who knew them.

Price, David. *Magic: A Pictorial History of Conjurers in the Theater*. Cornwall Books, Cranbury, New Jersey, 1985.
A heavily illustrated history book with descriptions of magicians and tricks that are not available elsewhere. Out of print.

Sachs, Edwin T. *Sleight of Hand*. Fleming Book Company, Berkeley Heights, New Jersey, 1946.
One of the ten most important books on magic, first published in the nineteenth century and still relevant.

Silverman, Kenneth, *HOUDINI!!!* HarperCollins, New York, 1996.
The definitive biography of the most famous magician of all time.

Steinmeyer, Jim. *Hiding the Elephant*. Carrol & Graf, New York, 2003.
A lively historical account, this book mixes together the important players of magic's golden age and reads like a novel.

Tarbell, Harlan. *The Tarbell Course in Magic*, volumes 1–8. D. Robbins, New York, v.d.
A complete course in magic that has remained popular (and in print) since its initial publication in 1927—for good reason.

Vernon, Dai. *Early Vernon*. Ireland Magic Co., Chicago, 1962.
Some of Vernon's subtlest and most disarming secrets.

Vernon, Dai. *Malini and His Magic*, edited by Lewis Ganson. Harry Stanley, London, 1962.
Vernon's versions and interpretations of Malini's tricks are worth studying.

Waldron, Daniel. *Blackstone: A Magician's Life*. David Meyer Magic Books, Glenwood, Illinois, 1999.
The best biography of this titan of stage magic.

Willmarth, Philip Reed. *The Magic of Matt Schulien*. Ireland Magic Co., Chicago, 1959.
Learn the close-up magic and philosophy of magic of this master magician.

WITHOUT THESE...

Despite the fact that a single name—well, in this case, two names—generally appears on the title pages of books, no published work, and certainly not this one, is truly the work of one person.

The first thank you goes to my phantom collaborator and co-author, Mr. Mysterio. Wherever you are, and whomever you're deceiving, know that your dream of completing that big book of tricks has been realized.

As for those who remain on this side of the veil, I have more than a few gratuities to pay in print. Thanks to Adam Rubin for being a constant sounding board, idea machine, and otherwise contractually obligated friend. Thanks to Mark Levy for passing along a lead and giving me a shove forward. To my family: Who could ask for more indulgent, supportive, and encouraging parents (to say nothing of an overly smart and sympathetic sister, and an endlessly encouraging grandmother) than I? To the Quirky individuals in two cities who steered me down the right road on the course to publication: Eloise Flood, Jason Rekulak and Sharyn Rosart. To the mighty Tony Dunn, an illustrator who's seen it, read it, drawn it, and asks the right questions. A thousand thanks are owed to all of the above—for starters.

And, of course, to everyone else who assisted in ways both major and minor, knowingly and unknowingly, including those that generously contributed ideas and effects, or offered a quick check of a credit or historical tidbit. Here's a deep bend at the waist and a tip of my hat to: Stan Allen, John Bannon, Benjamin Barnes, David Ben, Julie Eng, John Fisher, Martin Gardner, Richard Hatch, Sara Karp, Richard Kaufman, Kostya Kimlat, John Lovick, Sandy Marshall, Jr., Kevin McGroarty, Max Maven, Tomás Medina, Anita and David Meyer, John Moehring, P. T. Murphy, Tom O'lenick, Patrick Page, David Parr, Graham Putnam, George Schindler, Allan Slaight, David Solomon, John Sturk, Arthur Trace, Dan Waldron, Michael Weber, Meir Yedid, and Herb and Phyllis Zarrow.